The Mountie

from **Dime Novel**

to **Disney**

The

Michael Dawson

Mountie

from **Dime Novel**

to **Disney**

Between the Lines

The Mountie from Dime Novel to Disney
© Michael Dawson, 1998

Between the Lines gratefully acknowledges financial assistance for our publishing activities from the Ontario Arts Council, The Canada Council for the Arts, and the Government of Canada through the Book Publishing Industry Development Program.

Every reasonable effort has been made to find copyright holders. The publisher would be pleased to have any errors or omissions brought to its attention.

Canadian Cataloguing in Publication Data

Dawson, Michael, 1971 –
     The mountie from dime novel to Disney

Includes index.
ISBN 1-896357-16-4

1. Royal Canadian Mounted Police — Public Relations — History.
2. Royal Canadian Mounted Police — In motion pictures.
3. Royal Canadian Mounted Police — In literature.   I. Title.

HV8157.D38 1998   659.2'93632'0971   C98-930683-6

Cover and text design by Gordon Robertson
Cover collage by David Laurence

Goofy cartoon: Aislin—*The Gazette*; map: RCMP Centennial Souvenir Programme; still from *Rose Marie*: Glenbow Archives, Calgary, Alberta, NA-2947-1; watercolour: RCMP Centennial Calendar, courtesy of the Regina Chamber of Commerce; Estevan gravestone: Glenbow Archives, Calgary, Alberta, NA-2009-2

Printed in Canada by Transcontinental

1 2 3 4 5 6 7 8 9 10   05 04 03 02 01 00 99 98

Between the Lines, 720 Bathurst Street, #404, Toronto, Ontario, M5S 2R4, Canada
(416) 535-9914   www.btl.on.ca

Every saint has a past and every sinner has a future.

— OSCAR WILDE

If the culture of the nation is only so much wool,
then the eyes over which it is pulled must belong to sheep.
And so everything disappears, except the possibility of farming.

— PATRICK WRIGHT,
On Living in an Old Country

Contents

Preface

Like a suspect tracked through the vast reaches of the Arctic tundra, I too have felt the cold, relentless stare of the Mountie. Any attempt to distance myself from this project was constantly subverted by the appearance of a Mountie on television, in department stores, in my mailbox, on my office door, on my Christmas tree, and even in a travel agent's office in Vienna. Sometimes the Mountie was plastic, and sometimes he was acrylic. But always, it seemed, he was there.

To conclude this project and thus escape the Mountie's gaze I came to rely on many people for advice, moral support, money, supplies, and occasionally a place to sleep . . .

This book began as my Master's thesis. As a graduate student in the History Department at Queen's University, I have benefited from the wisdom and support of a great many people. Ian McKay has been an extremely enthusiastic and supportive supervisor. His sound advice on research, secondary literature, and writing (he pleaded with me more than once to write "more like a Mountie and less like Mackenzie King") is much appreciated. His interest in my work and his insights into Canadian history and cultural studies have been crucial to the completion of this project—and to my enjoyment of graduate school. Karen Dubinsky did not, I think, expect to be perusing local bookstores for *Dale of the Mounted* novels when she began teaching graduate students. I consider myself extremely fortunate that I began my Master's degree at Queen's just as she arrived. Her patience with me as a scholar and her support for this project were far beyond what any graduate student could expect. Her graduate course on

Sex and Gender in Historical Perspective opened up an exciting world of historical research and debate for me. Sandra den Otter allowed me a great deal of latitude in creating my third doctoral field and offered enthusiastic support while I attempted to balance the early years of my Ph.D. with the writing of this book. I would also like to thank the members of my thesis examining committee for their helpful comments. Bryan Palmer, in particular, offered constructive and enlightening comments. Many thanks also to my undergraduate professors at the University of British Columbia, especially Bob McDonald and David Breen.

Bill Beahen, Stan Horrall, John Bentham, and the staff at the RCMP Public Affairs Directorate were most co-operative. I thank them for taking the time to answer my many questions. The staff at the Glenbow Archives in Calgary were also very helpful.

Russ Johnston, Jeff Grischow, and many other roommates and travelling companions have heard more than their fair share about this manuscript, and their support is much appreciated. Iain Brown suffered through this project at the thesis stage and deserves special consideration for that dark February evening in 1995 when, exhausted and frustrated by his own work, he joined me in attaining a new level of procrastination by alphabetizing the contents of our freezer.

I am grateful to my colleagues at Queen's for their encouragement, support, and comic relief, as well as for the many Mountie souvenirs that have come my way over the past few years. I would especially like to thank Catherine Adam, Angela Baker, Ross Cameron, Lara Campbell, Elise Chenier, Lorraine Coops, Gord Dueck, Ross Fair, Joy Frith, Catherine Gidney, Alan Gordon, Jeff Grischow, Martina Hardwick, Helen Harrison, Doug Hessler, Paul Jackson, Russell Johnston, Richard Kicksee, Dan Malleck, Alan MacEachern, Todd Mc-Callum, Glenn McKnight, Roger Neufeld, Dave Plaxton, Andrew Sackett, and Robbin Tourangeau, and Elsie Watts.

Roger Neufeld generously shared with me some of his research notes on the *Manitoba Daily Free Press*. Thanks also to the History Department staff (past and present) that helped make the department an enjoyable place to be:

Yvonne Place, Judy Vanhooser, Cindy Fehr, Norma St. John, Debbie Stirton-Massey, and Cindy Butts.

Many other people have given me help and support along the way: Chris Gittings, A.B. McCullough, Mimi Martin, Len Kuffert, Sara Posen, Gary David, and Scott Chamberlain. For "on the road" accommodation I would like to thank Willy and Alison Lyon, Dave Seglins and Bay Ryley, Vic Huard and Kathy Sutherland, and Bob and Ann Louise Plaxton. Back home in British Columbia, Jeff and Joanne Triggs and Scott and Jodi Phillips sent along primary sources as well as their encouragement. Thanks also to the Rawlings clan for books, support, and parsnips.

I am grateful to Bill Baker at the University of Lethbridge for a useful critique of the manuscript in its thesis form and for his encouragement over the past few years. Persse McGarrigle, most recently of University College, Limerick, also provided unwavering support.

Many thanks also to the folks at BTL. Jamie Swift showed unwavering patience in a rookie author and contributed ideas for revisions. Paul Eprile and Marg Anne Morrison were encouraging, while both Paul and David Peerla offered useful suggestions on how to improve the thesis version of the manuscript. Robert Clarke dazzled me with his editorial abilities. Writers Reserve Grants from the Ontario Arts Council were invaluable in allowing me to complete the manuscript.

B.C. and federal student loans made my Masters degree possible. Funding from the School of Graduate Studies at Queen's along with Teaching Assistant assignments from the History Department were also significant and much appreciated sources of financial support. Conference Travel Grants from the School of Graduate Studies also allowed me to present earlier versions of chapter 2 at the 1995 Imperial Canada Conference hosted by the Canadian Studies Department at the University of Edinburgh and the 1996 Canadian Historical Association conference in St. Catharines, Ontario.

An earlier version of chapter 2 appeared as " 'That Nice Red Coat Goes to My Head like Champagne': Gender, Antimodernism and the Mountie Image, 1880—1960," in *Journal of Canadian Studies* 32,3 (Fall 1997).

Catherine Gidney has been a tower of strength throughout this project. Her support, advice, and criticism (of the book!) are very much appreciated. And, finally, I would like to thank my parents for their love and support. This book is for them.

It is customary at this point for the author of a book, having thanked many people, to accept full responsibility for the errors, omissions, and opinions within it. I am quite willing to honour this custom. All I ask is that those readers who maintain that the reading or "decoding" of a text is simply another "encoding" or the production of an entirely new text accept at least half of the blame.

Michael Dawson
Kingston, Ontario
April, 1998

The Mountie

from **Dime Novel**

to **Disney**

Introduction:
Of Mice, Mounties, and Historical Magic

> How do you separate the idea of a Canadian writer and a Canadian
> publisher wanting to do a children's book about the history of this
> force we all admire so much and which we feel proprietary about . . .
> how do you separate that—which seems to be legitimate—from some
> company in . . . I'll just say Hong Kong without meaning anything . . .
> making stupid little dolls and getting rich on the backs of our image?
>
> – Peter Gzowski, *Morningside*, Sept. 4, 1995

In June 1995 my underwear became the subject of a national debate. In newspapers, coffee shops, even on Parliament Hill, heated exchanges were erupting across the country. I felt besieged by questions. Some seemed quite straightforward. Were these boxer shorts legal? Where were they manufactured? Were they licensed? Other critics, however, demanded deeper contemplation. What vision did my underwear offer of the country's future? What did they say about Canada's national soul?

I own a pair of "Mountie" underwear. I didn't buy them. Like most of the Mountie souvenirs that adorn my office wall, they were a gift. They were designed by the Montreal artist Marc Tetro, whose art appears on coffee mugs, T-shirts, bookmarks, and a variety of other souvenirs. These souvenirs, straightfaced news reporters informed the Canadian public in summer 1995, were soon to be policed by an internationally known organization with

The timeless charge of the majestic Musical Ride. (RCMP Centennial Calendar. Reprinted with the permission of the Regina Chamber of Commerce.)

more economic clout than many sovereign nations. Disney now "owned" the Mountie.

But it wasn't just *the* Mountie that Disney now "owned," many Canadians lamented. It was *our* Mountie, and over the next few months Canadians eagerly expressed their opinions. Some thought the deal was a sell-out; others thought it was long overdue. Several CBC commentators and representatives of the Council of Canadians lamented the selling of a national icon to a U.S. firm and what was seemingly an attempt to cut out Canadian businesses from the profits.[1] Michael Valpy, a *Globe and Mail* columnist, expressed his concern that a national police force legally controlled its own image and questioned the sanity of welcoming aboard what he termed two of the country's "most unreconstructed, loose-cannonball capitalists, Bill Pratt and Bill Mulholland," to co-ordinate the deal as members of the Mounted Police Foundation. Alan Fotheringham in *Maclean's* magazine suggested that insufficient public outrage about the deal was a sign of Canadians' apathy in the 1990s.[2] About two years after the deal, former Alberta premier Peter Lougheed—a staunch supporter of free trade—lambasted the Disney deal while decrying the "Americanization" of Canada.[3]

Conversely, supporters of the deal championed the Force against "shoddy, two-bit, third-rate souvenirs that flood our country from [other] nations."[4] They also supported the deal as a money-saving measure for the cash-strapped federal government.[5] Others celebrated the supposed "family-values" orientation of Disney and the effect this might have on the image of the Force itself. Syndicated columnist William Gold adopted this position:

> You can be very sure that the Mounties reporting to Superintendent Disney will not be publicly portrayed as burning down barns in Quebec. No, the people who today so jealously guard Walt's legacy will leave that type of caper to the originals.
>
> The images will not imitate life down such byways as a once-upon-a-time chapter in a misguided fight against Quebec separatism. There will be happier endings provided free of charge.

Indeed, if we leave everything to the Disney people, they'll soon wrap up the Case of the Air India Bombing and maintain forever pure the force's reputation for always getting its man.[6]

Gold's opinion was shared by the editors of Fredericton's *Gleaner*: "Without question Disney symbolizes family and quality. Those are the qualities that the RCMP were looking for to ensure their reputation for professionalism and proper conduct is not sullied by cheap products."[7]

Yet those opposed to the deal maintained that it was a national disgrace for a symbol of Canadian nationhood to be auctioned off to a U.S.-based multinational corporation. The Mountie, they argued, was a part of our heritage. It was part of who we were as Canadians. For the most part even supporters of the Disney deal agreed with this point. Their argument hinged on the notion that because the Mountie was *ours*, Canadians had to do their best to protect it from misrepresentation and embarrassment. If the best way to do this was to call in a major U.S.-based multinational entertainment conglomerate, then so be it.

The Mountie, of course, was never just *ours*. Since the inception of the North-West Mounted Police in 1873, the image of the Force has been used by Canadians and non-Canadians alike. Mountie novels, especially prominent from the 1880s until the 1920s, were written by American, British, and Canadian authors. Hollywood dominated the Mountie movie industry from the 1930s to the 1950s. Throughout the twentieth century U.S. as well as Canadian companies enlisted the Mountie image for commercial purposes. Later, in an attempt to boost Canada's balance of payments in tourism and other industries during the 1970s and 1980s, the federal government got into the act and embarked upon a promotional program that saw Mounties escorting Canadian officials throughout the world. So why this feeling, in the summer of 1995, that the Mountie was somehow "ours"?

The image of the Mountie has a history as long as the Force itself, and questions about RCMP tradition clearly touch a nerve. Public outcries greeted attempts in 1931 to drop "Mounted" from the name of the Force as well as an attempt in the early 1970s to replace "Royal Canadian Mounted Police" with the more bilingually friendly "Police Canada." In the early 1990s the wearing of turbans in the Force ignited a major controversy when Constable Baltej Dhillon, a Sikh in British Columbia, was granted permission to wear one while on duty. Debate over this break with the "traditional" uniform of the Force appeared in newspapers across the country as well as in Parliament and was even the occasion for a book.[8]

The Disney debate made one thing clear: even in the 1990s, many people considered the Mountie to be an important national symbol. The steel-chinned, scarlet-clad horseman was worth writing about in newspaper columns and discussing on television because he supposedly said something about who Canadians were. Yet what it is he actually says about us is not discernible from the Disney debate itself. The debate about the Disney deal has, in fact, obscured many important aspects of the Mountie image. Portrayed as a battle between Canadian and American business interests for control of the image of Canada's national police force, the history of this image has been over-looked—and with it the lessons it holds for students of English-Canadian nationalism and political culture. In short, the debate centred upon who owned the symbol, rather than upon its meaning; and despite all of the rhetoric from both sides of the debate about the importance of defending "tradition," the symbol they were arguing about was very much a product of the early 1970s. This "treasured symbol" of Canada's heritage was, in many ways, not even a quarter of a century old. The Mountie, like national symbols generally, has been as created, edited, and revised as anything Walt Disney could have come up with.

(RCMP Centennial Calendar. Reprinted with the permission of the Regina Chamber of Commerce.)

A Battle For The Past: The Contested Terrain of RCMP History

History is useful. I am convinced of this. It is harder, at times, to convince others. Several years ago, when I worked as a bank teller during the summer, customers frequently asked me what I was studying in school. "History," I answered. Sometimes they nodded approvingly. Often they greeted my response with something like, "History? That's not very useful." Or, more pointedly, "What kind of a job are you going to get with a history degree?" That is a good question, but in actual fact, in our everyday lives most if not all of us do *use* history; and, what's more, we often employ the past to further our own ends.

In his 1961 polemic on the historical craft, E.H. Carr offered the intriguing scenario of Mr. Jones and the unfortunate Mr. Robinson—a scenario that, had it occurred in their jurisdiction, the RCMP would certainly have been called upon to investigate: "Jones, returning from a party at which he has consumed more than his usual ration of alcohol, in a car whose brakes turn out to have been defective, at a blind corner where visibility is notoriously poor, knocks down and kills Robinson, who was crossing the road to buy cigarettes at the shop on the corner."9

Carr employed this anecdote as part of an all-out assault on the notion of "chance" in history, but the scenario he created is one in which the *usefulness* of history is clearly evident. It is quite easy to imagine a court case resulting from Robinson's mishap. That court case would very much be a battle for the past, with each lawyer attempting to have her or his version of events accepted as the truth. What, for example, was the cause of Robinson's death? Was it the faulty brakes? Mr. Jones's intoxicated state? Incompetent city planners? We might even blame Mr. Robinson's nicotine dependency, or the cigarette manufacturers for creating the craving that convinced Robinson to cross the road to get to the store.

What is true of the accident scene and the courtroom is just as true of the nation. A convincing argument about the nation's past is a weighty ally in soliciting support for a particular vision of the future. Not surprisingly, then, supporters of various ideologies and policies are often engaged in battles for the past. Frequently these battles concern a nation's long-standing institutions.

In Canada issues such as free trade and distinct society boast highly visible opposing sides clamouring to offer their particular view of the past—a view they offer as evidence of the lucidity of their position. Thus, battles rage on about the meaning of the Constitution. Battles rage as well over Aboriginal treaty rights, the role and shape of public education, and many other issues. Yet, surprisingly, no major public battle rages over the history of the Royal Canadian Mounted Police, an institution called upon continually by the federal government to implement (sometimes very unpopular) governmental polices and legal decisions.

In my research on the history of the Force, I have consistently come across two very different versions of the RCMP's past. These two versions indicate clearly that despite the apparent lack of public debate, somewhere behind a veil of silence the battle for the RCMP's—and the country's—past goes on. The competing versions of RCMP history demonstrate how the Force's accomplishments, setbacks, and duties have been drawn upon to substantiate ideological positions on issues as varied as nationalism, immigration, sexuality, and Aboriginal rights. The RCMP's past has proved to be a very *useful* one indeed.

A Classic Story of the Mounties

The classic version of RCMP history was most pronounced in the first half of this century. It goes something like this:

The Royal Canadian Mounted Police played an important role in the emergence of Canada as a prosperous and united nation. Introduced to the world by Prime Minister John A. Macdonald in 1873 as the North-West Mounted Police, this group of men ensured that the "Peace, Order, and good Government" detailed in the British North America Act by the Fathers of Confederation would continue to prevail.

In the 1870s, shortly after Confederation, Canada's newly acquired Northwest Territories were on the verge of anarchy. The activities of American whiskey smugglers had converged with what an RCMP report referred to as "a certain amount of tribal warfare" on the part of the Indian population.[10] The future of the region was cast into doubt: "The whisky robbed the savage Plains Indians of all reason. They burned farmhouses and murdered settlers. Ranchers were found scalped, with barbed arrows in their backs. White women were dragged off naked, to be the slaves and mates of Indian warriors. Children disappeared. The torture stake was put to horrible use."[11] In the face of such wanton Indian violence, aware of the bloody and expensive wars in the American West, and anxious to safeguard the future of the West as an area of settlement, the Canadian government took decisive action.

In 1873, in response to this growing concern about law and order on Canada's recently acquired plains, and specifically in response to the massacre of Canadian Indians by American whiskey traders in the Cypress Hills, the federal government created the North-West Mounted Police. In the summer of 1874 the Mounted Police, less than three hundred strong, began the long trek westward on horseback from Fort Dufferin, Manitoba, to the foothills of present-day Alberta. Their mission: to establish forts from which the land was to be tamed. As historian P. B. Waite put it: "Few yet knew the magnitude of the task that lay ahead of the Mounted Police. . . . The far west, the vast reaches of grassland in southern Alberta (it had no name yet), was in American hands. . . . Southern Alberta and Saskatchewan were unofficially the provinces of American traders from Fort Benton."[12]

During this "March West" the men overcame tremendous hardships. Relief from cruel drought came only in the form of harsh thunderstorms. Mosquitoes and locusts filled the air. The heat combined with the pace of the Great March to debilitate both man and animal. Nonetheless, the Mounties, with "the high standard and strict discipline of a crack regiment," quickly "chased out the unscrupulous whiskey traders who had crept in from south of the border and were demoralizing the Indians." Soon "the chiefs were properly grateful for their new peace and security."[13]

The tiny Force supervised Canada's vast western lands. Determinedly pursuing a strategy of calm negotiation, in which force was always seen as a last resort, these men purged the plains of American whiskey traders and both pacified and protected the Indian communities. Indeed, "The Force so impressed the Indians that a series of Treaties was concluded, and the Government was enabled to assume control of the aboriginal inhabitants of the country."[14] This "control" came just in time, for during the 1870s the once-abundant plains buffalo disappeared: "Had there been no strong and just authority in the land, the Indians would have been driven by starvation to warfare against the whites."[15] The Reserve System, policed by the RCMP, saved both Indians and whites from this sad fate. The real achievement was that "these nation-building Police set their seal to the great treaties which provided for the future of the Indian tribes and at the same time extinguished the title of the tribes in order to open up a new empire for higher civilization."[16]

With one crisis averted, the Force had little time to rest on its laurels. Pursuing the objective of providing for "each development in advance," the Force was there to keep the peace when the Canadian Pacific Railway was built, uniting the new province of British Columbia with the rest of the country. In doing so the Force found itself face to face with labourers under contract to build the CPR, "many of them rough men, trained elsewhere to dislike and fear the Indians." Yet order prevailed.

Maintaining order meant that some brave men paid with their lives:

> When Sergeant Charles Colebrook of the Duck Lake detachment rode out to arrest the dangerous Cree outlaw Almighty Voice, the Mountie advanced with one hand raised in the sign of peace. His pistol was in its leather holster. He was not frightened by the bad reputation of Almighty Voice. At short range Almighty Voice shot him through the throat. The Sergeant fell dead.[17]

For almost two years the Force pursued Almighty Voice, who, before he was finally apprehended in 1897, ambushed and killed two more Mounties. The Force faced similarly unruly characters during the Yukon Gold Rush, and despite the pressures of development on the Canadian frontier—and with the exception of the 1885 Riel Rebellion—once again "perfect order . . . prevailed."[18]

Assistance to settlers was another ingredient of this "perfect order." Faced with the challenges involved in setting up homesteads on the prairies, settlers of many descriptions sought the help of the Mountie: "To his role of policeman were added those of doctor, counsellor and friend to those seeking homes in the new land." [19] The last great test for the Force on the prairies came in 1919, when "the West was seething with labor troubles, and radical extremists, hoping for the support of the demobilized troops and relying upon a disaffected foreign element in the population, were openly preaching the doctrines that had overthrown the government in Russia and, as a means to effect a similar revolution in Canada, were advocating the declaration of general strikes." [20]

On June 21, 1919, the mettle of the Force was put to the test. In a 1940 book approved by the commissioner of the Force, R.C. Fetherstonhaugh provided a detailed account of the critical clash between the Force and labour in Winnipeg. On that fateful day, "Out from the Police barracks, with instructions to prevent the [workers'] parade and restore order with the use of as little force in the process as possible, trotted fifty-four mounted men under Inspectors Proby and Mead, followed by thirty-six men in motor trucks under the command of Sergeant-Major Griffin." As the police came into view, "The strikers roared defiance, and almost at once a barrage of bricks, bottles, and heavy stones beat upon the Police from all sides." During this ambush, Inspector Proby was "struck from behind . . . and owed his life to Corporal Newnham who felled a foreigner in the act of aiming at the disabled officer with a revolver. Corporal Wynne and Constable McQueen also fell, were beaten, and were dragged by rescuers to safety in nearby shops." Constable McQueen, "by a strange coincidence," was taken "into the undertaking parlor where, silent and majestic in death, lay the body of that old stalwart of the Force, Major-General Samuel B. Steele." Here was a rich historical symbol of the great tradition of the RCMP, passed on from father to son:

> Perhaps the disciplined spirit of the lion-hearted old veteran, who lay so peacefully beneath the folds of a Union Jack, was with the Mounted that day. For the discipline of the Police was as superb as at any time of crisis in the Force's history. Time and time again, as brickbats beat upon them, as shots cracked from revolvers hidden among the crowd, and as they suffered in the hand-to-hand battles that raged all around, [Inspector] Proby might

(RCMP Centennial Calendar. Reprinted with the permission of the Regina Chamber of Commerce.)

justifiably have ordered his men to fire. But his orders were to shoot only as a last resort and, until three of his men went down in a charge and the murderous crowd closed in to effect the kill, he did not consider that shooting was essential.

Eventually the police had no choice but to open fire. But even then, Proby "gave the order to fire at the strikers' legs only when a warning volley into the air had proved ineffective." Once the police took action, the battle was soon over:

Savage as the mob had seemed while battering at—and to some extent being battered by—the vastly outnumbered men in red, the rioters had no stomach for a fight in which the odds were not overwhelmingly on their side. So the shouting and tumult died down, the rioters slowly dispersed, and the battle-scarred Police, too weary as yet to realize the magnitude of the work they had accomplished, were left as victors on the stricken field.

Within days the strike was called off and sympathetic strikes throughout the West were cancelled.[21] The Bolshevik threat to peace, order, and good government had receded, and order prevailed once again.

While the RCMP is most famous for its accomplishments in the Canadian West, it has also frequently defended Canada against foreign moral and political dangers. The Force sent a contingent to South Africa during the Boer War and took an active part in both world wars, and it was also intimately involved in preventing terrorist activities by foreign elements on Canadian soil. When Igor Gouzenko defected to Canada in 1945 with evidence of Soviet spy operations, the Mounties were there to protect Canadian sovereignty: "The men assigned to the Gouzenko case were members of the Security and Intelligence Branch of the RCMP, a specially trained group of men whose members have increased from a mere handful . . . to a . . . strength of several hundreds."[22]

The legendary Superintendent Samuel B. Steele poses 110 years before his appearance in a televised Heritage Minute. (Glenbow Archives, Calgary, Alberta, NA-1506-1)

In 1940-42 the RCMP schooner *St. Roch* "became the first ship to navigate the hazardous Northwest Passage from West to East and, on completion of the return journey [in 1944], the first to traverse the Passage in both directions." [23] Canadian sovereignty in the North was thus ensured.

An Unofficial Story of the RCMP

A second version of RCMP history has also been in circulation for many decades: a dissenting, left-wing story of the RCMP. That retelling goes something like this:

The myth of the heroic Mountie conceals the actual history of a Force that repressed Native peoples, spied on and crushed working-class organizations, discriminated against women, and persecuted homosexuals. The Force has been little more than an instrument of coercion, siding with elites against marginalized Canadians. Often acting in conjunction with the federal government, but occasionally acting alone, the Force has been more concerned with its own departmental aggrandizement than with true public service. Working within a police force with a strong military tradition, the Security Service branch has spied upon law-abiding Canadians, while regular members of the Force have often crushed peaceful protests. Throughout its history, the Force has been the federal government's instrument of choice for controlling, eliminating, and even killing its opposition.[24]

In 1874 the Force worked quickly to carry out its primary duty: to clear the Plains Indians out of the way, making room for "white" settlement. After providing an intimidating presence during unequal treaty negotiations, these "agents of civilization" were instrumental in setting up reserves and enforcing a "pass system," which prohibited Indians from leaving their reserves without written permission from the local Indian Agent. Instigated in 1885 in response to the Northwest Rebellion, the "pass system" was perpetrated—somewhat ineffectually—until 1904, despite the Force's awareness that "the system rested

Amicable Advances!

on no legal foundation." Pressured by government officials, the Force set aside its concern that "the lack of a legal basis in this case undermined the validity of all NWMP operations," and "on their daily patrols" officers "sent back any people found off the reserves without passes." [25] In short, the Force regulated the Canadian version of Apartheid.

Having cleared the way for settlement, the Force was "soon defending the interests of the corporate friends of the government . . . particularly the CPR, against Indians, settlers and their own employees." According to Lorne and Caroline Brown, "In any dispute between the CPR and the Indians or the CPR and its own employees, the police automatically sided with the corporation and often made no attempt to hide the fact." [26] The Mounties' response to the Winnipeg General Strike was of a piece with this repressive tradition. Confronting a peaceful parade organized by returning war veterans but banned by the mayor:

About 50 Mounted Police swinging baseball bats rode through the crowd twice. When two of their riders were unhorsed, they drew their revolvers and fired volleys into the crowd. Mike Sokolowiski, who appears to have been only a spectator, was killed instantly of a bullet through his heart, and Steve Schezerbanower was fatally wounded. Dozens more in the crowd were wounded. Mounties and specials wielding clubs then cleared the streets.[27]

Brutal incidents like this were not uncommon. The RCMP was used to break strikes and prevent rallies throughout Canada. One of the bloodiest of these occurred in 1931 in Estevan, Saskatchewan. Members of the Force shot three men dead while breaking up yet another workers' parade. One man was shot through the heart as he attempted to smash a fire engine with an axe.[28] Faced with owning up to an incident in which "non-participants had been struck by flying bullets," the RCMP and local authorities conspired to alter civic documents in order to shift as much blame as possible onto the miners.[29]

The RCMP's concern with the "Red" threat was not confined to workers. The Force closely monitored university students. It often placed left-leaning student groups under surveillance, and occasionally directed its efforts at actively undermining the groups' activities.[30] In a 1941 article, "Tools for Treachery," Commissioner S.T. Wood made clear his position on the possibility of subversion:

Many may be surprised to hear that it is not the Nazi nor the Fascist but the radical who constitutes our most troublesome problem. Whereas the enemy alien is usually recognizable and easily rendered innocuous by clear-cut laws applicable to his case, your "Red" has the protection of citizenship, his foreign master is not officially an enemy and, unless he blunders into the open and provides proof of his guilt, he is much more difficult to suppress. Since Communism was outlawed, most of his work is carried on under cover of other organizations and associations pretending to be, or in reality, loyal to the Constitution. It is important to remember this for the

reason that this type of fifth column activity is least understood by our Canadian people, and yet is doing most harm at the present time.[31]

That Commissioner Wood could make this statement in the midst of the Second World War suggests just how dedicated the Force has been in persecuting Canada's left-leaning citizenry.

During the Second World War the Force was particularly concerned with securing sweeping coercive powers to prevent enemy activities on Canadian soil, namely the Defence of Canada Regulations. Negotiations pitted the Department of National Defence [DND] and the RCMP against "liberal elements hoping to preserve as much individual freedom as possible."[32] The extent to which these two organizations were successful in guiding government policy is illustrated by the justice department's appeal to no less a figure than Ernest Lapointe in its attempt to oppose "a regulation so violently repugnant to the fundamental, constitutional rights of a British Subject."[33]

The appetite for repression continued after the war. This time homosexuals were a favoured target. The DND and the RCMP addressed the threat of homosexual civil servants, and their perceived vulnerability to Soviet blackmailing, with an unsettling level of enthusiasm. This position "derived in large measure from each organization's internal policy of automatically discharging all discovered homosexuals."[34] Again, the policy debate "was characterized by liberal-versus-hardliner disagreement,"[35] with the Force taking the hard line of repression against more tolerant voices.

Having gained support for its initiatives, the Force formed a separate unit to deal with the security threat posed by homosexual Canadians. By the 1960s, of the nine thousand RCMP files concerning homosexuality, only one-third concerned government employees. As usual, the Force sought to make use of

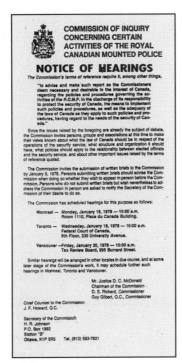

Just over a century later a very different notice appeared in newspapers, soliciting evidence for an investigation into RCMP wrongdoings.

the latest technology in monitoring the population:

In conjunction with this investigation, the federal government sponsored a research project that sought to "detect" homosexuality through the photographic measurement of eye movement of people shown hetero- and homoerotic pictures. . . . Dubbed the "fruit machine" by the Mounties, the project amounted to a four-year effort to enlist science in the cause of state security.[36]

Far from being a proud symbol of Canadian democracy, the Mounties were all too ready to trample on civil rights and share information with U.S. authorities. In fact, "The Mounties were in the habit of giving the FBI information on Canadian political subversives to which even federal cabinet ministers were denied access."[37]

Whenever the Force failed to convince the government to take its view concerning a particular policy, it simply did as it pleased, as was revealed during the 1981 Royal Commission Concerning Activities of the Royal Canadian Mounted Police. With respect to the activities of the RCMP on university campuses, the Commission stated:

We have reached the conclusion on the basis of . . . evidence that the RCMP in the late 1960s embarked, without government approval, on a significant programme to upgrade and improve their contacts with university faculty members. . . . It appears to us that this programme was in conflict with the instructions received by the RCMP in 1961 that no new operations were to be conducted and that only established sources were to be used. It was also in conflict with government policy enunciated by [Prime Minister] Pearson in 1963 that there was no general surveillance of university campuses. In our opinion, [it] was designed to circumvent the policy of the government and it was inaccurate to claim that such procedures complied with government policy.[38]

Given the penchant of most Royal Commissions for euphemism, this was a forceful condemnation indeed.

The Commission paints a similar portrait of the Force's surveillance of the Parti Québécois. The Commission concluded, "The [RCMP] Security Service has acted beyond its mandate by receiving . . . information and retaining and using it." Thus the Commission concluded, "There is therefore evidence that since the 1975 mandate and public announcements about surveillance of legitimate political parties, the Security Service has actively sought information about the P.Q., unrelated to the Security Service mandate." [39]

Overall, revelations of "wire tapping, fake communiqués, breaking and entering and other RCMP misdeeds," including arson and brutality, have done much to undermine "our illusions about an all-wise and benevolent police authority." [40]

Just the Facts . . . but Which Ones?

Telling stories means making choices. Writing a history means selecting a beginning, middle, and an ending as well as selecting "appropriate" evidence to support the story.[41] These two "Stories of the RCMP"—both woven from factual evidence—offer very different versions of the Force's past.[42]

The first version of the RCMP's past was really the dominant history of Canada. It was the inspirational story of how brave young men overcame great hardships to build a great nation. This interpretation of RCMP history played a large role in the emergence of the Mountie image as a sought-after commodity, both in the entertainment industry and in the business world in general.

According to the second version of history, RCMP activities have been marked by incidents of repression and intimidation directed towards Canadians. Often challenging less extreme elements within the government in order to get its way, the Force has carried out and enforced state victimization of minorities and the repression of the left, often using tactics of dubious legality and questionable morality.

Because both of these narratives are more or less "accurate," and their inaccuracy lies in their selectivity rather than outright invention, why did one become the classic, "official" version and the other "unofficial"? Why did one prevail over the other?

The first story gained its dominant position because it was supported and enhanced by popular writers during the first half of the Force's existence. It was buoyed by government publications and firsthand accounts by former Mounties, all of which acted as resources for those wishing to learn (and write) about the Force. The second story, arising chiefly from the perspective of more marginalized members of society, lacked these resources for research and distribution, and so its dissemination remained limited in scope until the 1970s.[43]

A quick tour of a postcard rack or the Canadiana section of a bookstore suggests that even today the Mountie remains a popular national symbol. Given that the Force's history obviously prompts radically divisive opinions, how is it that the RCMP has been able to survive as such a prominent and popular Canadian symbol for well over a century? It is far too simplistic to assume that the Force alone has been responsible for its ascent to the status of a national treasure. While the Force certainly had a role in promoting the positive aspects of its past, it alone could not guarantee itself a positive public image. Besides, as we shall see, the Force has had less control over its image than is often assumed.

Today's vision of the Mounties, as embraced and perpetuated in books, postcards, and even television shows, is very different from the two historical versions I have just outlined. The left-wing critique of the Force is hardly the basis for a national symbol. "Fruit machines," internment camps, and burning barns are not the stuff of national mythologies. Yet the once popular classic story

The trials and tribulations of the Mounties during their Great March West were recorded by artist Henri Julien, who accompanied them on their trek. . . .

of the Mounties, which highlights the taming of savage Indians and untrustworthy immigrants, is nowhere to be seen on bookshelves and postcard racks today. The Force's past has been renovated in the past twenty or thirty years, largely because of the need for the RCMP to maintain its place of prominence in English-Canadian culture—because of the need for English-Canadians to remain comfortable with their country's past.

History-Making and Nationalism

My aim in this book, then, is to examine the history of the Mountie image—and of the police force it represents—in order to see how it has been reinvented

. . . Great marches such as the Chinese Long March, Mussolini's March on Rome, and the Boers' Great Trek in southern Africa (or even unsuccessful marches like the Charge of the Light Brigade) . . .

and reshaped over time. To understand the changing nature of the Mountie image and Canadians' attachment to it, I have found it useful to draw upon three major contributions to the history of nationalism. Interestingly, these studies suggest that Canadians are not alone in inventing and reinventing their national symbols—or indeed their nation.

One body of historical scholarship that has increasingly informed my work is the British writing often termed the "Invention of Tradition" school. This body of research has concentrated on questioning established national rituals and symbols. These historians have shown that such supposedly timeless traditions as the Scottish kilt and British coronation rituals are of quite recent origin. These inventions, Eric Hobsbawm argues, "occur more frequently when a rapid transformation of society weakens or destroys social patterns for which

'old' traditions had been designed."[44] Invented traditions offer the reassuring element of precedent and the assurance that time, and perhaps even history, are on *our* side.

Another useful contribution to the study of nationalism is Benedict Anderson's concept of the "imagined community." In his interpretation of the history of nationalism Anderson observes, "All communities larger than primordial villages of face-to-face contact (and perhaps even these) are imagined."[45] They are "imagined" because there is such a limited capacity for contact between members of these "communities." Anderson suggests that "print capitalism . . . made it possible for rapidly growing numbers of people to think about themselves, and to relate themselves to others in profoundly new ways."[46] He argues, in part, that the advent of the newspaper and the novel provided a common body of knowledge and a common sense of belonging among members of the same territory.

More recently developed media such as radio and television would presumably have similar effects. For example, in Canada two people can grow up living thousands of kilometres apart, yet they can share many common memories and a common outlook on politics, the environment, sports, or other issues. This community exists to a great extent through media such as *The Globe and Mail* or CBC Radio. The recent flurry of praise (accompanied by not a few tears) for longtime CBC radio personality Peter Gzowski attests not simply to his skill as a broadcaster, but also to the large community of listeners who shared the daily experience of his *Morningside* program. Paul Henderson's series-winning goal in the 1972 Canada-Russia hockey showdown is another example of an experience "shared" by millions of Canadians who were nowhere near each other at the time of the event, yet who feel, as those of us too young to "experience" the goal ourselves are constantly reminded, that they have shared an event of national significance.

A third insight into nationalism is represented by the British historian Raphael Samuel, who concentrates on the structure of "national histories." His main targets are the renowned British historian Geoffrey Elton and the curriculum of the British school system. Samuel emphasizes the exclusive nature of many national histories in circulation. Through the use of "a unified subject matter, consecutive narrative, familiar landmarks, well-marked periods and a sequence of cause and effect," historians often produce a tight, orderly story of a nation that speaks only to the experiences of a very limited number of its citizens.[47] Such histories tend to turn out happy stories of peaceful progress that omit many of the conflicts and catastrophes that are just as much a part of national pasts as great discoveries and periods of sustained economic growth. The classic story of the RCMP is a good example of the type of "continuous national history" that Samuel and others oppose.

Invented traditions, mythic symbols, and orderly stories are crucial to the manufacturing of nationalism because, as Benedict Anderson reminds us, nations themselves are invented. In his examination of national memory,

Anderson explains how crises or conflicts that at first seem to stand out as inconsistencies in a nation's inherent cohesion are recalled as "reassuringly fratricidal" conflicts between members of the same nation. Anderson uses the famous "English" example of the Normans meeting the Saxons at the Battle of Hastings in 1066 to illustrate his point:

> English history textbooks offer the diverting spectacle of a great Founding Father whom every schoolchild is taught to call William the Conqueror. The same child is not informed that William spoke no English, indeed could not have done so, since the English language did not exist in his epoch; nor is he or she told "Conqueror of what?" For the only intelligible answer would have to be "Conqueror of the English," which would turn the old Norman predator into a more successful precursor of Napoleon and Hitler. . . . Norman William and Saxon Harold thus meet on the battlefield of Hastings, if not as dancing partners, at least as brothers.[48]

Conflict and bloodshed are thus reinvented as reassuringly fratricidal growing pains, and the English nation begins its slow but steady climb to greatness—a common theme in national histories.

English-Canadian Nationalism

There are, no doubt, many different ways of defining "English-Canada," including ethnic, linguistic, and geographic meanings. Each of these definitions by itself is too neat and tidy for my liking. More useful is the approach suggested by Philip Resnick, in which all of the previously compartmentalized definitions play a part in a working definition of English-Canadian culture. For Resnick this culture is largely the "English-language culture of Canada," to which people of non-Anglo-Saxon origin have contributed and which is concentrated in the "very extensive terrain, essentially outside Quebec and populated by nonaboriginals, that has English speakers as its dominant group."[49] Such a definition does not preclude divisions within English-Canada (for example, divisions based on race, class, gender, or region), nor does it suggest that such a culture is static and unchanging; but it does make clear the existence of, at least to a certain extent, a shared English-Canadian culture. Like many cultures, the most direct expression of this culture comes in the form of nationalism.

Resnick suggests that the "two key elements that have characterized English-Canadian nationalism since Confederation" are a "love-hate relationship with the U.S." and an "identification with a reasonably strong central government."[50] The CBC epitomizes these two elements. Another institution that meets Resnick's two criteria is less obvious, though potentially more divisive: the Mounted Police.

In the mythic Mounted Police there is a *central* authority that tamed the west and in doing so provided the nation with a tradition for decency and paternalism that Canada's neighbour to the south could not match. One story that arose from the Mountie myth was Canada's careful and fair treatment of the Aboriginal peoples, particularly in comparison with the treatment meted out by the law and order forces of the United States. Another was the rugged individualism of the (English) Canadian Mountie and his triumph over the American criminal. The story of Sam Steele's work in the Yukon is probably the best known of this genre. A recent television *Heritage Minute* features Steele staring down an unruly American miner and escorting him out of town. The television series *Due South* (of which more later) offers a more contemporary angle on this theme. In such stories, the American becomes the "other" against which English-Canadian superiority can be confirmed and celebrated. Eric Hobsbawm's observation that "nations do not make states and nationalisms but the other way around" underscores my point.[51] Mythologies, like the one surrounding the Mountie, are instrumental in forming a cohesive bond of shared English-Canadian sentiment—a sentiment essential for English-Canadian nationalism given Canada's proximity to the United States and the necessity of developing some response to an increasingly boisterous Quebec nationalism.

While much of the Canada-Quebec debate has been conducted around the issue of language rights, English-Canadian nationalism has had to rely on a different framework to enclose, and protect, its sense of common purpose. Again, Resnick's observations are helpful here. He compares the struggles of nations to maintain their distinctiveness in the face of other nations which speak the same language: "Much as Austrians or German-speaking Swiss faced with the Germans, Walloons or Quebecois faced with the French, or Argentineans or Mexicans faced with the Spanish, English Canadians must invoke cultural traits, geographical location, or political institutions to make a case for their particularity."[52]

The image of the Mounted Policeman has been one way in which English-Canadian identity and nationalism were articulated and expressed. Because he (and it has historically been a "he") is the bearer of national essence, the Mountie is almost a sacred figure: a critical narrative outlining his limitations, or a break with RCMP tradition, could be seen as an attack on Canada itself.

French-Canadians have not shared English Canada's reverence for the Force. The RCMP, as an agent of the federal government, was involved in too many of the controversial events that brought French-English tensions to a head for the French-Canadian public to embrace the Force as their own. Indeed, the French-Canadian reaction to the Force's exploits suggests that the Québécois view of the RCMP differed greatly from the classic view held in English Canada.

While the Quebec press approved in principle the creation of the Force, coverage was not extensive and the press was quick to bemoan its "weak French-speaking representation."[53] In response to the 1885 Rebellion, the press was at first critical of Riel and the Métis, but when more facts emerged from out west, the tone of the press changed abruptly. Reports stressed the odds against the Métis and criticized the police for provoking the fight at Duck Lake as well as for losing to the vastly outnumbered Métis. One newspaper accused the Force of spreading hatred and dishonour, while another suggested that the Mounties were "indulging in the traffic of Indian women."[54] With Riel appropriated as a martyr to the French-Canadian nationalist cause, memories of the

Rebellion hindered acceptance of the Force in the eyes of the French-Canadian public.

The Quebec press was more supportive of the Force during the Winnipeg General Strike. The "spectre of Bolshevism could be easily detected in every editorial, despatch or release" at the time. Yet complaints were also voiced concerning the reorganization of the Force in 1919 and 1920. Commenting on a parliamentary debate about the merger of the RNWMP and the Dominion Police, an editorial in *Le Droit* observed:

> If one is to believe the Government and the Western M.P.s, the immigrants established in the West are allegedly revolutionaries and undesirable citizens because of whom a close to two thousand policemen force should be maintained. I suspect that these immigrants' crime is not wanting to become anglicized and refusing to send their children to public schools. In that case millions of policemen would not be sufficient to convert these immigrants.[55]

Viewed with suspicion by those promoting provincial autonomy, the Force's image was further tarnished in Quebec as a result of its role in enforcing conscription during the Second World War.[56]

If the day-to-day activities of the Force failed to garner a ringing endorsement from the Quebec media, the Force's role in French-Canadian literature fared little better. Researching this question in 1971, Gilles Langelier was unable to find any French-Canadian novels in which a Mountie was the hero. When the Mounties appeared at all, they came in mainly as "part of the setting in North-West adventure novels."[57] While French-Canadian literature largely ignored the Force, the Mountie was the central character in many English-language stories. The frequency with which French-Canadians were assigned the role of villains in English-language novels and films focusing on the Mounties made the genre's popularity among Francophones highly unlikely.

The Mountie, then, is central to the English-Canadian identity, even though writers, movie producers, and business executives from outside Canada have played a large role in creating and sustaining the mythic Mountie. While imagined communities emerge through shared experience and a shared body of knowledge, such communities—particularly in the twentieth century—are not isolated from other cultures. After all, our identities as individuals are shaped as much by those we meet as by ourselves. Canada, throughout the era of the Force's existence, has been strongly influenced by the United States, and so too has English-Canadian nationalism, which is very much a product of such interaction. As historian Alan Smith argues, "The dialectic between national and continental forces is a principal structuring element in the country's history."[58]

Resnick's more recent work suggests that the Canadian attitude towards the United States has become an increasingly important component of English-Canadian national sentiment. From the Second World War on, Resnick observes, "The dilemma of English-Canadian identity had clearly become that of differentiating itself from the United States."[59] This sentiment developed during the particularly tumultuous decade of the 1960s:

> The wave of English-Canadian nationalism that hit during that period—the critique of American policy in Vietnam, of American domination over the Canadian economy, trade union movement, magazines, publishing, university curricula, and much besides—struck a responsive chord. And it coincided with a number of changes internally—the deepening of the welfare state, the extension of the postsecondary education system, the celebration of Canada's centennial and Expo 67, the emergence of a new generation of English-Canadian novelists and playwrights, artists and filmmakers less interested in making it in the United States than in addressing the Canadian experience on its own terms.[60]

Not surprisingly, during that same era English-Canadian nationalism and the image of the RCMP underwent a metamorphosis. English-Canadians have long drawn upon the Force's experiences to tell a story about themselves—about what it means to be Canadian. Yet as the makeup of English Canada (and Canada as a whole) has changed over time, so too has the story.

Stories about the past are crucial to the modern phenomenon called *nationalism*. As nations change, so does their history. Our past, like our government buildings and our highways, is often in need of renovation. A clear example of this was the renovation of the Mountie's image in the 1960s and 1970s. Faced with growing criticism of RCMP exploits in a world increasingly prone to questioning authority, what I describe as the classic Mountie myth would no longer suffice. The Canada of the 1960s and 1970s possessed radically different demographic and social characteristics than did the Canada of the first half of the century. By the early 1960s, one Canadian in four was of neither British nor French origin, and the country was abandoning such British symbols as the Red Ensign.[61] Political concerns dictated that the story of the Force be renovated to bring it up to date.

Yet a complete break from the classic story of the Force was hardly desirable or even possible. The result was a new, progressive, and inclusive story of Canadian nation-building with the Force as the central protagonist. Seeking to establish the RCMP in the eyes of Canadians as a technically modern and socially progressive police force, and simultaneously to preserve its celebrated past, the Force and its supporters wove a new narrative combining these new and old elements. The year 1973, marking the one-hundredth anniversary of the Force, offered the perfect opportunity to showcase this "new and improved" history. In doing so, contributors mined the past for a usable story—a history that would reclaim the glory of RCMP accomplishments while adapting this tale of glory for a contemporary audience.

Having undergone this metamorphosis, the mythic Mountie was well prepared for his—or in a few cases, her—present duties in the postmodern global marketplace—alongside Pocahontas, Hercules, and other mythic heroes purged of their original pasts.

2

Fiction and Film: The Mountie as Antimodern Crusader, 1880–1960

A letter came to a citizen the other day with the address: Mr. _____, Winnipeg, Manitoba, Indian Territory, where the Mounted Police are.

– *Manitoba Daily Free Press*, Feb. 22, 1879

In the annual report of the Mounted Police, published not long ago, underneath all the heavy restraint of official language, there is enough romance for a library of novels.

– Vincent Massey, "Good Neighbourhood," in *Good Neighbourhood and Other Addresses in the United States*, 1930

This 1899 wash drawing by Arthur Heming offers a classic image of a Mountie firmly controlling his rearing horse. For most of the twentieth century the Force's popular image was remarkably consistent. By the 1960s, however, alternative images of the Force were rearing *their* heads. The Force's attempts to rein in these alternative histories led to the 1973 Centennial celebrations, and then to the infamous Disney deal. (Glenbow Archives, Calgary, Alberta, NA-180-1)

National heroes are made, not born, and the mythology surrounding the Mountie is no exception. In 1873 the North-West Mounted Police was formed and sent forth to prepare Canada's newly acquired Northwest Territories for resettlement. Reaction to the Force's early efforts at preparing the territory for its role in Sir John A. Macdonald's vision of an industrialized and modern Canada was mixed. Articles and letters in the *Manitoba Daily Free Press* in the 1880s and 1890s, for example, suggest that on the whole the public's attitude towards the new police force was ambivalent at best. Readers of the *Free Press* could hardly have envisioned a day when Canadians in general would come to see the Mountie as a fitting (and flattering) symbol of their country.

FICTION

AND FILM:

THE MOUNTIE

AS ANTIMODERN

CRUSADER,

1880-1960

32

A newspaper report in 1886 told of a constable stealing a fellow officer's watch and fleeing to the United States. One article, in June 1886, detailed the exploits of a Mountie who was soon to be arrested for stealing government property. Several others that same year focused on members of the NWMP deserting the Force. One report of desertions went so far as to suggest, "Judging by the reports of desertions from the NWMP, the ranks must be getting pretty well thinned." Another article that year commented: "Deserters are quite common in the NWMP just now. The redcoats are skipping across the line in good shape. Uncle Sam is a very attractive personage."[1] Mounties fleeing to the United States hardly formed the basis for a budding national symbol.

Hints of growing dissatisfaction within the Force meant that, at times, the Force's administration came under fire. In one case an editorial blamed the "family compact" between NWMP Commissioner L.W. Herchmer and Northwest Territories Lieutenant Governor Edgar Dewdney for "the greatest dissatisfaction [that] exists in the ranks of the Mounted Police." The writer complained that the "efficiency of the force is being daily impaired by a system of tyranny and incompetence."[2] Earlier reports suggested that dissatisfaction and desertions resulted from a lack of supplies and from overwork.[3] One interview with a Sergeant Major Francis, "late of the Mounted Police," quoted the former officer as saying that the men were "very badly" clothed and the forts "badly built." Francis went on to complain that these poorly fed men were far too busy with non-military duties. He noted, "Any man can buy an [Indian] woman for a horse at any time."[4] Again, this was hardly the stuff that legends are made of.

The *Free Press* of the time was very much a mouthpiece of the Liberal Party, and as such not inclined to give the NWMP, a creation of a Conservative government, the benefit of the doubt when rumours of inefficiencies or illegalities arose. Malcolm Cameron, a Liberal Member of Parliament, implicated members of the Force in his charge that government officials in the West were committing adultery and worse with young Indian women. Defenders of the Force blamed the immorality of the Indian women for such problems, and, as Sarah Carter observes, "Any critical reflections upon the behavior of early government officials and the police in Western Canada did not survive beyond the controversy of the 1880s."[5]

For a time, then, inefficiency, irresolution, and impropriety seemed as much a part of the image of the Force as fairness, perseverance, and self-control. Still, the Force did have its defenders. Some reports celebrated its success in controlling the whiskey trade.[6] One praised the Mounties' ability to deal efficiently with the rough and tough "desperados" who inhabited the west.[7] An 1880 article in the *Free Press* paid tribute to the "gentlemanly" conduct of the Force, which it described as being made up of "young men of a very good class."[8] In due course these more positive reports began to hold sway, and a body of literature soon emerged to overshadow the Force's mediocre beginnings and the rather mixed reactions to the Force's early work. While the critical view of the Force never disappeared entirely, a romanticized, or idealized, view of the Mountie would take over and dominate public opinion with little difficulty until at least the middle of the twentieth century.

Keith Walden, who has made by far the greatest contribution to the study of the Mountie myth, focuses his explanation on the vast changes that took place in Western society at the turn of the century: "As comprehensive authority disappeared, western society longed that some universal standards of truth and morality could be found. It was this yearning, more than anything else, that produced the symbol of the Mounted Policeman."[9] Modernization, urbanization, secularization, and other transformations combined to make the late nineteenth and early twentieth centuries a time of great apprehension.[10] Many of the stories concerning the Mounted Policeman contained themes that directly or indirectly responded to these changes: the mythic Mountie became, then, part of a general response to modernity.

The Mountie was chosen to be the starring protagonist in hundreds of novels written mainly between 1880 and 1920; and historical realities—and the debates that had appeared in newspapers like the *Manitoba Daily Free Press*—were quickly discarded in favour of a romantic hero and a happy ending. For the authors, the Mountie became a popular character because, like most mythical figures, he was politically useful. The popular novelists were lamenting the passing of Victorian manliness and traditional hierarchies in the face of modernity, and the Mountie became a staple figure in their efforts. A police force brought into existence in 1873 to usher in modernity on the Prairies thus quickly had its image appropriated by authors uneasy with all that modernity promised.

The real trials and tribulations of a Force burdened with the task of pacify-ing the Prairies in order to help make Canada a successful modern industrial nation were not central to the novels that reshaped the image of the Force. Instead what emerged were heroic stories of individual accomplishment eagerly consumed by an audience uneasy with the rapid social, economic, and cultural changes they saw around them. Middle-class concerns with modernity perme-ated the stories. The Mountie addressed threats to Victorian hierarchies and sought, in his fictional duties, to combat threats to Anglo-Saxon middle-class hegemony, threats including immigrants and French Canadians, while encour-aging the reader to defer to a social order that encouraged female passivity and rigid class distinctions.

In many stories the Mountie did not follow the letter of the law but used his common sense and compassion to do the "right" thing. Significantly, the Moun-tie's knowledge and authority were kept exclusively male during an era of in-creased female emancipation. In the fiction, the very way that new Mounties were welcomed into the fraternity of power demonstrates this tension. Walden makes note of the apprenticeship system without considering its gendered characteristics:

> At a deep subconscious level, the popular image of the relationship between the Mountie and his officer often described the traditional relationship between the hero and his cosmic ally. This invested the officer with an authority that could not be questioned, an authority symbolized by rank but legitimized by something far beyond it. It was the authority of a father passing on the secrets of existence to a son, who one day would teach the same lessons to his son.[11]

The close relationship in Mountie fiction between senior officers and new recruits suggested a way to ensure continuity between the generations and thus preserve the dominance of the old guard.[12] An unseen hierarchical order, with an obvious gender ideology, is thus upheld. As a result so too are "traditional"

FICTION

AND FILM:

THE MOUNTIE

AS ANTIMODERN

CRUSADER,

1880-1960

34

gender roles, which are tied closely to the stability of the hierarchy. The icon of the well-meaning, honourable Mounted Policeman encouraged the maintenance of the status quo. As Walden explains, the mythic Mountie was a welcome symbol of reassurance in a time of great apprehension: "Only symbols and myths could transcend the limitations of rationality and logic and provide the fundamental reassurance that order was not repression, that identity was not invention, and that progress was not just change."[13]

As a symbol, the Mountie allowed all of these abstractions to be flawlessly fused into one person. These characteristics and motivations combined to produce several recognizable themes indigenous to Mountie literature at the turn of the century.

The Fiction

Fictional stories about the Mounties were a clear case of art imitating life so that life could imitate art. Whereas real Mounted Police officers in the 1870s relied upon their own activities and behaviour to set an example for others to follow, the authors of Mountie fiction created a mythic hero to provide a similar example.[14]

This Mountie literature contributed powerfully to Canada as an "imagined community." Because representations of the Mountie in these books varied so little, readers in Vancouver, B.C., Hamilton, Ont., or Lower Sackville, N.S. all shared roughly the same image of the Mountie. Mountie novels provided a shared experience and a shared body of knowledge for people who would never meet each other.

Between 1890 and 1940, authors produced well over one hundred and fifty Mountie novels. These "boys' adventure stories" ranged between one hundred and four hundred pages long and were published by large firms in Toronto, New York, and London. Some, like the many works of James Oliver Curwood, were illustrated, while others relied solely on the written word to evoke the image of the scarlet-clad hero. These novels were part of a growing literature that painted a portrait of a slowly disappearing society, and they held that society up as the ideal for both the present and the future. Intertwined with the emphasis on "traditional" masculinity was an emphasis on Anglo-Saxon superiority and "proper" deportment.

Mountie literature closely paralleled other masculine adventure stories, particularly British stories of colonial adventure and Maritime sea stories. Both of these genres boasted young protagonists who achieved manhood through devotion to authority and by overcoming physical trials. These "real men" were invariably white, and their achievements were an example for others. Their heroes avoided the dangers of "overcivilization" and effeminacy.[15] While hardly a realistic portrayal of the Force's exploits, Mountie fiction was part of a growing trend in Canadian historical writing of the time: an infatuation with the Canadian West.[16] The exploits of the Mountie thus reflected antimodern concerns and offered inspiration to all who believed "traditional" social roles should be maintained.

Classic Themes of "Mountieness"

Most Mountie stories revolved around the same specific themes. Antimodern concerns emerged in representations of the Mountie's physical description, his "coming of age," his relationships with women, and in the authors' practice of ascribing "feminine" characteristics to particular inanimate objects.

The authors of these stories illustrated the ideal characteristics of the Mounted Policeman through physical description. Apparently fearful that society's elite had become flabby and susceptible to challenges from immigrants and workers, writers spared no effort in differentiating the Mountie from the various criminals or antagonistic secondary characters in the stories, establishing the Mountie's superiority with a firm hand. Many fictional Mounties resembled Z.M. Hamilton's Sergeant Major Churchill, described as "one of these splendid specimens of manhood who have made that wonderful force famous." Over six feet tall, Churchill was "lean and wide and as straight as a dart" and much sought after by the women at local dances.[17] In many of

FICTION

AND FILM:

THE MOUNTIE

AS ANTIMODERN

CRUSADER,

1880-1960

36

these stories, the body was the mirror of a person's standing and respectability.

Yet physical strength was not all. Mountie manliness was upheld more by conduct than by brute strength. John Mackie, in his 1895 novel *Sinners Twain*, contrasted unco-operative and selfish officers with the ideal Mounties, who were "gentlemen by birth and education, splendid, all-round, good-hearted fellows as one could wish to meet."[18] Even Mounties of "slight build" could successfully complete their missions.[19] Refinement was a common trait, and many of the fictional heroes displayed a "high quality of breeding and conduct" by demonstrating their musical skills as well as their interest in art and dancing, even on patrol.[20] This was an endorsement of the ideal of Victorian manliness and its characteristics of sexual self-restraint, chivalry, and gentlemanly behaviour. The Mountie literature constructed a masculine ideal associated not just with particular physical traits but with those of a man, and more specifically of a refined, physically fit, Anglo-Saxon man. The Mountie was always of Anglo-Saxon extraction.

The Mountie's enemies (by extension, the enemies of true Canadian manhood and therefore threats to traditional hierarchies) were not part of this physical and cultural fraternity. Corporal Downey's suspect in "Routine Patrol," for example, was "a large man, unprepossessing and ill-kempt, with a month's growth of beard"—a villain who failed to fit the class ideal of refined appearance.[21] Some authors went to great lengths to contrast the Mountie's refined, gentlemanly, and "white" appearance with that of "foreigners."[22] As Walden observes of this early twentieth-century genre, "The number of foreign villains in Mountie novels was astounding."

Benton of the Mounted pitted his energies against the likes of Harry Shapiro and Joseph Lipinski, who entered Canada from Chicago. Inspector Renfrew, "the whitest man on earth," foiled the evil designs of Kid Canceolinni of Milwaukee, Tom King, a Chinese-Italian from Seattle, and Dago Frank Shwarzcropft from Toronto. Sergeant Alan Baker had to contend with John Siebielski, Pete Gonzales and Chink Woolley who was one-quarter Chinese.[23]

Mounties were distinguished from other men, particularly villains, by the *degrees* to which those others adhered to class, ethnic, and gender ideals. An example of this is the case of the "half-breed" character Bateese in James Oliver Curwood's 1921 novel *The Flaming Forest*. Bateese's exploits included several demonstrations of amazing physical strength, yet such merely physical feats could not save him from ridicule on the part of the hero, Sergeant Carrigan. While watching Bateese's efficiency in "smoothing the pillows and straightening out the rumpled bed-clothes," the Mountie could not restrain himself "from chuckling at this feminine ingeniousness of the powerful half-breed."[24] Americans, French "Half-Breeds," Eastern Europeans, and Chinese immigrants would all take turns occupying the role of "the other," over which Anglo-Saxon superiority was confirmed.

Implicit in the physical descriptions was the assumption of the Mountie's heterosexuality. While the sex life of the Mountie never made its way to the forefront of the story, female characters were around just often enough to confirm the Mountie's interest in them and, thus, his suitable sexual orientation.

Quite often the Mountie achieved or obtained manhood by undergoing various trials. All myths of the "hero" follow much this same approach, but the theme of "coming of age" was particularly prevalent in Mountie literature. Occasionally it was the wilderness (almost always gendered female) that provided the test against which a raw recruit could establish his manhood. A fine example is that of Phillip Raine from James Oliver Curwood's 1921 novel *The Golden Snare*. Raine arrives in Canada a weakling, but with time in the wilderness he improves considerably:

> Philip doubled up his arm until the hard muscles in it snapped. He drew in a deep lungful of air, and forced it out again with a sound like steam escaping from a valve. The *north* had done that for him; the north with its wonderful forests, its vast skies, its rivers, and its lakes, and its deep snows—the north that makes a man out of a husk of a man if given half a chance. He loved it.[25]

The "north"—or, more precisely, the Northwest—often played the vital role of "masculinizing agent" in these stories. It was the true test of a man's

FICTION

AND FILM:

THE MOUNTIE

AS ANTIMODERN

CRUSADER,

1880-1960

38

hardiness. The Mountie, in overcoming the trials and tribulations of the environment, showed he was ready for anything; yet he retained his refined and gentlemanly qualities too. The Mountie's adversaries could not match his dual nature: they either lacked his hardiness in the face of nature's challenges, or his upstanding Victorian demeanour. As Carl Berger has demonstrated, the motif of the North has long been an important ingredient in Canadian imperialism and nationalism, particulary concerning its virulent opposition to Eastern European immigrants in the late nineteenth and early twentieth centuries.[26]

The Mountie, then, served as a vehicle for those wishing to put forward ideals to which young boys could aspire if they hoped to become real men. Many of the trials undergone by the Mountie were prerequisites for reaching manhood. Moreover, masculinity and imperialism were related: antimodern concerns in Mountie novels paralleled a concern with an increasingly threatened empire in boys' literature in Britain.[27] Although many other male characters figured in these novels, the Mountie alone subscribed to the ideal role of chivalric and fearless guardian of British order, and was therefore raised above all other men.

No examination of the Mountie would be complete without an exploration of the relationships between female characters and their Mountie heroes. Women in these stories were included to highlight the Mountie's character and were most often objects to be rescued from some peril. Most often women provided great demonstrations of gratitude towards the Mountie. For instance, in Harwood Steele's 1923 novel *Spirit of Iron* a Mountie's future wife responded:

> You're the first real *man* I've ever met. Oh, it isn't just that nice red coat—though that goes to my head like champagne. . . . Every girl has dreams, too. "Someday," I dreamt, "I'll meet a real, real, man—brave, strong, chivalrous, with great, yes, great ideals—a fairy Prince, a knight of the Round Table." They say they don't live now—Oh, but they do! Perhaps the armour's gone but they are knights and Princes just the same.[28]

A passage like this reflects a nostalgia for a lost world of romance and an antimodern yearning for tangible experience. It also suggests that the proper

place for women in society was not one of equality with men—some Canadian women had finally gained the right to vote in federal elections five years before Steele's book was published—but that of waiting patiently for their interests to be served, if and when men decided to act upon those interests.

If the Mountie's relationship with women was almost always based on chivalric service to them, the response often came in answer to the women's cries of distress. The actual resolution of crises was left to the Mountie, just as "tradition" dictated. Just as important as the depiction of female dependence was the reassuring image of the lone Mountie, single and apparently celibate, who went on with his tasks, giving no sign that he required or even desired the love of a woman. Women required men to solve crimes, protect them from villains, and uphold the rules of society—but men required nothing vital from women. The relationship of the sexes in a Mountie novel was in no way recip-

rocal. Women were generally left on the side-lines as static characters and prevented from playing an active role in the stories.

Still, in the surrounding text many of the objects to be upheld or overcome are gendered female. First, and least surprising, the Dominion and the Empire that the Mounties serve are female. These books often explain the entire *raison d'être* of the Force, then, as a male body protecting and serving the female; and the Mountie also has to contend with Mother Nature and the wilderness. One of Corporal Downey's comrades in James B. Hendryx's 1926 novel *Downey of the Mounted* nicely sums up this phenomenon:

In your heart, and in mine, Downey, our wilderness has taken the place of love of woman. It chains us to its bosom with the invisible chains, as the love of woman chains men to their hearths and their firesides. And it is wondrously like a woman—this great North of ours—with its passions, and its storms, and its unutterable longing. With its pitiable helplessness, and its unreasoning demands.[29]

In this passage, as in most Mountie books, the men all occupy active roles while the female-gendered objects are mystified and deemed helpless. An illogical, "emotional" wilderness that is conquered by the calm and rational Mountie: this allegory drew upon the constructed notion that men are more rational than women.

The books thus defined the Mountie fraternity in many ways: through descriptions of appearance and deportment; through displays of courage and determination that brought them acceptance as men, not boys (and never women); and through their chivalrous service to helpless female characters. The purpose of this fraternity was to uphold the trinity of "Duty, Law, and Order."[30] The Mountie embodies a kind of premodern *noblesse oblige* in helping others, although in doing so he prevents others from helping themselves. Women and men not fitting the gender, class, and ethnic ideals of the Mountie, and thus generally excluded from the ranks of the actual Force, functioned in Mountie novels as passive problems. Thus, after the story is happily resolved the message remains that problems and solutions are to be defined only by "traditional" leaders. Faced with the tumultuous world of turn-of-the-century Canada, this was a comforting thought for many.

Ralph Connor (the pen name of Charles W. Gordon, a Presbyterian minister based in Winnipeg) was undoubtedly the most influential Canadian writer of Mountie narratives. Indeed, Connor was "the most successful Canadian novelist in the early 20th century."[31] His books "sold 5 million copies and caught the imagination of a generation" with protagonists winning "victories for the temperance movement and the Church."[32] As David Marshall argues, Connor never lost sight of his general objective—to evangelize Canadians: "What was important to [Connor] was not that he had written a good story, but that he had written an effective sermon that reached many. By writing novels, [Connor] did not think he was abandoning the Christian ministry; instead he thought he was expanding it."[33]

Connor's personification of this evangelical ideal is the Mountie—a logical choice, perhaps, at a time when many antimodernists were contrasting a "muscular Christianity" to the supposed feminization and overcivilization of organized religion. In *A Tale of the Macleod Trail*, Connor's Corporal Cameron starts out as a down-and-out football player in Edinburgh who is out of shape, out of money, and deep in drink. Undergoing the necessary trials of manhood in Canada, Cameron is transformed into a typical Mountie. Salvation, temperance, maturity, manliness, and lawfulness: Cameron attains them all by becoming a Mountie, a man who not only enforced the law, but also embodied it.[34]

As the tremendous social transformations of the turn of the century led to middle-class worries about the future, the Mounted Policeman thus emerged as

FICTION
AND FILM:
THE MOUNTIE
AS ANTIMODERN
CRUSADER,
1880-1960

42

the personification of Christian social harmony and conservative gender, class, and ethnic ideals. He was a symbol of divinely ordained hierarchies, against which ethnic minorities, subordinate classes, and feminists could struggle but never prevail.

As such, Mountie literature was an expression of Canadian antimodernism. Antimodernists, or "reluctant modernists," as George Cotkin terms them, were attempting to preserve aspects of Victorianism; and they worked to combine these aspects, however uneasily, with modernity. These "self-appointed custodians of culture" hoped to "develop and disseminate their cultural values to the population at large."[35] Class divisions and cultural heterogeneity meant that their hopes for cultural unity would remain unfulfilled. Ironically, consumerism, a force that "horrified the custodians of culture," soon emerged to promote social and cultural unity—but in a very different way than what the antimodernists had planned. Jackson Lears explains:

> By exalting "authentic" experience as an end in itself, antimodern impulses reinforced the shift from a Protestant ethos of salvation through self-denial to a therapeutic ideal of self-fulfillment in this world through exuberant health and intense experience. The older morality embodied the "producer culture" of an industrializing, entrepreneurial society; the newer nonmorality embodied the "consumer culture" of a bureaucratic corporate state.[36]

Born of antimodern dissent, the mythic Mountie would come of age in the consumer culture of the twentieth century.

In 1912 former prime minister Wilfrid Laurier wrote to Ralph Connor to thank him for a Christmas copy of *Corporal Cameron*. He told Connor that he found his books "particularly attractive . . . because they will preserve a special phase of our national history, and customs which are rapidly passing away."[37] While Laurier here reflected concerns about the "customs" that dominated Mountie literature of the period, he need not have worried about their impending disappearance. Many aspects of the mythic Mountie survived largely intact into the Cold War era.

Mountie Movies and the Dawning of Consumer Culture

Where the classic Mountie novels led, the movies followed. Mounted Policemen would appear as central characters in over two hundred and fifty feature films. These movies strayed little from the usual storyline of the novels: Mountie falls in love with girl; girl falls in love with—or is related to—alleged villain; Mountie discovers alleged villain is actually innocent; Mountie arrests evil person (usually an ethnic minority) for crime; Mountie and girl live happily ever after.

Two of the most popular Mountie films, *Rose Marie* and *North West Mounted Police*, bore a strong resemblance to the earlier works of fiction. But by the time these films appeared, a plethora of early Mountie movies had distributed, ever more widely, an image of the Mountie that contained many remnants of its antimodern predecessor, consolidating the fictional Mountie's position as both a mythic hero and a commercial success. As Pierre Berton has observed: "The movie Mountie was almost invariably brave, noble, honourable, courteous, kind, and trustworthy—all the standard Boy Scout qualities, to go with the hat. . . . He is the quintessential hero and he always wins. He gets his man and he usually gets his girl (or nobly gives her to another)."[38] The 1910 movie *Riders of the Plains* concerned "the capture of a band of Indian horse-thieves." *Nomads of the North*, released in 1920, included "a brave, honourable Mountie forced to choose between Duty and Love (the heroine), the Canadian north as landscape, and the inevitable French-Canadian villain."[39] In *The Eternal Struggle*, Constable O'Hara and Sergeant Tempest must arrest a woman they both love. Berton summarizes their dilemma and its resolution:

> Holed up in the supply station with the other two, Tempest finally breaks. He wants O'Hara to flee to safety with the girl: "I can't stand this any longer! It's torture. . . . Listen to me, Bucky, I'm going to let her go. Go! I give her to you."
>
> But O'Hara is the stronger of the two: "Every fibre of my being, every beat of my heart cries out for you," he tells the girl. But he knows his duty.

FICTION

AND FILM:

THE MOUNTIE

AS ANTIMODERN

CRUSADER,

1880-1960

44

"She is not mine and she is not yours," he reminds Sergeant Tempest. "She belongs to the Crown and she's going back!"

As a woman in a Mountie movie, the "girl" belonged to pretty much anyone but herself.

At least thirty films followed the same theme. Berton provides a useful synopsis:[40]

Mountie is ordered to bring in his

sweetheart's brother	9 [movies]
sweetheart's father	6
sweetheart	5
the man his sweetheart *really* loves	4
own brother (apart from twin)	3
best friend	3
twin brother	2
sweetheart's sister's boyfriend	1

Such soap-opera plot twists simply underscored the Mountie's triumph over the arbitrariness of his personal feelings. A premodern ideal of chivalrous service to the Crown ensured that justice would be done no matter how complicated the situation.

In the 1936 version of *Rose Marie*, starring Nelson Eddy and Jeanette MacDonald, Rose Marie is a temperamental opera star anxious to help her brother (played by James Stewart), who has fled into the woods after killing a Mountie. Sergeant Bruce is assigned to apprehend the Mountie's killer. Rose Marie ventures into northern Quebec to help her brother, but is no match for the locals. They make life rough for her, and a storekeeper's response to the theft of her money is reminiscent of the earlier literature: "That's the trouble with those half-breeds. You can't trust 'em." When Sergeant Bruce comes to town, the local women attach themselves to him immediately, but he has his eyes on Rose Marie. He tries in vain to woo her. Even in filling out the stolen property report, he is clearly on the make: "Sex . . . decidedly. Complexion . . . lovely." The poor guy even sings to her in a canoe, but only makes things worse for himself by calling her the wrong name in the second verse of "Indian Love Call."

Rose Marie is no fool. Quick to recognize his motives, she inquires into his past. Their exchange reveals much about the period's view of Native people. While watching Indians wearing Prairie headdresses dance around west-coast totem poles in northern Quebec, Bruce explains how he spent six months with the tribe. Rose Marie asks if there were any white women for him to sing to during this spell in the north. He points out an Indian woman and responds: "No one but Cassie . . . and when I caught myself singing to her I went home." The Hollywood Cassie was the latest in a long line of Indians and "half-breeds" that stretched out from the earlier literature.

Rose Marie goes on to illustrate her incompetence in the wilderness by almost drowning in a river and by running away from a wild animal that she claims was chasing her. It turns out to be a deer. She even styles her hair before sleeping. Sergeant Bruce, who despite days in the bush looks as handsome as ever, is now clearly indispensable on her quest to help her brother. At last they do find her brother and Bruce arrests him, despite his growing fondness for the guilty man's sister. Once feisty and independent, Rose Marie returns to the opera disheartened, but she is now far more pleasant company for her co-workers than she was before her adventure. All is not lost, though: the two main characters meet again and live happily ever after when Bruce's voice interrupts her uninspired performance of "La Tosca," and the two of them are united to sing "Indian Love Call" to end the film. She has clearly become a better person for her trip into the north and her contact with a Mountie.

Nelson Eddy's character is no Rudolf Valentino, but he does make concessions to the social mores of the time. He is more aggressive and self-assured, but no less chivalrous than earlier Mounties. Hollywood made the Mountie more comfortable in the role of leading man, but it did not fundamentally change the officer's pristine, gentlemanly image.[41]

Most Mountie movies were U.S. productions, and occasionally American content would pervade the storylines. A good example of this was the 1940 film

FICTION

AND FILM:

THE MOUNTIE

AS ANTIMODERN

CRUSADER,

1880-1960

46

Nelson Eddy and Jeanette MacDonald in the 1936 classic *Rose Marie*. Eddy's character retained gentlemanly traits from the Mountie novels, but also tipped his hat to the increasingly relaxed sexual mores of the time. (Glenbow Archives, Calgary, Alberta, NA-2947-1)

North West Mounted Police, starring Gary Cooper and Madeleine Carroll and directed by Cecil B. de Mille. This movie too had some characters in common with the earlier literature: a Scotsman who feels it is his duty to keep the Empire together and cannot fight against the Queen, a seductive but evil "half-breed" woman, and "Shorty," a "half-breed" too simple to know whether his new baby is a boy or a girl.

This film contained some inventive departures from the standard novel plots. The most obvious of these was an American rewriting of history: a Texas Ranger named Dusty Rivers arrives on the scene and plays a key role in quelling the 1885 Riel Rebellion. The Ranger, played by Cooper, and a Mountie named Jim Brett, played by Preston Foster, end up competing for the interest of the same woman. This woman, April, is the sister of Ronnie Logan, a Mountie who deserts the Force when tricked by the evil seductress "half-breed." Mountie Jim rides with six other Mounties into Big Bear's camp, where he forces the chief to kneel down before them in order to be recognized as leader of his people again. The Texan then manages to destroy the rebels' Gatling gun and ensure victory for the Force. (The real rebels of 1885 had no Gatling gun of their own, though they faced one carried across the country by the Canadian militia).[42] In the end the rebellion is quashed with the aid of the Texas policeman. Louis Riel (on screen for less than five minutes) and a fictional leader named Jacques Corbeau are both arrested. Mountie Jim gets the girl while Ranger Rivers takes Corbeau back to Texas to face an earlier charge. If Sergeant Bruce and Sergeant Brett were more forward and comfortable with women than earlier Mounties, they retained their chivalric credentials by always remaining gentlemen, the embodiment of Victorian manliness.

If some movies drew their contexts out of invented historical circumstance, others boasted improbable storylines that found fault with white settlers for the strife and tension that dominated the Hollywood version of nineteenth-century Canada. The backdrop of the 1939 Shirley Temple film *Susannah of the Mounties* was the building of the CPR line across the Prairies. According to the film, the Force was caught between wild Indians and greedy and impatient railway managers. Susannah is a young girl who clears up the misunderstanding between the Indians and the Mounties and delivers the Inspector's message that the CPR managers are to blame. This was not, by any means, a story that suggested that the Force was allied with the Indians against the railway. After all, one character sported a toupee in order to stave off death when the warring Indians arrived in search of scalps. The film did, however, build on the tensions of nineteenth-century expansion—tensions that would disappear when English Canadians reinvented their past in the 1970s.

As the twentieth century moved along, the Mountie remained linked to his experience on the old frontier, a reassuring icon of continuity. The movie Mountie seemed most comfortable on horseback, no matter what his mission entailed: once more, a reassuring combination of traditional chivalry and modern law enforcement. This formula was so powerful that the movie producers could not resist using it in even the most unlikely circumstances. In one episode of *Dangers of the Canadian Mounted*, a movie serial with a post-Second World War setting, a Mountie on a horse chases a car down a highway to rescue the heroine,

FICTION
AND FILM:
THE MOUNTIE
AS ANTIMODERN
CRUSADER,
1880-1960

48

who is tied up in the front seat. In another episode the hero, Sergeant Royal, again on horseback, chases a small First World War-type plane that is taxiing down a field. He hops off his horse and onto the back of the plane. In this case a helpless woman who needs to be rescued is in the open back seat of the plane.[43]

In *The Cyclone* (1920), the chase scene was even more unlikely: after discovering the location of a Chinese gambling den, the Mountie "returns to headquarters, gets into his dress uniform, leaps onto his horse, and gallops off to make the bust. He rides noiselessly up three flights of stairs and then crashes through to the cellar, still on horseback, to capture the lawbreakers."[44] Some Mountie movies deviated from the standard model. According to Berton's account, "Movie Mounties always shot first and asked questions later,"[45]—a tendency that indicates Hollywood's incorporation of the Mounties into the myth of the wild American West. When directors did stray from established myth, they often found themselves so completely misinterpreting the appearance and exploits of the Force that the movies took on a comical effect. Yet such exceptions did not overthrow the basic plot line of Mountie movies: a lone Mountie, Anglo-Saxon and refined, saves a woman in peril by frustrating the evil designs of the villain (usually a caricature of an ethnic "other," often French-Canadian).

The Cold War Mountie: Towards a Reconciliation with Modernity

While the popularity of Mountie movies peaked in the 1930s, the classic Mountie myth was by no means exhausted. The standard formula entered the 1950s through a revival of its original form: the novel. If Mounties chasing runaway cars (and planes) on horseback seemed a little out of keeping with postwar realities, the Cold War again offered the fictional RCMP regular employment. The threat to Canada was no longer American whiskey traders or Indian horse thieves: it was now swarthy Eastern Europeans and communist sympathizers intent on world domination.

Between 1951 and 1962 Toronto author Joe Holliday wrote nine children's stories about the fictional hero "Dale of the Mounted." Each book featured the scarlet-clad hero saving various parts of Canada (by and large excluding Quebec) from foreign subversives. As with earlier novels, character descriptions helped to differentiate the Mountie from his opponents. For example, Giorgy Kovass, the Hungarian spy in Holliday's Cold War thriller *Dale of the Mounted: Dew Line Duty*, was burdened with the following description: "Giorgy Kovass was a chunkily-built man. His hair was thick and unkempt. . . . His skin, dark and swarthy, had an unhealthy tone, and his lips, thick and jutting, held a touch of cruelness in the arrogant way they thrust outward."[46]

FICTION

AND FILM:

THE MOUNTIE

AS ANTIMODERN

CRUSADER,

1880-1960

50

Karl Reiger, Kovass's accomplice, had yellowing teeth and a variety of other unattractive characteristics: "Reiger, his jowls plump and beefy, was badly in need of a shave. He had a small, sharp aquiline nose. His hair was thinning, as a centre bald spot testified. His skin bore an unhealthy pallor. Two beady, black eyes peered out from beneath shaggy eyebrows, and they held a glint of cunning."[47]

The hero Dale was five-foot-eleven and 163 pounds. He was fit and attractive, though not a threatening physical force—about two times per book he was knocked unconscious by his antagonists. His success depended upon outsmarting his opposition. Before entering the Force he had lived in Toronto with his decidedly middle-class parents and two siblings. His uncle had promised Dale a position in his aircraft manufacturing plant if the youngster's dream of becoming a Mountie did not work out.[48] But of course it did. Neither the Hungarian antagonists nor the two Polish spies in the original Joe Holliday novel were any match for Dale of the Mounted. His superior traits were often related to his civilizing manner to confirm a superiority that was both racial and political.

In *Dew Line Duty* a group of Hungarian immigrants arrives in Canada and suspects Kovass of being a spy. They attempt to take matters into their own hands only to be prevented from doing so by the Mountie. "One of the angry crowd pushed forward and spoke rapidly and savagely in Hungarian." Then, as the crowd physically attacked Kovass:

Dale's jaw tightened. "You tell these people," he informed the interpreter, "that this is Canada. I know they've had a rough time in Hungary, but in this country they've got to obey our laws, our way of doing things.". . .

There were mutterings and some rumbles of discontent, but the crowd made way as Dale led the man out.[49]

This was essentially a Cold War re-enactment of the story of the Force's experience in the Yukon six decades earlier. Equally reminiscent of earlier themes is *Dale of the Mounted in Hong Kong*, in which Dale is sent to the Far East to "find out every method that's being used to smuggle Chinese into Canada."[50] In both cases, as threatening strangers swarmed in, the Force ensured justice, maintained Canadian sovereignty, and upheld the right.

In *Dale of the Mounted: Atlantic Assignment*, Dale tracks down Joe DeMarco, a Canadian born in Toronto of Balkan descent, who is trying to sabotage Canadian Navy vessels. DeMarco, Dale discovers, is being blackmailed by the dictatorship of an unnamed Balkan country. *Dale of the Mounted: Atomic Plot* finds Dale in Chalk River, Ontario, protecting a visiting Pakistani scientist. Dale was quite excited about this assignment, we are told, because it "was to be his first experience meeting anyone from the other side of the world; from the mysterious, the exotic, the unusual Far East areas."[51] The scientist's visit is interrupted by an Indian-led terrorist attack on the power plant, with Dale solving the case that leaves his "dark-skinned" colleagues baffled. Again, one of the conspirators had been blackmailed from abroad.

Each Dale of the Mounted novel contains lengthy "educational" digressions that outline the basics of nuclear physics, Naval operations, and other male-dominated occupations. Gender roles are consistent with the earlier novels. Dale always exercises proper Mountie deportment: he enjoys the piano, drinks non-alcoholic beverages, and is polite to a fault. None of the villains live by this code. There are few active female characters.

Holliday's mythical Force also provides reassurance to, and sanctuary for, men opposed to the "new" woman. As with the earlier literature, these books defined suspected criminals in the Cold War era through their relationships to women. This is the case with Harry Savage, a factory worker. The evidence points to Savage as a prime suspect until his family life is revealed: "Very popular with the other fellows. Married. Got two youngsters. There's

FICTION

AND FILM:

THE MOUNTIE

AS ANTIMODERN

CRUSADER,

1880-1960

52

something fishy here." Even Dale's mother affirms the Force's ability to provide "the best training in the world for a young man." Again, as in the earlier literature, women often provide demonstrations of gratitude towards the Mountie: the female stenographers who had previously worked with Dale "made it a point to ask him for a snapshot when he got his uniform."[52] And, once again, Mounties are somewhat bashful in response. In *Dew Line Duty* a Constable Sweeney makes somewhat nervous and reserved comments about a particularly attractive movie star: "That blonde in that picture last night—you know—the one with the—ahem—neat figure, ho-hum."[53] Indeed, the Dale of the Mounted series affirmed the traditional masculine values of valour, strength, and honour even as it delivered lessons on such modern topics as aerodynamics, surveillance techniques, and the complexities of Interpol.

In general the Cold War novels transported the classic Mountie from his original duties on the plains to a starring role in defending Canada from the Eastern Bloc with remarkably little change in his character or mission. Still, there were two major exceptions to this continuity. Dale of the Mounted was more closely identified with modern technology than were his earlier counterparts, and his assignments saw him defending Canadian sovereignty rather than a more amorphous Imperial sentiment.

Conclusion

Not all of the RCMP's popularity can be attributed to fictional sources. Real achievements, in particular successful apprehensions of criminals in the North, brought the Force well-deserved tributes. Yet the evidence suggests that fictional representations of the Force greatly outweighed the impact of these real achievements.

A study by T.A. Culham in 1947 found that most of the books the public read about the Force were classified as fiction and consisted primarily of adventure stories. Culham's analysis of information gathered from several public libraries concerning the circulation of books on the RCMP suggests that the reading audience preferred fiction over non-fiction by a two-to-one ratio. His questionnaires produced a similar result. The popularity of Mountie fiction was also confirmed by publishing information. Between five and six thousand copies of Harwood Steele's fact-based 1936 book *Policing the Arctic* were produced, while over one hundred thousand orders had been placed for James Oliver Curwood's fictional *The Valley of the Silent Men* before it was even published in 1923.[54]

From the 1890s until the 1950s, books and films—as well as TV programs and comic books—depicted Canada's federal police force as a daring group of individuals who brought British justice and fair play to the less civilized peoples of the world: Native peoples, Eastern European immigrants, and French-Canadians. In coming to the aid of damsels in distress, these square-jawed Victorian gentlemen also rekindled the spirit of Medieval chivalry. Despite the homage paid to the wonders of technology in the later fiction, the mythic Mountie remained a heroic individual, not a member of modern bureaucratic organization.

The fictional stories of RCMP achievements quickly overshadowed the rather mixed reviews received by the original Force during its first decade of existence. In the Force's eyes, such antimodern mythologies continued to overshadow its achievements in the following decades. The mythic Mountie's popularity remained high long after the turn of the century, because the RCMP officer had come to epitomize what many English-Canadians considered to be the ideal: in confirming Anglo-Saxon superiority and the righteousness of Imperial destiny, he appeared impartial, always successful, and unfailingly polite. The end result was an intense demand for uniforms, photos, and endorsements from the architects of the new consumer culture that had been one of the main targets of antimodernism in the first place.

3

The Mountie and the
Culture of Consumption, 1930-70

We should be what we are—Canadian and not a mixture of all the
nationalities who come to us.

> – E.H. Adams, addressing the Canadian Chamber of
> Commerce on the need to bolster the tourist industry
> by stationing uniformed Mounties outside federal
> buildings, Vancouver, B.C., Sept. 9, 1937

Why oh why . . . do we insist on giving the whole world the impression
we have nothing but mounties and Indians in Canada?

> – E.P. Robertson to the editor of the *Niagara Falls Evening
> Review*, July 20, 1961, after witnessing Canada's contestant in
> the Miss Universe Contest appear in a Mountie uniform

Born of antimodern sentiment, the mythic Mountie was soon gainfully
employed by new business professionals. As consumerism and advertising came
of age in Canada, the business world quickly picked up on the strategy of iden-
tifying products with the Mountie image.[1]

In the interwar years, the expanding world of advertisers anxious to win
over consumers, spent a great deal of time and effort studying the potential
audiences. In doing so, advertisers reached two major conclusions. First, it was
important that advertisements "reflect public aspirations rather than contemporary realities." Consumer products and leisure pursuits were supposed to

Antimodern symbol greets
modern tourists in Banff,
Alberta, in October 1929.
(National Archives of Canada,
W.J. Oliver, PA57239)

help people escape from the problems and complexities of the modern world, not remind them of their daily anxieties. Second, despite consumers' affinity for new technological gadgets, the buying public still harboured a general uneasiness about the effects of modernization on older forms of community and on the sense of individual achievement and control. Advertisers thus sought to offer up the wonders of technology to consumers in ways that "gave the appearance and feel of a personal relationship."[2] One way of meeting this challenge was to infuse ads with reassuring and comforting premodern symbols. As one of Canada's most recognized romantic icons, the mythic Mountie quickly became a highly sought-after advertising tool.

Yet tension was often evident between businesses and individuals who sought to employ the Mountie image for their own ends, and a police force anxious to avoid any public relations scandals. During the first half of the twentieth century, RCMP activities concerning the Mountie image were restricted to routine and administrative matters. They did not attempt to challenge the image itself. The Force's administrative response to requests for uniforms, tourism initiatives, photographs, and public appearances was a combination of fatalism and cautious co-operation. But on the issue of advertising and endorsements, the Force was to take up a firm position.

Central to the image of the Mounties—and the ideal for any police force— was an image of impartiality. With the Force's image in great public demand, it was deemed necessary to make legal restrictions on the use of that image, particularly in commercial endeavours. Photographs of the Force were often in great demand—and often this demand was from south of the border. U.S. photographers identified Canada's police force with its classic image. In 1949 a photographer in New York state wrote to the RCMP indicating that he sought "one or two of the Mounted Police who have fine physiques and photographic features" and wanted to photograph such men in uniform and on horseback in Banff, Alberta. After being informed by Commissioner S.T. Wood that the RCMP did not keep horses in Banff, he abandoned the project, explaining that "the absence of horses would mitigate against the very type of pictorial effect I would work for." Wood had approved the project upon the condition that the pictures not be used in "advertising for sale of commodities."[3] Commissioner Wood had long been weary of the liberties taken with the Force's image by those seeking to profit from its popularity. As early as 1942 legal restrictions on its use had been introduced.[4]

In 1957, when the Canadian Kodak Company wrote asking to use photographs of members of the Force in its advertising, RCMP Liaison Officer C.H. Bayfield informed them that in refusing their request the commissioner was "bound by the provisions of the RCMP Act." Bayfield's letter to the company included a lengthy quotation from the Act itself:

> 37.(2) Every person who uses, without the authority of the Governor in council, the name "Royal Canadian Mounted Police" or "RCMP" or any other combination of letters relating to the Force, or any pictorial simulation or representation of a member of the Force in trade marks, business identifications, business advertisements, or any similar marking or advertisement, is, on summary conviction, upon the complaint of any member of the Force, liable to a fine not exceeding two hundred dollars, or to imprisonment, with or without hard labour, for a term not exceeding six months, or to both fine and imprisonment; but no such complaint shall be laid without the consent in writing of the Commissioner.[5]

The law was enforceable only within Canada, but when one entrepreneur sought permission to make plaster models of Mounties, a Liaison Officer informed him (in somewhat contradictory language): "American manufacturers generally have invariably respected our wishes."[6] Even a wallpaper company hoping to produce a design suitable for young men's rooms received a warning that such photos "may be used only for the purpose stated in your letter and that neither they nor the Force may be involved in any advertisement of the product."[7]

Clearly the RCMP found it necessary to remind and warn companies of its legal right to protect its image. In its correspondence with these firms the Force itself invariably warned the companies not to use the photographs for advertising or for any other purposes that it had not previously approved. Sometimes, as we've seen, excerpts from the RCMP Act were included in correspondence to the companies. On other occasions the respondent merely alluded to the Act. In his letter to a company wanting to use the image of the Force on a pamphlet for a company convention, Liaison Officer M.J. Keough made his point clear: "I would like you to know that in the past several persons and organizations who used the name and pictures in a way that was undignified besides using them for advertising purposes, caused very strict legislation on this same subject to be adopted."[8]

The Force was only rarely called upon to enforce such legislation, although an incident in 1961 did rally the officers to action. In January of that year W.H. MacKay, president of the International Playing Card Company of Windsor, Ontario, wrote to the commissioner complaining that he had discovered that a Japanese company was using the Mountie image on its cards. He asked how this could be allowed, because his own company had been required to obtain the Force's permission. In addition, the Japanese deck contained the notation "RCMP Canada" which, MacKay argued, was illegal. Moreover, he lamented, "The Japanese reproduction does not do justice to the subject matter, and the pack itself is of poor quality." A liaison officer, E.A.F. Holm, wrote back to MacKay promising to look into the matter, yet reminding him that "the provisions of our Act would have no application in Japan."[9] The matter was then turned over to the RCMP's Legal Section for investigation. In April an Inspector Gorman informed MacKay that the Japanese firm was indeed contravening the RCMP Act by manufacturing playing cards using a design that had been authorized to another firm. An investigation was underway to amass evidence to support prosecution of the firm. Upon investigation, however, it was discovered that the sale of the illegal cards had not been widespread. This, combined with the Force's lack of a legal recourse in Japan, meant that the RCMP would not be recommending prosecution to the minister. MacKay wrote back to Holm thanking him for his interest in the incident, and expressed optimism that the investigation of the company would probably have a "restraining effect on this type of merchandise."[10]

Although RCMP endorsements were out of the question, and the use of the Force's image was now legally monitored, business opportunities still remained.

Companies simply found other ways of linking their products with the Mountie image. In the 1940s, for instance, the Mountie remained a sought-after symbol of Canada's limitless potential—for Americans. In 1948 the Monsanto Chemical Company of St. Louis, Missouri, succeeded in gaining the permission of the Force to have a Mountie appear on the cover of its company magazine. Inside, a feature article on Canada entitled "Canada Has Her Sleeves Rolled Up" celebrated the takeover by Monsanto's Canadian division of a Seattle-based company called Laucks.[11] As control of the Canadian branch plant passed from Seattle to St. Louis, the Mountie offered a comforting symbol of continuity, if not economic imperialism.

The Mountie's appeal to a U.S. audience was not lost on Canadian companies. The Canadian Pacific Railway sought to capitalize on it as well. Long identified with the settlement of the Canadian West, the CPR in the 1940s was well aware of the importance of the U.S. market. In 1948 a CPR public relations officer succeeded in convincing the Force to allow *The Saturday Evening Post* to photograph a Mountie in Banff for use in an article on the company. The photographer was "highly anxious to include a photograph of a member of your Force to add not only color to his subject matter" but also because the Mountie is "characteristically Canadian to all American readers."[12]

Almost twenty years later, in 1964, Johnson's Wax drew on the Force's co-operation to include a Mountie in a film to be shown to the company's employees. The script, "Canada and Johnson's Wax," was sent to the RCMP for approval. An excerpt suggests that the company was well aware of both the Mountie's appeal and the conflicting nationalisms within Canada:

> Here in Ottawa, Ontario, capital of Canada, the Parliament Buildings with their resemblance to London's Houses of Parliament, bear mute testimony to the English heritage of the country (as [d]o the red coats of the famous Canadian Mounties). But just across the Ottawa River lies Hull—in the French-speaking Province of Quebec—a quick reminder of the dual culture of Canada—English and French. This bilingual culture, unique in North America, is a fact which Canadian marketing men must never forget.[13]

The Mountie was still identified with the British culture of Canada. He had emerged, after all, in literature and film, confronting scheming French-Canadian villains who supposedly made up the other half of this "dual culture." Banned from using the Mountie in conventional advertising campaigns, Johnson's Wax and other businesses were quick to find other ways of capitalizing on the Mountie image.

The Red Serge

The scarlet and gold uniform continued to be worn by fictional heroes long after it had been relegated to ceremonial duty by the Force itself, and the RCMP received constant requests concerning its famous uniform. These requests, reviewed individually, required the approval of the commissioner. Many requests came from movie directors aware of the drawing power of the movie Mountie. Pierre Berton has outlined the Force's frustrations with Hollywood's depictions of the Mounties in his *Hollywood's Canada*. The Force's relationship with Hollywood can perhaps best be summarized in an exchange between Hollywood cowboy actor Tom Mix and Commissioner A.B. Perry in 1919. In responding to a request from Mix, Perry outlined his concerns at length:

> Personally I have heretofore hesitated in supplying Film concerns with our uniform, because [in] any pictures where members of this Force have been represented, it has rather tended to hold the Force up to ridicule than otherwise; as the actors usually present a very unsoldierly appearance, such as: Ill fitting uniform, long hair, drooping shoulders, incorrect hats and make a practice of saluting one another whether wearing headgear or not.[14]

Yet Perry still sent the requested articles along—a response typical of the Force. While many uniforms were sent around the world for state occasions and ceremonies, there was also a domestic demand for the Mountie uniform. This was a tricky business. Showing up at a costume party in Melbourne, Australia, dressed as a Mountie was one thing; wandering the streets of a Canadian city dressed in a police officer's uniform was quite another. In 1939 one poor fellow in Toronto was arrested for impersonating a police officer. It turned out he was merely in his Halloween costume.[15]

Citizens mistaking other citizens for members of the Force was not simply a matter of public safety. The Force also had its image to think of. In a 1939 memorandum to the commissioner, Supt. Vernon Kemp recommended that the Force lend a uniform to the Hart House Players Guild for use in a play: "Provided the play is not derogatory to the Force . . . it would be wiser to co-operate in order that a faithful protrayal [sic] rather than a caricature would be assured." Commissioner Wood was not receptive. He informed Kemp that the Force had recently adopted a policy of "refusing to assist theatrical concerns and parties, professional or otherwise" by loaning "articles of uniform."[16]

Within a year, though, Wood's position seems to have softened. Groups or individuals wishing to rent a uniform were required to first approach the Force. The commissioner would then review the application and, if he approved, send it along with a reply, much like one sent in 1941 by Commissioner Wood to W. T. Randall, chair of the Canada Night Committee of the American Water Works Association Convention in Toronto. Randall had in mind a Mountie sing-a-long to celebrate "Canada Night."

If you propose that the octette are to sing in RCM Police costumes rented for the occasion from some theatrical costumer and you will agree that the persons concerned are not to parade around, and that they will not appear on the streets and as far as possible will take off the uniforms as soon as they have sung their parts, and you will give me a guarantee that there will be no reason for the American visitors to imagine that any of the singers or all of them are members of the Force, I shall have no objection to the costumer renting you the uniforms you require for the occasion in question, and you may produce this letter as your authority to the

In 1932, two Mounties were present at the first International Legion Convention at Waterton National Park in Alberta. RCMP commissioners received frequent requests for Mountie appearances at such gatherings. (Glenbow Archives, Calgary, Alberta, ND-27-42)

costumer, provided there is attached to it a second letter making further stipulations.[17]

Despite his approval, Wood's concern was evident. Lending uniforms or allowing costumers to rent them out to the public often left the commissioner with an uneasy feeling. Occasionally his concern was warranted.

In 1947 the secretary for the Hespeler, Ontario, Old Boys' Re-Union for that year requested permission to rent Mountie uniforms for the Dominion Day Parade. Wood reluctantly approved the request and informed the secretary, R. Travers, "that we have had so many complaints of people representing themselves as members of the Force, involving prosecutions, that

I feel unless your Committee gives strict orders regarding these uniforms, it may lead to embarrassment of yourselves and this Force."[18] Wood's discomfort with these arrangements meant that a patrol was made by "O" Division to observe the parade. What they found disturbed them greatly. In his report to the division, Constable N. Craig noted that the uniforms, rented from Malabar Costumers in Toronto, were "unkempt, stained and ill fitting and presented a very poor appearance." This was not the image the Force wanted to promote. Craig continued, "From the general conversation overheard at the time of the parade the aforementioned squad of men were taken to be regular members of the RCM Police and comments passed about their appearance were not complimentary." Thus, the commissioner's two main fears were realized. Unfortunately, the worst was still to come. Craig's final statement must have sent his senior officers reeling: "Men in these rented uniforms were seen later in the day on July 1st, consuming beer at the Canadian Legion Branch."[19]

Eventually the Force entered into an agreement that made Malabar Costumers the sole company permitted to rent out Mountie uniforms in Canada, and a concrete policy concerning uniform rentals was in place by the mid-1950s. The Malabar Costume Company of Toronto had branches in Montreal and Winnipeg. The agreement ensured that the company would not rent a uniform unless the customer could produce "written permission from a representative of [the] Force." The RCMP would not approve requests for uniforms to be worn "in a public place such as a parade."[20]

At times the Force went to great lengths to monitor the use of Mountie costumes. Amidst all of the resources and effort required to protect Canada during the Cold War, the Force still found time, in 1956, to enlist civil servants in the task of monitoring uniforms as far away as Belgium.[21]

However, the Force's reluctance to permit the wearing of the uniform by civilians could be overcome. One of the more bizarre cases of RCMP co-operation involved two Belgian Counts who toured the world in 1958 as part of a wager. They had been challenged by a friend to accomplish unusual things around the world, and part of the bet involved being "photographed wearing RCMP

uniforms and mounted on RCMP horses." The counts were being followed on their trek by *Life* magazine. A representative of the magazine pleaded with the Force to make an exception in the case of these men. Admitting that "this would amount to what is strictly illegal use of the force's uniform," he suggested that the magazine had in mind "only a good-humoured gag, though in the best of taste." He concluded by stating that he was "quite sure that the whole thing would be excellent public relations for the RCMP, and we would of course stress that it was arranged with your cooperation."[22]

The commissioner acceded to the request, and Assistant Commissioner J.R. Lemieux's letter to a Belgian civil servant summarizes the events. Arrangements were made to have the two counts photographed in uniform and on horseback. Lemieux sent the photographs to the Canadian official in Belgium so that he could show them to Dino Vastapane—the man who had wagered with the two counts—to authenticate their success. "Under no circumstances" was the official to let the photographs out of his hands. Nor was he to reveal to the Belgian press how the photographs had been taken: "These instructions are very specific and they are to be obeyed to the letter," Lemieux warned.[23] Cooperation and a sense of good fun were one thing, but they could not come at the expense of the Force's reputation.

Several years later the Malabar company got into hot water with the Force when a photograph of a "phoney" Mountie appeared in the Toronto *Telegram*. A 1964 Lions Convention in Maple Leaf Gardens was unsuccessful in gaining RCMP permission for a member of the Force to appear on stage, so the conventioneers simply rented a costume from Malabar and had someone impersonate a Mountie. This was a clear breach of the agreement between Malabar and the Force, because the Force had not authorized the wearing of the uniform. According to an unamused Toronto *Telegram*, the man on stage "gave himself away as a phoney when he gave [a] three-fingered Boy Scout salute." Not only had Malabar rented out a uniform to an organization without RCMP permission, but it had also done so after having received a clear warning against doing so. The Force complained to the manager of Malabar, who promised to heed the Force's wishes in the future.[24]

The Mounties making one of their many parade appearances (Vancouver, 1953). (City of Vancouver Archives, CVA 180-2242. Reprinted courtesy of Pacific National Exhibition.)

The mythic Mountie of novels and films had helped create a demand for Mountie costumes that was clearly causing the Force some administrative headaches. Yet, as Commissioner Wood's softening position suggested, the public relations benefits were obvious, too. In fact, so famous was the Mountie uniform that when, in the early 1950s, receptionists at Ontario government tourist Reception Centres began wearing red, white, and navy blue uniforms, their appearances led to inquiries as to whether they were "lady Mounties."[25]

Demand for the uniforms was sustained through the identification of the Mountie as a symbol of Canada. In the late 1950s, for instance, a uniform was used in a CBC-TV musical sketch ridiculing an American tourist attempting to converse with a Mountie on duty. The script for the sketch went:

> American tourist walks on with hat, binoculars, camera, sunglasses, loud shirt, cigar. He is chewing gum.
>> He says "Hi Mac!".
>> No answer.
>> American—"Nice day".
>> No answer.
>> American—"Pretty darn hot though".
>> No answer.
>> American—"What gives around this burg today? By the way I'm executive Vice-President of Walterburgers, New York. We manufacture all them paper cups."
>> No answer.
>> American—"But I guess that don't mean nothing to you".
>> No answer.
>> (American looks at him with interest for the first time).
>> American—"Say, what do you do for a living?".
>> Reaction—to black.[26]

This sketch was clearly designed to appeal to the anti-American strain of English-Canadian nationalism—pitting the pushy, self-centred American against the staid, disinterested symbol of Canadian law and order. The writers drew on the trope of the annoying tourist, contrasting him with the venerable Mountie. This was familiar territory for the Mountie: confirming Canadian superiority over the less civilized characteristics of American visitors, and Americans in general. By the 1960s American culture, rather than the cultures of Native peoples or Eastern European immigrants, was taking centre stage as the "other" over which the Mountie demonstrated English-Canadian cultural superiority. Ironically, this image, used so often to assert Canadians' superiority over their U.S. neighbours, was highly sought-after by American visitors to Canada.

A Tourist Icon

In 1937 the Canadian Chamber of Commerce met in Vancouver for its annual meeting. In his address to this gathering, E.H. Adams chose to focus on what many were coming to see as a panacea for the country's economic ills: tourism. In outlining his suggestions on how to improve the tourist trade, Adams called on the delegates to make more use of the Mountie's popularity. "Too often," he suggested, "we Americanize our attractions under the mistaken idea that the tourist from across the line will feel more at home."

He continued: "The tourist does not want to feel at home. He wants to feel that he is in a foreign country and to get the thrill attached to such travelling. . . . How often have we . . . heard visitors ask 'Where are the Mounties' . . . whose deeds of valour and endurance are spoken of in fact and fiction throughout the world[?]"

Visitors from the United States, he opined, expect "to find something that is romantic or different to anything they have seen at home . . . something that is traditionally British."[27] A decade and a half later a request by the CPR seeking photographs "for inclusion in the Canadian Pacific Railway's official photographic files for ultimate distribution with a view to 'selling' Canada as a tourist magnet" underscored the staying power of the Mountie symbol.[28]

A 1952 editorial in a Niagara Falls newspaper illustrates how important the Mountie remained to proponents of tourism. When Ottawa mayor Charlotte Whitton opted to remove the Mountie from the cover of her city's tourist booklet in favour of a cover jointly depicting Samuel de Champlain, an Indian, and the Rideau Canal, she hoped to demonstrate that "Ottawa has other things to offer besides Mounties." The editorial writer was sceptical: "Give an American tourist the picture of a modern Mountie and ten-to-one the tourist will take off in pursuit of a live model, camera posed, but give the same tourist a picture of Champlain and he will probably ask: 'Who's that guy?'"

The Mountie, the editorial continued, was essential to the tourist industry because he "symbolizes Canada just like Uncle Sam symbolizes the United States." As such, the writer called upon Mayor Whitton to "relegate ancient Champlain back among her memoirs and put back the Mountie to his rightful position at Canada's front door."[29]

Offered to the world as something quintessentially Canadian, the Mountie had became an attraction that visitors to Canada expected to see. In 1964, for instance, the Tourist Industry Group of the Victoria Chamber of Commerce approached the B.C. Minister of Recreation and Conservation about setting up a Mountie tableau in a tourist information centre. The Minister thereupon made a formal request to the Force:

> This group has approached us on numerous occasions with the request a Mountie be stationed at the Parliament Buildings so that those visiting Victoria would be able to see and photograph them and as this was impossible, this new proposal has now been submitted. It is felt that the Mountie has been selected as a symbol of Canadian identity and Canadian unity and those visiting the City seem to expect to find this symbol. The colourful uniform too, of course, adds a great appeal to the photographer.[30]

Over the course of the twentieth century, businesses had been responding to the public demand for the Mountie in a variety of ways. Some sought uniforms to bring customers to watch their movies. Others hoped the presence of

As part of its billboard campaign to attract American tourists to Vancouver, the Vancouver Tourist Association drew upon one of Canada's most famous icons — the Mountie — to offer American visitors a unique and authentic travel experience. (City of Vancouver Archives, Add MSS 633, File 21, #1937)

real Mounties would live up to the preconceptions of American tourists and convince them to spend their holiday savings in Canada. These were highly orchestrated attempts by movie directors, local businessmen, and others to profit from the romantic mythology surrounding the Force. Yet there was another, less organized, demand on the Force's time too: a constant stream of requests by individuals, some tourists, some not, for their very own photograph of a Mountie.

The Positives and Negatives of Photography

The sheer number of requests for photographs of Mounties left some commanding officers seeking guidance from the commissioner and making suggestions of their own as to how to deal with the delicate matter of publicity. C.E. Rivett-Carnac, then an assistant commissioner, occasionally voiced his concerns to Commissioner Wood. As commanding officer of "F" Division in Regina in 1949, he noted the delicacy required in handling such requests: "The point with photographers . . . is that we have to give them something to send them away satisfied and without friction being caused, but at the same time have to reduce what we do give them to such an absolute minimum that they cannot take undue advantage."[31] Two years later, while commanding "E" Division in Vancouver, Rivett-Carnac outlined the Force's chief dilemma regarding its image in a memo to Commissioner L. H. Nicholson concerning a request for slides of the Force by a Mr. Tanner of Victoria Photo Supply Ltd.: "If we do not give Mr. Tanner our co-operation," he warned, "there is nothing to prevent him taking pictures of anyone he sees in uniform and using these for the purpose he requires." The result, Rivett-Carnac continued, "might be highly detrimental from the standpoint of the results achieved and instead of being a credit to the organization, might be the reverse." A response from Deputy Commissioner C.K. Gray suggested agreement on the matter. Rivett-Carnac was authorized to co-operate with Tanner in securing the slides, but was to ensure that any photographs taken be approved before being distributed.[32]

The editing of such photographs seems to have been a common practice by the Force. Even View-Master reels were not beyond its corrective hand. In January 1956, in approving the View-Master proposal from a Portland, Oregon, company, the Force made two observations. First, it regretted that one photo seemed to include a puddle of engine oil in the foreground—hardly acceptable for a photograph of the RCMP "Highway Patrol." In a letter to the company, the Force requested that another picture be used, but officially left this matter to the company's discretion. Second, it told the firm that its highway patrol officers carried out their duties in a brown uniform, not wearing the famous scarlet tunic, but suggested this was "a minor point and no harm will be done if this picture is left in the series." The letter to the company also included a historical outline of the Force and "descriptive information on each scene."[33]

The historical outline sent to Portland suggested that the RCMP was beginning to find fault with the "classic" Mountie myth. The account described the Crime Detection Laboratory and the Identification Branch, reflecting the Force's pride in itself as a modern, efficient law-enforcement apparatus—a side of the Force often overshadowed by the romantic myth. Another description, entitled "RCMP and Indian," suggested that the Force was not completely satisfied with earlier versions of its relationship with Native peoples in Canada:

Since its first meetings with the Western tribes, the Force has enjoyed peaceful relationships with Canada's Indians, for in the van[guard] of the small force were men who quickly won the respect and confidence of the chiefs of the 30,000 natives that peopled the Western plains. This situation was to stand the Force in good stead in the ensuing years when, on more than one occasion, catastrophe was averted by the staunchness of Canada's Indians. (The slide shows a member of the Force conversing with a Chief outside his tepee.)[34]

The difference between this summary of events and the history of RCMP-Native relations as it appeared in popular literature on the Force is striking. By 1956 Indians were not wild men willing to scalp innocent settlers. They were becoming "staunch" allies of the Force.

As requests for photographs and public appearances continued to flood in to detachments across the country, some officers sought a clear-cut policy on dealing with such requests. In 1956 Superintendent J. H. T. Poudrette, commanding "A" Division in Ottawa and thus responsible for RCMP duties on Parliament Hill, wrote to the commissioner asking permission to issue a Post Order to guide his underlings. Pointing to the division's location in Ottawa and the duties of its Protective Branch, Poudrette wrote, "We receive constantly at all levels requests for permission to photograph our members."[35] After some tinkering by the commissioner's office what emerged was a code of conduct for Mounties in dealing with the public.

Post Order No. 11 outlined the rules governing RCMP contact with its adoring public for members of "A" Division in Ottawa. "Regarding visitors, tourists and the like," members of the Force were urged to "graciously co-operate *as long as it does not interfere with their duties.*" Co-operating officers were to "pose with dignity and proper bearing, being sure that such photos will not portray them improperly dressed or in ridiculous poses." Thus, "They should discourage tourists who wish them to pose showing uncalled-for-familiarity, such as with [an] arm around a female's waist, etc." Approval from the Officer in Charge of the Protective Branch or the Officer Commanding "A" Division was required for any photograph to be used for "*professional purposes.*" The order summarized the overall policy of the Force towards the professional use of its image:

(a) The Commissioner has no objection to pictures of a member of the Force being used commercially, providing:

(1) It is strictly as a souvenir or gift item (such as Post Cards) and providing that nothing is said or done in displaying or selling them which would indicate or imply that they have RCMP sponsorship or approval;

(2) The photograph, before being so used must be forwarded by the person or firm concerned to the Commissioner for examination and approval;

(3) The photograph will not be used directly or indirectly for advertising or publicity purposes.

At all times members were to use "common sense regarding the setting and background of the shot which, in itself might tend to make a picture ludicrous or to imply advertising, such as posing in front of an advertising poster or shop." Ever conscious of the RCMP image, the orders also included the following command: "When a photo is taken at a Post where more than one member is on duty, the member in charge will detail the member whose appearance for the purpose will be of most credit to the Force."[36]

The "appearance" of the Mountie has always been central to his appeal. His manly and respectable appearance in the classic literature of the Force differentiated him from his antagonists and identified him as suitable for the task of administering justice. Public relations exercises adhered rigidly to this novelistic formula. An incident in April 1960 makes this point clear. On April 22 a Mrs. Baldwin of Malak Studios called the Force "requesting the presence of a member of the Force in Review Order in front of the Parliament Buildings . . . to be photographed with the new Canadian Mother of the Year." The same request had been received the year before and, given the guidelines of Post Order No. 11, "A" Division had presumably responded positively. Unfortunately, the previous year's crew had failed to consider the exact nature of proper appearance for a Mountie when meeting the Canadian Mother of the Year. In her 1960 request Baldwin "remarked that they would prefer to have a younger and less paunchy specimen to photograph this year and mentioned that they were not at all happy with the physical setup of the member we detailed last year." The commissioner approved this request and "A" Division was informed of the corrective measures to be taken.[37]

Perhaps news of this incident travelled quickly, for in June of that same year, in a confidential memorandum to W.G. Hurlow, officer in charge of the New Westminster Sub-Division, regarding a *National Geographic* request to photograph a Mountie, Assistant Commissioner D.O. Forrest suggested that Hurlow select a man "from a point of view of his appearance in uniform, rather than his police experience and ability." Hurlow's choice was a corporal whom he described as "about 6' tall, weighing about 190 lbs., and is a slim, proportionately built individual of athletic appearance." This was a man who fit the Mountie myth. His "official bearing and a pleasant personality" sealed the deal.[38] Members of the Force were now receiving orders from their superiors calling on them to actively resemble what were considered the more positive aspects of the classic myth. The Force was becoming complicit in its own commodification.

Even books stressing the romantic image of the Force received the RCMP's co-operation. The publishers of Alan Phillips's *The Living Legend* received permission from Liaison Officer Bayfield to use a photograph of the Musical Ride on the back cover of the book.[39] The Force also loaned a Kodachrome positive to Joe Holliday for use in the *Dale of the Mounted* series.[40] This assistance to proponents of the classic myth rested uneasily with an RCMP warning to the Regina *Leader Post* a month later. The newspaper wanted to do a "features" page on the Force, and Bayfield informed the newspaper that in approving the request for access to the recruit training facility in Regina, he would like them "to insure [sic] that the finished article" was "entirely factual and not overdramatized."[41] This case revealed the tension between the Force's desire to free itself from the romantic image and its dependence on that same image for public relations reasons. The same tension dominated the *Dale of the Mounted* series, as the chivalric Mountie of the antimodern era was transported to the high-technology world of nuclear physics and naval operations. The Force had very few corrections to make in editing an extremely laudatory 1958 *Omaha World Herald* article stressing the modern characteristics of the Force.[42]

The tension between the classic Mountie and a more modern rendition of the Force was evident not just in traditional media like newspapers and books, but on television as well. In the U.S.-produced series *Sergeant Preston of the Yukon* (1955-58), Richard Simmons played the title role: a Mountie who in the tradition of the classic myth arrested evil-doers "in the name of the Crown" with the assistance of his dog, "Yukon King," and his horse, "Rex." His exploits brought him face to face with superstitious Indians, helpless women, and greedy prospectors, all familiar stereotypes from earlier films and novels.

Yet *Sergeant Preston of the Yukon* also contained hints of a new Mountie myth. In one episode, "Bad Medicine," Sergeant Preston finds himself in a battle against "ignorance and superstition" as a troublesome medicine man named

Kluk-Wan convinces the Chilkat tribe to forgo a white doctor's diphtheria vaccine in favour of his own traditional cure. Preston is aided by the chief's daughter in convincing the chief of the medicine man's folly; and in the end the Mountie apprehends Kluk-Wan and saves the tribe from what seemed a certain epidemic. Here a classic tale might have ended, but in the mid-1950s this Mountie story offered a further twist. As the show draws to a close, Kluk-Wan joins forces with the white doctor and announces in broken English, "My Medicine and White Man's medicine work together." Preston of the Yukon had not only saved the Chilkat tribe from certain death, but he also seemed well on the way to reconciling Native and European cultures.

The late 1950s saw the appearance of another television series about the Force, this one of Canadian origin, entitled simply *RCMP*. The program "dealt with the modern adventures of a three-man detachment in the fictitious town of Shamattawa, in northern Saskatchewan." The French-Canadian actor Gilles Pelletier starred as "the ever-efficient and always friendly Corporal Jacques Gagnier," who was assisted by Constables Frank Scott and Bill Mitchell. French-Canadian and English-Canadian officers thus worked together in the modern world to protect their "small town from the predatory ways of urban outsiders." While the program thus gave off hints that the classic myth was slowly giving way, *RCMP* by no means ushered in a dramatic change in the Mountie's image. The series lasted but one season, though it continued to appear occasionally in syndication.[43]

Conclusion

In 1969 Eaton's celebrated its one-hundredth birthday as one of Canada's leading department stores. As part of the celebrations for this achievement, management made sure to invite Mounties to the party. More specifically, Eaton's approached the Force with the aim of setting up an RCMP display in various stores to mark the centennial. With the co-operation of local RCMP detachments, the company set up displays in a number of cities in Western Canada.

Eaton's representatives, well aware of the Force's official opposition to its image being used for commercial purposes, promised that no selling would be connected with the displays. Yet, rather conveniently, the company's merchandise display manager, W.J. Hepplewhite, informed Superintendent Peter Bazowski that the displays were not going to be concentrated in a central place, but instead would be spread throughout the store. Hepplewhite was quick to assure the Force, "This is because of a space problem and not to get customers into various corners of the Store."[44]

The Force accepted this explanation. What the RCMP did not accept so easily was the content of the proposed displays. The Force wanted displays that offered a more modern, up-to-date version of its achievements and characteristics. Inspector G.A. Kennedy recorded the concerns of Commissioner M.F.A. Lindsay in a memo:

> The only criticism we have with the proposed layout is that perhaps too much stress is being placed on past history. While we realize the importance of this, particularly from the public point of view, we would prefer that the central theme be more on the portrayal of a force that is completely modern; one that has at its disposal all of the latest scientific aids that are associated with law enforcement agencies today.[45]

A compromise was reached, and as the "Eaton 100 Police Show" program trumpeted, the displays offered "the story of the Royal Canadian Mounted Police—the past, present and future."[46] This compromise between past and present was a portent of things to come.

Yet there was another compromise in this case as well, one that would have surely raised the ire of those early writers of Mountie fiction so concerned with the coming evils of modernity. The mythic Mountie, who had first emerged through antimodern dissent, was now clearly enmeshed within the web of Canada's consumer culture. Constant requests for uniforms, photographs, and public appearances had attested to the continued popularity of the classic image. While the government had banned the use of the Force's image in advertising, companies had found other ways to take up and profit from the Mountie image. These means ranged from uniform rentals to tourism campaigns and included toys, wallpaper, and photographic layouts in company magazines. The mythic Mountie, who had once stood on guard against the evils of overcivilization, now stood as a backdrop to consumer goods in a department store.

4

A Moment of High Nationalism
(and Tension), 1968-73

The whole world seemed to be reinventing itself and showing its
modernity in Montreal.

– William Thorsall, editor-in-chief,
The Globe and Mail, on Expo 67

In 1963, at the height of the Cold War, Prime Minister Lester Pearson held his
first meeting with U.S. President Lyndon Johnson. As with all such meetings,
this one was preceded by a gift exchange. Pearson presented Johnson with an
English saddle, "a gift hard to explain given the fact that LBJ rode western."
Unimpressed, the President suggested that, perhaps, his wife could use it. She
was thrilled, and noted in her diary, "Just like the Royal Canadian Mounted
Police use. . . . Those men who were always the symbol of romance and daring
adventure in my childhood."[1] Even in Texas, the classic Mountie myth still had
power in the early 1960s.

As a president of the United States, Lyndon Johnson is closely associated
with the era of conflict and cultural upheaval that was "the sixties." Issues such
as civil rights and the Vietnam War polarized American society. Canada too
faced an upheaval of its own that included the Quiet Revolution in Quebec as
well as student and antiwar protests. Yet in the midst of this upheaval was a
moment of high nationalism. Canada's centennial celebration of 1967 called
forth a previously muted expression of national pride. As William Thorsall of

The latest in a long line
of graduating Mounties.
(RCMP Centennial Calendar.
Reprinted with the
permission of the Regina
Chamber of Commerce.)

The Globe and Mail explained in an editorial marking the thirtieth anniversary of the celebrations, Expo 67's comfortable idealism was misleading: "In one sense, Expo 67 misled us in its happy-face, generic idealism. It obscured the precise moment in Canadian history when the repressive myths of Canadian nationhood were breaking up, and a whole country of peoples and individuals was seeking liberation from the defining authorities of their youth."[2] The social forces that spoiled Canada's birthday party would also have a dramatic impact upon its national mythologies.

An Awkward Inheritance

At first glance it might appear that the classic, romantic myth of the Mountie would hardly have been difficult for the Force to live with. The fictional Mountie appears in such a positive and heroic light that he would seem the perfect fit for any celebration of the Force's accomplishments. He would also seem to work well in tandem with the many supposedly "factual" histories produced about the Force, most of which were so one-sidedly positive in their treatment that unsuspecting readers could be forgiven for confusing them with the Mountie novels.

By the 1960s, however, certain characteristics of the mythic Mountie, along with many recent incidents in the Force's history, had rendered the classic version of the myth problematic. It was now difficult to reconcile Donald Creighton's assertion that the Aboriginal "chiefs were properly grateful for their new peace and security" with the increasingly prominent arguments of Native rights advocates. Nor was it easy to reconcile the depiction of women as helpless and subservient to their Mountie heroes with the increasingly resonant voice of second-wave feminism. For many people, the political and demographic reality of the 1960s and 1970s rendered the gender, class, and ethnic stereotypes prevalent in Mountie fiction untenable. The role of the Mountie, too, had changed. Given the new flag and talk of patriating the Constitution, Canadians were less comfortable with a hero who was seen to be serving the British Empire, the monarchy, and the white man's burden. Moreover, with the exception of the *Dale of the Mounted* series, a large gulf existed between the rustic setting of Mountie fiction and the day-to-day police work of the actual Force. Time had passed the classic Mountie by, though he was so closely associated with the Force that simply putting him out to pasture with his horse was unthinkable. Somehow the Force and its supporters had to bridge the gap between its present reality and its mythic past. To do so would require a much more active policy for monitoring the use of its image. More importantly, it would also require an intervention into the production of Mountie mythology. Here was the challenge faced by the Force as it approached its own centenary, in 1973.

While the romantic image of the Mountie remained central to movies and stories about the Force long after the antimodern period, in the 1960s some less flattering portrayals of the Force had begun to appear. One of these was imported from the United States in the form of a television cartoon character named Dudley Do-Right.

Created by Alex Anderson and Jay Ward in 1948, Dudley Do-Right premiered on a segment of *The Bullwinkle Show* in 1961 and appeared on ABC in his own series in 1969 and 1970, in a total of thirty-nine episodes broadcast on network television. Each was four and a half minutes in length.[3] Do-Right, though originally inspired by Nelson Eddy's character in *Rose Marie*, was possibly the most incompetent police officer television audiences had ever seen.[4] The show itself was a send-up of the old Mountie melodrama. Supervised by Inspector Fenwick, Dudley battled his arch enemy, Snidely Whiplash, who was constantly kidnapping Dudley's best gal, Nell, Inspector Fenwick's daughter. There was no tension between duty and love here as there had been in the classic fiction of the Force. Indeed, there was no tension at all. While Dudley fawned over Nell, she was in love with his horse. In these Mountie stories, the Mountie neither outsmarted nor outmanoeuvred the villain. Whiplash either escaped or was apprehended by accident.

The transition from a competent and daring Mountie to this comic, clumsy, slow-thinking variation was not the only difference between this show and previous renditions of the Mountie myth. The very characteristics that dominated the classic story of the Mountie were now held up for ridicule. Hence Do-Right's studio biography. This "nauseatingly unsullied figure" was born in Toronto, where he "attended the DeLacey School of Good conduct and Decorum." There, we are told, he often won the school's exemplary behaviour award, yet was "affectionately known to his classmates as 'Fink' Do-Right." He went on to attend McGill University, "where he majored in Personal Hygiene and minored in Good-Citizenship." Seeking employment upon graduation, Dudley turned to "that one organization pure enough to meet [his] standards—the Mounties!" Described as a "stickler for regulation," he is "the only Mountie known to starch his underwear and socks and to adjust his hat with a plumb-bob and a mason's level." In addition, "he has been known to jail a pregnant spaniel for violating the anti-litter law."[5]

Jay Ward's contributions to the 1963 April Fool *TV Guide* confirm this view of the cartoon Mountie: in it Dudley is described as "stalwart, clean-living, chaste, dense—and a crashing bore." Ward describes his creation as "equally sickening off screen and on." In fact, "He even wears a bathing suit in the shower, he's so modest!" In addition, Do-Right is credited with helping to found "The Mounties, Canucks and fur Trappers Anti-Smut League and Madrigal Society."[6] The characteristics of ideal manhood that had been central to the classic Mountie were now portrayed as passé and out of step with a new, more "hip" ideal of male deportment. The Mountie ideal was becoming ridiculous.

Do-Right's exploits on the TV screen backed up this reputation and, in the process, called into question many of the assumptions central to the classic Mountie myth. Do-Right's antagonists were neither Native nor recent immigrants. They were fellow Caucasians, Snidely Whiplash and his gang.[7] Whiplash had an uncontrollable urge to kidnap women and tie them to railroad tracks. It was Dudley's duty to save Nell from this fate. Often, though, it was Nell who saved the bungling Dudley and in the process further undermined the classic myth of the Force.

In one episode, Nell and Dudley exchange duties. Nell pursues Snidely Whiplash while Dudley becomes a homemaker. Inspector Fenwick, fearing that his daughter's success as a Mountie could lead to women's suffrage, aids

Dudley in helping the criminals escape. In another show Inspector Fenwick, seeking to discourage Nell's interest in policing, sends her off to "read a book." Unfortunately for Inspector Fenwick, the only books she has access to as the daughter of an RCMP inspector stationed in the Canadian Northwest are law books. When the Inspector and Dudley finally succeed in capturing Snidely Whiplash, Nell draws upon her recently gained understanding of the legal code to offer a spirited defence of Whiplash and secures his release to spite her father. While a Mountie's red coat did not go to Nell's head "like champagne," as it had for female characters in earlier fiction, Nell had no trouble "seeing red" whenever she faced sexual discrimination.

Besides offering a new role for female characters, the Dudley Do-Right segments offered a very different view of the Force itself. Along with Do-Right's mistakes and misadventures, the sterling image of the Force as a whole was lampooned. In one episode, Dudley's horse is called into action to win back the RCMP post in a poker game. The Inspector had gambled the mortgage away to Snidely Whiplash. This was hardly an image the RCMP would endorse, yet there is no indication that the Force took action against the producers of the series. In fact, the only action taken against the series seems to have been by the U.S. Forestry Service, which opposed the "Stokey the Bear" episode in which a "700-pound cinnamon-colored bear wearing a mountie hat" wandered around *starting* fires after being hypnotized by Snidely Whiplash. It aired only once, in 1961.[8]

Do-Right's exploits in comic books strayed little from those on television. A 1973 "Rocky and Bullwinkle" comic entitled "Stolen Luck" saw Dudley raise the ire of Inspector Fenwick by failing to pay proper respect to Lance Sturdyman, the first commander of the post. In a few short pages, Do-Right then manages to almost hang himself raising the flag, injure the Inspector by mistaking live ammunition for blanks, cause an explosion by confusing gun powder with baking powder during kitchen duty, and then, in pursuit of Whiplash, forget his compass and circle the fort endlessly only to stumble across his arch-enemy in his own barracks.[9]

Another, equally famous, send-up of the classic Mountie was the "Lumberjack Song" sketch performed on the British comedy program, *Monty Python's Flying*

Circus. The sketch, which first aired in 1969, centred upon a cross-dressing lumberjack who sang about his exploits in the Canadian wilderness. The lumberjack was accompanied by a choir of singing Mounties made to appear increasingly uncomfortable with each successive verse of the song. No longer content to leave the Mountie singing love songs on horseback or in a canoe, in the context of the 1960s, entertainers were now parodying these authority figures. Whereas antimodern writers had once drawn upon the Force's exploits in an attempt to stave off challenges to traditional institutions and hierarchies, Jay Ward, the Monty Python troupe, and others were now doing just the reverse: they drew upon the image of the Mountie to call such authority into question.

In Canada by the mid-1970s, writers such as Rudy Wiebe, Ken Mitchell, and others used the Mountie image to "comment ironically on their own society," focusing their works on the plight of the country's Aboriginal population.[10] In 1973 in Wiebe's *The Temptations of Big Bear*, a description of the Force suggested that the classic image was no longer quite so dominant:

> The North West Mounted Police were not all handsome, clean-cut, and six feet tall. Some told barrack-room stories that would have made a Victorian daughter blush; more got drunk on the whisky they confiscated. Some were young Canadians wild for adventure, others British regulars looking for jobs when imperial wars were scarce and who believed that the proper job for Indians, as for Untouchables, was to have them sweat polishing high boots.[11]

While preparations for the centennial celebrations preceded the publication of these words, it was difficult to miss the growing hints that the public was becoming weary, and skeptical, of the classic image of the Force.

The Force and the 1960s

Even if the RCMP at times felt helpless to interfere as directors in Hollywood or fiction writers closer to home romanticized the Force and its achievements, why did it accept its sorry lot so easily? Former RCMP historian Stan Horrall proposed one explanation. As early as 1931, he wrote, Commissioner James MacBrien had decided that "the romance of the West had gone far enough," and "the Force should project a new image as a modern, efficient law-enforcement body." According to Horrall's account:

> As a start [MacBrien] suggested the dropping of the word "Mounted" from the title of the Force. From the protests that greeted this suggestion, it was apparent that Canadians cherished the legendary Force and would not give it up easily. Although the myth was sometimes an encumbrance the Force came to realize that it reflected a very positive image, and certainly one that made excellent public relations.[12]

MacBrien's intervention would be followed by many more complaints from the Force that Hollywood romance was overshadowing the RCMP's modern, professional identity, accompanied as well by public outcries defending the traditions of the Force, including objections that greeted the termination of its equestrian training.[13] Commissioner W.L. Higgitt, in his foreword to the 1969 issue of a public memorandum outlining the history and present duties of the Force, made his stance on the matter clear: "Although the public has never lacked for reading material, motion picture and television productions dealing with the RCMP, it is unfortunate that in many instances the Force has been used merely as a background for some absurd fiction leaving the public completely mystified as to its true function."[14] As inspirational and widespread as the image of the mythic Mountie had been in the past, the day-to-day activities and accomplishments of a modern police force remained absent from public understanding.

The RCMP's 1973 centennial celebrations became an attempt to bridge the old and the new. In constructing the story that dominated the centennial, organizers were greatly influenced by the political climate of the time. As comfortable as elements of the classic image of the Mounted Police had once been for the Force, those organizing the centennial were well aware that renovations were necessary.

In the Canada of the 1960s, the classic image of the Force was clearly anachronistic. The arrival on the political scene of an increasingly powerful Native rights movement reflected a new era in which growing public sympathy towards Canada's indigenous peoples now precluded essentializing "the Indian" and the "half-breed" as the enemy.[15] The "second wave" of the feminist movement further disrupted the classic myth. Many women would have seen any attempt to resurrect the devoted damsel in distress waiting for her Mountie as comic, if not offensive.[16] The recommendations of the federal government's Royal Commission on Bilingualism and Biculturalism also played a part in the shift, as did the subsequent reaction of "many ethnic groups who found this dualist image . . . offensive" and "sought official assurance that their own aspirations and interests would not be overlooked."[17] The end result was a policy of multiculturalism within a bilingual framework. Gone, then, were the days when "Chink Woolley" was an acceptable depiction of a Chinese-Canadian in a novel or when dimwitted but devious French-Canadians were welcome depictions of francophones in film. By the 1970s, even one of the legendary villains in the classic RCMP tale of Canadian history, Louis Riel, leader of the Métis resistance in 1869 and 1885, had been fully rehabilitated and was seen more as a hero than a rebel in popular and academic writings on the West.[18] These changes in the country's political culture meant that it was time to update the classic story of the Force.

The era of the 1960s was also one in which, according to historian George Mosse, "Police forces assumed a special significance." Mosse argues that as a result of civil disturbances, "The word 'police' was transformed into a slogan: for some the guardians of the law became the enemies of the people, while for others they represented the last bastion of besieged society."[19] While the Force might have taken some consolation from the location of the most famous of these clashes between demonstrators and police—the United States—questions were being raised about its own handling of dissent.

This questioning of RCMP tactics had touched a nerve within the Force as early as the late 1940s. Former Commissioner C.W. Harvison had been frustrated by media dissatisfaction with the Force's handling of the Gouzenko affair. Complaints in the 1950s and 1960s about "gestapo tactics," too much secrecy, and objections to the use of informers meant that the Force's image was indeed starting to tarnish.[20] If these criticisms removed some of the shine from the Force's image, revelations a decade or so later meant that some of the protective layers of this image were in danger of peeling off.

The beginning of the 1970s was not a good time for the Force's public image. The political impact of the use of the War Measures Act and the arrests of Québécois nationalists on questionable grounds promoted a sense of caution in the Force. It was also a time when the media were beginning to explore the relationship between the Force and Aboriginal Canadians, particularly those on reserves. In October 1970 an RCMP officer shot a fourteen-year-old Native boy named Michael Muskego just outside Saskatoon: the resulting public enquiry raised doubts about the Force's competence. In late 1971 a Chilcotin Indian, Fred Quilt, was allegedly beaten in Alexis Creek, B.C., while in police custody.[21] To a Force very much aware of and, in its own opinion, dependent on its public image, such episodes—so far removed from the classic chivalric tradition—were a nightmare. So were public demonstrations by Native peoples and teenagers protesting police brutality.[22] In January 1973, just as the centennial was getting underway, three RCMP officers in White Rock, British Columbia, were facing charges of attempted arson.[23] Lorne and Caroline Brown's *Unauthorized History of the RCMP*, published in 1973, was yet another dent in the Force's armour.

Perhaps the most damaging blow was levelled by a former member of the Force in the July 1972 issue of *Maclean's*. Disillusioned after fourteen years of stellar service, Jack Ramsay quit the Force in 1971 and felt obliged to go public with his views. He documented dozens of disgraceful incidents perpetrated by Force members, including rampant drinking, the forging of crime statistics, and perjury under oath. His was a ringing condemnation of an organizational structure that forbade candid communication within:

> The force still has fine policemen, men who serve in the old tradition, but it's fast losing public respect, and in trying to regain it the RCMP is much more concerned with polishing its image than with pursuing its ideal. As a result, morale has fallen so low that alcoholism and suicide have become serious problems. And many of the force's officers only make things worse. Some of them are so inept they can maintain discipline only by fear; they mistreat and pressure the lower ranks who in turn, often persecute the public. Especially during my last seven years on the force, I watched fellow members lying, falsifying records and ignoring suspects' rights until I came to dislike putting on the famous scarlet tunic, because it made me feel like a hypocrite.[24]

This kind of coverage, in a major newsmagazine, underlined how merely polishing up the romantic legend would not be enough to overcome the Force's tarnished image. Substantial renovations were necessary. The Force was well aware of this, and so too was the business community.

Along with its past sins and recent indiscretions, the Force also had to contend with a federal government very much trying to reinvent Canada as a bilingual and bicultural nation—an effort that sometimes provoked a very negative response from the public. In 1972, for instance, rumours began to circulate about the Trudeau government's plans to replace the Force's "Royal" name with the more easily translatable "Police Canada." The public outcry against this break from tradition dominated editorial pages in spring 1972, particularly in the West. B.C. Attorney General Leslie Peterson was so incensed by the federal initiative that he threatened to cancel the Force's contract if its name was changed, and the Trudeau government quickly abandoned its plans.[25] The lesson to be learned was that any severe break with the Force's tradition could quickly turn into a public relations disaster.

In general, the political climate of the 1970s dictated that the Force display its history without relying on an "other" against which its members would be favourably compared. As a result, the Force faced a dilemma. On one side was an increasing amount of direct criticism of the Force's activities. This, combined with the general questioning of authority of the 1960s, meant that the organization badly needed some sort of public relations initiative. Yet the Force could hardly rely on the classic myth that had served it so well in the past, given that new governmental initiatives brought in to address the changing ethnic and linguistic face of the country had caused this classic myth to lose much of its utility. Indeed, parts of it were very much a hindrance.

Still, some authors continued to add to the classic genre. Organizers looking for advice on how *not* to celebrate the centennial given the political culture of the time needed look no further than Delbert Young's 1968 book, *The Mounties*. Young's laudatory history of the Force drew upon many of the tropes of the classic myth. The Métis were lazy and uninterested in working the land. The government starved non-Treaty Indians into submission. "Howling, jeering" strikers battled the Force in the Winnipeg General Strike—a strike that Young frankly admitted led to the reorganization of the Force. The RCMP worked hard to bring the "near-stone-age" Eskimos "into the twentieth century." Evil Doukhobor extremists had to be subdued by the Force. Almighty Voice and Igor Gouzenko, soon to be exorcized from the 1973 centennial by Commissioner Higgitt and the Centennial Advisory Committee, were front and centre in Young's tribute to the Force. This was no way to celebrate a birthday.

Instead of relying on Young and other like-minded authors who still clung to the classic myth, the Force turned to the advertising and public relations experts who spent so much of their time and energy monitoring and moulding public opinion. The architects of consumer culture who had been in such a rush to capitalize upon the classic Mountie were now going to be intricately involved in refashioning his image.

Organizing the Centennial

Sometime during 1968 a letter arrived at RCMP headquarters in Ottawa. It contained no legal documents, nor was it a terrorist threat. It was a letter from a private company asking what the Force was planning to do to celebrate its upcoming centennial. Over the next few months, more and more letters arrived from other companies as well as from individuals. All suggested the necessity of a one-hundredth birthday party for Canada's federal police force. Many of these letters came from souvenir manufacturers intent on profiting from such a celebration.[26] According to John Bentham, the RCMP officer in charge of the centennial's Flare Square exhibit in Calgary, the Force was not initially convinced of the need for a large and expensive commemoration. However, the obvious public support (particularly in the West) soon won over the sceptics.[27] Given the context of the 1970s, it is not surprising that the Force heeded the advice of the public on this matter. After consultation with government bureaucrats, the RCMP set up a steering committee to co-ordinate the centennial effort.

In planning for this 1973 centennial, organizers and supporters chose not to rely on the RCMP's classic image. Instead, they renovated the Force's history to

Jerry Potts, a mixed-blood guide, helped the force find its way across the Prairies during the legendary March West. His achievements are honoured in Mountie literature but, as the following quotations demonstrate, the ways he has been remembered have changed over time:

R.G. MacBeth, 1921:
"a short, heavy-set, taciturn man, half Scot and half Piegan . . . became a splendid help to the police."

T.M. Longstreth, 1955:
"This dark, stubby, slope-shouldered son of a Scot fur-trader and a Piegan squaw was not much to look at, but he had gifts that amounted to genius."

S.W. Horrall, 1973:
"the son of a Blood Indian woman and a Scottish trader . . . a short, strongly built man . . . his knowledge of the plains and his uncanny sense of direction was to become an invaluable asset to the Mounted Police."

(Glenbow Archives, Calgary Alberta, NA-1237-1)

make it more in tune with the times, setting up a highly centralized organizational branch to co-ordinate the celebrations. The branch, in conjunction with numerous private firms, developed the centennial's dominant narrative to reflect the Force's desire to adapt to the political climate of the time.

If the classic story of the Mounties was no longer guaranteed a sympathetic audience across the country, it also had less and less relevance for members of the Force itself. The Force of the 1970s shared few characteristics with either the Force of 1873, or its representation in popular literature. In enforcing federal statutes and fulfilling contract agreements with all provinces but Ontario and Quebec, the Force was responsible for upholding laws that varied from drug law enforcement to overseeing the Migratory Birds Convention Act. It fulfilled its duties through operational divisions set up in each province, plus 41 subdivisions and 689 detachments. By 1972 the commissioner (with the assistance of two deputy commissioners and six assistant commissioners) presided over a total of 13,726 members.[28]

The RCMP had undergone dramatic changes since the 1950s. For instance, when historian Stan Horrall first joined the Force in 1956, the emphasis at the Depot Division in Regina, site of basic training, was on foot training and equitation. After graduation, an officer lived in a barracks and could be transferred from one place to another without warning. The city police forces they came into contact with were invariably better paid. After three years in the Force, Horrall left to study history at universities in Canada and Dublin, Ireland.[29] When he returned to the Force as its historian in 1968, he encountered a police force in which training was now practical, technical, and academic (equitation was no longer mandatory). Restrictions on the right to be married or divorced were on the way out, and a de facto union had resulted in shorter working days and a grievance system. The RCMP was still committed to public service, but its methods of carrying out its mandate had changed considerably in a relatively short period of time.[30]

The RCMP was also an organization committed, out of necessity, to secrecy. This was a characteristic that sometimes sat awkwardly alongside the aim of the centennial: publicity. When Commissioner Higgitt wrote in the "100th

Anniversary Edition" of the RCMP organ *Scarlet and Gold*, "I certainly hope that all Canadians will join with us in celebrating our 100th birthday and thereby get to know us even better," he was probably not being purposefully deceitful.[31] However, those organizing the centennial celebrations worked exhaustively to ensure that the public got to know the RCMP in a limited and predetermined way. Two key and interrelated characteristics would structure the RCMP's centennial program. One was the markedly centralized and secretive way in which the program was run. The other was the high level of political awareness exhibited by the organizers concerning such issues as national unity, fiscal responsibility, racial tolerance, and the mounting criticism of the Force's recent legal transgressions. Both characteristics had implications for the new narrative and helped account for the Force's deft handling of the political challenges it confronted.

A submission to the Treasury Board outlined the objectives of the centennial program. The RCMP presented four key aims: to stimulate "public awareness" of the Force's contributions to the "settlement and growth of Canada"; to "improve" the public's understanding of the Force's present duties; to further communication between the Force and the Canadian public; and, finally, "to encourage participation in Centennial celebrations across Canada by members of the Force, all Canadians and tourists from abroad."[32]

Yet, in summarizing the benefits of the proposed program, the submission quickly turned to economics, with the Canadian government Travel Bureau predicting, "The return from tourist dollars alone is expected to exceed fifty million dollars."[33] The centennial program was approved in part because it was profitable:

> The Canadian Government Travel Bureau has advised the Commissioner that these imaginative and large scale plans will add to the quality of Canadian life in 1973. Additionally, the Centenary of the Force will divert Canadian travel money to Canada, attract many visitors and help increase employment in our already massive tourist and travel industry. We have been advised also that for every dollar spent on the Centenary, the financial return would be ten fold to the Canadian economy.[34]

Two different rationales emerged in this submission: public service, which permeated the stated objectives of the program, and economic utility, which justified its actual implementation. The planners apparently gave no thought to which areas or social groups would benefit economically from the centenary celebrations; they simply assumed that the country as an organic community would benefit.

With the backing of the Solicitor General, the Force submitted a detailed outline of its expected centennial-related expenses to the Treasury Board. Expenses for 1972-73 and 1973-74 would come to no more than $3,118,000.[35] The highest single expense, $755,000, appeared under the title "Musical Ride—Young Canadians." The Force maintained, "In addition to fostering Canadian pride and unity . . . this presentation would greatly assist us in meeting our objectives set for the overall Centennial Program."[36] This program, indeed, would evolve into the Centennial Review show and become a key instrument in renovating the Force's history.

The plan earmarked a total of $366,325 for "Professional Services," which were "required for research, planning, publicity, design and coordination." The Force received permission from the Treasury Board to enter into contracts with no fewer than four consulting firms.[37] It set aside an additional $563,100 for "Exhibits and Displays." Combined with a further $353,000 for "Launching Ceremonies and Other Events Including Assistance to Divisions," these moneys allowed the Force to take its centennial message across the country by employing stationary displays in large centres while sending mobile exhibits to smaller towns and villages. The proposed campaign could blanket the country.

The original steering committee for the centennial was composed mainly of members outside the ranks of the Force, and the pace of preparations picked up considerably when the steering committee fell by the wayside in late 1972 and the Force itself took over the planning. A memorandum from Chief Superintendent D.T. Saul to Assistant Commissioner Peter Bazowski regarding the organization of what would become the Centennial Review alluded to the reason for the quickened pace: "Until the complete overall responsibility for the Centennial program reverted to the Force, we were inhibited to a large extent by imposed guidelines with overtones that were to a greater or lesser degree in conflict with the views of senior management. This conflict made the process of blending the various activities into a cohesive program awkward to effect."[38]

For John Bentham, the steering committee had seemed far too interested in producing fancy logos and spending money.[39] Superintendent Don Saul thought the problem stemmed from the fact that members of the Force and its political masters were "diametrically opposed" in their views of how the centennial should be run.[40] With the Force now fully in charge of the program, Saul emerged as the head of the centennial celebrations, with extensive control over the program's activities. A veteran member of the Force, Saul had considerable experience in amateur theatre. He was chosen by Commissioner Higgitt to head the Centennial Review and was appointed officer in charge of the Centennial Branch. Saul chaired the Centennial Advisory Committee, and his signature was needed to approve any new ideas or to change any plans. When it came time to take the review on the road, Saul travelled with the troupe, acting as its executive producer.

Almost all of the presentations, exhibits, and written materials produced for the centennial were contracted out to private firms. Saul was the main link between these firms and the Force. After finalizing contracts and production schedules, the firms would remain in contact with Saul, periodically sending in preliminary plans and, later, more advanced drafts of their work. The Advisory Committee repeatedly reviewed these drafts until the project was completed. The firms were all well aware of the storyline that was to dominate the centennial, because they were sent a copy of the Force's official documents: *RCMP Centennial 1973: A "Background" For Editors*; and *An Historical Outline of the Force* (1967), which contained appropriate highlights of the Force's history. For the most part, though, the outside companies were generally of a mind with the Force on what was "appropriate" to celebrate. After all, as former Force historian Stan Horrall said, these firms were not looking to commemorate the Winnipeg General Strike on a souvenir plate.[41] Saul, as chair of the Centennial Advisory Committee, summarized its meetings and sent this information along to Assistant Commissioner Bazowski, underscoring items and issues that required the Commissioner's attention.

Sealy of the Mounted was on hand in 1973 to sell a Snidely Whiplash lookalike (and customers in general) on the idea of purchasing new mattresses. (Photo reprinted courtesy of Eaton's)

In cases in which Saul was not in a position to give final or official approval, the Commissioner's signature was necessary. Higgitt, appointed commissioner in October 1969, had joined the Force in 1937 and had served mainly in Saskatchewan, Ontario, and Quebec. During the early 1960s he served as "Liaison Officer for the U.K. and western Europe." In 1967 he became director of Security Services for the Force and was elected president of the International Criminal Police Organization (INTERPOL) in 1972.[42] Higgitt was highly involved in the centennial, particularly when communication with other government departments was necessary, and he kept a close eye on developments. The commissioner was not above intervening in the details. On one occasion he acted decisively to reverse a committee decision and ensure that at least some billings were placed in the "ethnic media" to advertise the Centennial Review.[43] These two men, along with Assistant Commissioner Bazowski, formed an RCMP triumvirate and controlled the centenary, seldom allowing even the simplest of decisions to be made without their involvement.

The Force historian, appointed in 1968, seemed somewhat peripheral to the day-to-day activities of the centennial. Although Horrall was not directly involved in the major organization-oriented decisions, his main duties revolved around checking films, displays, and other projects contracted out to private companies. To mark the centenary he also authored an official pictorial RCMP history, which became the most detailed rendition of the new 1973 narrative.

The private firms contracted to carry out the centennial project were well aware of the Force's desire to update its image. In a proposal for the Centennial Travelling Exhibit, Robin Bush and Associates acknowledged that the purpose of such an exhibit was "to make visible to Canadians the growth and dynamic changes that have kept the RCMP attuned to the sweeping social and technological innovation in Canada and the world during the century since 1873." The "main thrust of the exhibit" was "to show the men and the methods of the Force today with the friendship and respect of the communities, given perspective by highlights of its history through 100 years."[44]

Anxious to put on a good show, the firms tended, if anything, to exaggerate the Force's achievements. Luckily, the RCMP reserved the right to correct their

The Macdonald Lassie
Salutes the
R.C.M.P.
in their
100th YEAR

work, and the Force itself made the final touches to all such projects. As Lawrence Marshall's company neared completion of its script for an audio-visual presentation outlining the Force's history, Marshall acknowledged that it was "necessary for the Force to review the script for technical inaccuracies and perhaps for the possible addition or deletion of sections."[45] The Force's official historian went to work on the script, and most of his alterations concerned factual errors made by the company. In one spot the writers had incorrectly named the defendants in a trial. In another they incorrectly recorded the *St. Roch*'s date of departure on its record-breaking voyage. Interestingly, Horrall also corrected overblown accounts of the Force's achievements. He found that the company's version of the Great March West, for instance, was "a little exaggerated," and he noted in the margin that, contrary to the production, maps of the area had been in existence at the time of the March. He also cut out the company's claim that all members of the Force survived the March, indicating instead that Constable Parks had died en route. Horrall even tried to tone down the Force's mythical role in the Klondike by taking issue with the consultant's description of the Yukon fields, which were said to have "swarmed with 40,000 brawling, quarreling souls, all intent on getting rich—however they could." He noted, rather, that "Steele and other C.O.'s in Yukon repeatedly reported that the territory was as peaceful and law-abiding as any other part of Canada. . . . Few major crimes—most miners hardworking, law abiding." With a stroke of Horrall's pen, a cache thief named George O'Brien (who had killed several people) went from a "mass" murderer to a "brutal" one.[46]

Notwithstanding these differences over historical tone and descriptive nuance, Horrall and the company were fully in agreement about the central point of the whole exercise. The film's concluding words received no opposition:

> Today, the Mounties fulfill a wider range of duties than could have been imagined 100 years ago. Often in the performance of these routine duties, an incident blooms into an historical event.
>
> As a result, fact and fiction have combined to create a distinctive Canadian legend—one that is popular around the world.
>
> The RCMP has not been content to be a legend. It moves with the times to meet new challenges.
>
> The RCMP is *more* than a man in a red coat.[47]

That was exactly the message the organizers wished to convey to the public. The Force wanted elements of the old myth—honour, manliness, duty—without the storybook romanticism or the imperial fervour that had once given those penchants an antimodern meaning. Bridging the gap between past and present is never easy. Attempting to do so in the context of the early 1970s would prove difficult indeed.

Political Concerns: Secrecy and Publicity

On October 16, 1973, Superintendent Saul wrote to an Alberta rancher expressing "sincere thanks on behalf of the Force for your kindness in allowing us the use of your two West Highland Cattle as oxen" for the Centennial Review. He continued: "Pierre and Elliot were outstanding in their roles once we had convinced them it was necessary to harness them singly."[48]

Setting aside the rancher's symbolic victory for Western regionalism (many Albertans in the early 1970s would have welcomed an opportunity to harness Prime Minister Trudeau), the significance of this passage lies in Saul's involvement in a seemingly mundane and routine task. Saul, in charge of the entire centenary, answered only to Commissioner Higgitt except when decisions involved more sensitive departments, such as the Security Service. That he recruited even the oxen for the Centennial Review suggests his involvement in even the most basic of tasks. In 1973, nothing was left to chance.

One reason for this centralization, of course, was the necessity of keeping track of "manpower" and costs. However, the tight involvement of the triumvirate suggests the existence of other, less money-oriented concerns. The choice of costumes, the shipment of two horses to Winnipeg for a display in a Hudson's Bay store, even responses to requests for souvenirs from an adoring public: all these seemingly routine responsibilities fell upon the two highest ranking officers in the land and their appointed problem-solver.[49] Although reminiscent in some ways of Commissioner Wood's role in supervising the lending of uniforms three decades earlier, the centennial apparatus displayed a more "hands-on," interventionist effort on the part of the Force.

The operations of the program were as secretive as they were centralized. When two horses were late arriving for a centennial display in a Hudson's Bay store in Winnipeg, one member of the Force seems to have become panic-stricken. He sent off a secretive telex marked "Warning . . . Classified . . . YOUR TELEPHONE IS NOT SECURED." The telex noted that it was "imperative we move quickly to ensure continued good rapport [and] established reputation for efficiency."[50]

This was an organization uncertain of its public standing, anxious to maintain the best of a century-old tradition, and (thanks to recent revelations of scandals and other transgressions) particularly wary of the media. A May 7, 1973, "Confidential" memo from Saul to those involved in a Centennial Review rehearsal for the press indicates the seriousness of the situation in the eyes of the Force:

> Above all, be *reasonably accurate* in your statements to the press and, if necessary, one could always introduce the question to the person responsible for the portion of the show being discussed. . . . Probably questions that will arise frequently will be in terms of the purpose or objective of the Review show and in fact possibly our overall Centennial plans. I would think it fair to say the whole purpose of our activities is to reinforce our existing rapport with the general public. The show itself being a capsule review of our past 100 years and touring to accentuate the Centennial activities of the Force in those areas where we will be appearing.[51]

A MOMENT

OF HIGH

NATIONALISM

(AND TENSION),

1968-73

100

A more alarmist tone entered into Commissioner Higgitt's Administrative Instructions dated December 28, 1972:

> I need not stress the importance of this historic occasion. The program must reflect our usual very high standards of achievement. The fact that it is already under very critical assessment demands the full co-operation and enthusiasm of every member of the Force. This co-operation may well include concerted efforts on the part of many that would be considered beyond the usual call of duty under normal circumstances. However, the circumstances we now find ourselves facing, and which were not of our own making, are not normal. Thus, I have full confidence that all members will rise to the occasion so that as 1973 closes we will be able to take pride in what has been accomplished to celebrate our 100th birthday.[52]

While there is no paper trail explaining what these "[ab]normal circumstances" were thought to be, the memoranda surrounding a variety of controversial and highly political topics suggest that the Force was well aware of the effort needed not only to protect (and in many ways reclaim) its reputation, but

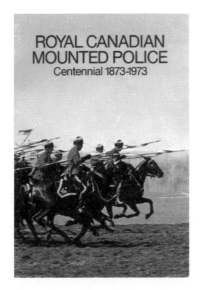

ROYAL CANADIAN
MOUNTED POLICE
Centennial 1873-1973

"The Charge." Symbolic of everything and nothing in particular, this image appeared on the front of the centennial souvenir program and in many other places during the 1973 celebrations.

also to avoid the political land mines faced by all police forces in the early 1970s.

Doing this meant overcoming a long tradition of reticence. A secretive hush had surrounded the Force almost from its inception and was "originally clamped on the Force to stop the unfavourable publicity resulting from complaints and criticism of members, many of which appeared in letters to the public press."[53] The Force was aware, early on, of the necessity of media approval in maintaining its authority. As Robert Thacker has observed, "The early reputation of the force rested largely on the treatment accorded it within the popular press."[54] This was also the situation in 1973. The Force remained extremely conscious of its public image, and the concern for secrecy had a measurable impact upon the narrative that dominated the centennial. As a result the people who developed scripts and lecture kits for use in RCMP exhibits exercised a great deal of caution in dealing with the activities of the Security Service. Saul stated this clearly in a memo to his superiors regarding one script: "One major area of concern in this script was the coverage given to our Security Service." Saul indicated that the Committee felt that the "Gouzenko affair should not be included" and that although "some mention of" the Security Service would be acceptable, perhaps the Committee should contact the Security Service itself to get "suitable substitute material." Commissioner Higgitt agreed. His handwritten note on the memo stated this in no uncertain terms: "Gouzenko *MUST* not be mentioned."[55]

The RCMP's most impressive moment on the world stage of the Cold War, and what could have plausibly been described as a spirited defence of Canadian sovereignty (a theme stressed *ad nauseam* throughout the centennial) was thus not included in the Force's centennial narrative, apparently on the grounds of national security.

Political Concerns: National and Regional Identities

To further emphasize the modern activities, organizers undertook a number of efforts to relate the Force's history to those communities in which the Force did not have a defined place in the local or provincial past. This is best seen in the Force's dealings with Quebec and Eastern Canada. In attempting to articulate the RCMP narrative to Canadians in different parts of the country, the Force was advised to make use of the ambiguous image of "the charge," with the scarlet-clad Mounties rushing forth on horseback. This equestrian manoeuvre was not necessarily associated with any particular historical event and therefore (it was fondly hoped) might be more acceptable to Quebec.

On March 21, 1973, a representative of Rolph-McNally Ltd. informed Saul that the "charge" would be ideal for the cover of the Centennial Review's souvenir program "because it has absolutely no background. It, therefore, represents all of Canada."[56] The Force apparently heeded this advice and "the charge" appears on the cover of the Centennial Review program and in numerous other places throughout the centennial. The "charge," along with the musical ride as a whole, was a particularly useful "invented tradition." The Force was able to draw upon its famed equestrian abilities without designating a particular enemy against whom the "charge" was directed. Because the exercise was entirely self-contained, it had a transcendental quality: it referred to no specific history about which Canadians might disagree with each other. Since there was no opposition to the "charge" to which members of the Canadian community could relate, it and other images were to be used in a narrative that could summon up "Canada," even though the performance had no real historical significance for the Force.

Early on, it was noted that dealing with exhibitions and performances in Quebec was going to require a unique approach. In the work of the centennial steering committee, the politics of language inevitably became an issue: centennial celebrations and presentations were to be held in both official languages where and when it was deemed appropriate, and the occasional lapse in this matter would bring a strong letter of protest from the Official Languages commissioner.[57]

A MOMENT

OF HIGH

NATIONALISM

(AND TENSION),

1968-73

102

In discussions surrounding the exhibit in Montreal, one consultant recommended that even "if the exhibit is bilingual, French should have priority."[58] Design and Communication, the firm hired to produce the Montreal exhibit, attempted to tailor it for French-Canadians, but when Information Canada refused to approve the firm's proposal, forcing the RCMP to drop the firm as a consultant, this approach was abandoned altogether.[59] The firm's letter protesting the cancellation of the project reiterated the importance of a distinct narrative for the Montreal exhibit: "An exhibition designed for Ottawa, Winnipeg or Vancouver cannot simply be translated and shown to French Canadians. The problem is different. The people are different. And so should the message be. The exploits of a Commissioner Macleod, of a Commissioner French or of a Captain Larsen have little impact on French Canadians."[60]

Apparently, the Force felt confident enough to stick with its original narrative and simply translate it into French for its Quebec exhibits and performances. The organizers made slight alterations (the Centennial Review was bilingual in Sherbrooke, but performed in French only in Rimouski),[61] but on the whole, the 1973 narrative was not altered in a special attempt to appeal to French-Canadians. A glance at the Force's own research on French-Canadian public opinion would suggest even a herculean effort to appeal to French-Canadians would have produced minimal results. A paper written by Gilles Langelier for the Force in 1971 made it clear that among other things, the role of the Force in hanging Louis Riel and implementing conscription in the Second World War prevented the Force from being embraced in Quebec as it had been in English Canada.[62]

Planners also made a determined effort to include the Maritimes. The Centennial Review was tied to local celebrations for the 125th anniversary of Fredericton, the bicentennial of Pictou, Nova Scotia, and the P.E.I. centennial marking the province's entrance into Confederation. Beyond the coincidence of also taking place in 1973, what the 100th anniversary of the Force had to do with any of these events was not clear; nonetheless, the association was made. Although one of its hired media agencies advised the Force on how to "exploit" P.E.I.'s characteristics and relate them to the Force, most of the Force's activities on the island seem to have consisted of making honorary appearances at various local events and competitions.[63] The two main expressions of the "dual centennials" seem to have been the "two gate posts at the entrance to L Division Headquarters" built by the province and the two signs erected at the province's ferry terminals welcoming "visitors to the province . . . with the accent on both the P.E.I. and RCMP centennials."[64]

One province that had no difficulty establishing a connection between its past and the history of the RCMP was Alberta. This province was not content to simply participate in the federally sponsored 1973 celebrations that marked the one-hundredth anniversary of the founding of the Force. In August 1972, Alberta's Minister for Tourism announced that his province "would place its full emphasis on 1974 since, historically, the centenary of the arrival of the NWMP had greater significance for Alberta" than the centenary of its inception. After a public competition, the public relations firm of Vickers and Benson was chosen "to co-ordinate the promotional support for the program."[65]

Following the lead of the 1967 celebrations marking the centennial of Confederation, organizers of the 1974 Alberta-RCMP Century Celebrations focused their efforts on the funding of community projects. "Parks, museums and senior citizens centres . . . comprised the most popular projects," although the organizers also supported the restoration of historical buildings as well as various artistic displays. One such project was a giant twenty-five-foot-high Ukrainian egg near the town of Vegreville, Alberta.

Other grants were used to boost the tourist trade in Northern Alberta while publicizing the "unique relationship between the RCMP and the people of native origin in Northern Alberta."[66] In one instance a cheque for $15,250 was presented to the Saddle Lake Indian Reserve for the "construction of an authentic Cree village, circa 1874."[67] The Alberta government's concerns with both Native Reserves and the rapidly expanding tourist business reflected political and economic concerns that were foremost in the minds of many governments.

A MOMENT

OF HIGH

NATIONALISM

(AND TENSION),

1968-73

104

Conclusion

The complexities involved in the formation of the story that came to dominate the centennial must be seen in the context of the realities of the 1970s. One apparent necessity, for instance, was that the Force not incur the wrath of the public on the grounds of financial mismanagement. The Force was obsessed with the need to appear thrifty and went out of its way to emphasize its financial responsibility and to ensure the public that the funds spent on its "100th birthday" were being spent responsibly.[68] While it analysed proposed commercial souvenirs to ensure their suitability *within* its celebrations, the Force still saw commercial products as a concern and refused to endorse them at all. This position would be softened considerably in the coming decades.

The RCMP's relationship with the federal government concerning such matters is particularly enlightening. On at least one occasion Commissioner Higgitt interfered in the production of souvenirs for members of the Force to ensure that such production met with the approval of the auditor general. In a more revealing example, Higgitt refused to endorse a federal government suggestion that a national souvenir competition be held to produce suitable mementos for the centennial. Higgitt acknowledged that the idea came from the Department of Industry, Trade and Commerce and was an attempt to improve the quality of Canadian souvenirs across the country. His main reservation was that he felt the public would not see this as a responsible use of the funding granted the Force.[69]

A number of other controversial topics made their way across Advisory Committee members' desks. The politics of language was one thing. Another was the location of exhibits, which was heavily influenced by federal-provincial politics: it was deemed inappropriate to house an RCMP exhibit at an otherwise ideal site in Quebec City because it was located next to Quebec's National Assembly.[70]

Equally explosive was anything to do with ethnicity. For instance, when auditions were to be held for singing parts in the Centennial Troop Review, which was to re-enact great moments in the history of the Force, the observations of

Inspector W.F. MacRae reflected the increasing resonance of multiculturalism: "It seems . . . that efforts should be made to recruit to the project, members representing the ethnic mix of the Force, such as Indians, an Eskimo . . . a negro and, if possible, a Japanese and Chinese Canadian."[71]

Such an endeavour would have to be tactfully and cautiously undertaken. As a letter from Stanley Public Relations informed Saul in March 1973, "Some concern was expressed about the way Indians—and Indian activists—would react to [the representation of Crowfoot in the Centennial Review] and to seeing a constable playing the part of Chief Crowfoot. Indian treaties have been in the news recently and I gather they are a hot subject with Indian communities in Western Canada."[72] In reviewing a submission from Lawrence Marshall Productions for an audio-visual presentation, the Centennial Advisory Committee recommended editorial changes based on the view that "specific mention of racial groups be omitted, i.e. Igor Gouzenko, Almighty Voice, Nazi Spy, etc."[73]

These political concerns would have a bearing on the story that dominated the centennial. The familiar theme of multiculturalism was a major part of the narrative constructed to renovate the image of the Force. Although a multicultural re-creation of the March West is a re-creation with a profound twist—a twist that decreases the resonance of the racial assumptions that obviously permeated the clearing of the West for settlement and the westward march of the British Empire—it was the order of the day in 1973. An emphasis on the bilingual makeup of the current police force encouraged the audience to overlook the near-monopoly of power held by the English-Canadians who had until recently controlled the RCMP and manufactured the opening of the West.

It is doubtful that any of the classic Mounties would have felt entirely comfortable in the Canada of the early 1970s. Significant demographic changes and recent federal policies were stimulating a new public approval of cultural diversity. A political culture that increasingly viewed the country's "welfare net" as a right, not a privilege, was also inclined to accept trade unions and, at times, celebrate rather than condemn the strikers of 1919. As well, the youth rebellions and protests of the 1960s bespoke a segment of society increasingly prone to

THE MOUNTIE
ENTERS THE
WORLD OF
POSTMODERNITY,
1973-97

106

A German prisoner of war is captured by the RCMP near Barnwell, Alberta in 1944. Such incidents, celebrated by supporters of the classic myth, were deemed too controversial to be highlighted in the 1973 Centennial Celebrations. (Glenbow Archives, Calgary, Alberta, NA-2746-12)

questioning authority. In this altered context the Force also found its image tarnished through public revelations of its recent legal transgressions.

Aware of the importance of good public relations, and with the Force's one-hundredth anniversary at hand, the RCMP's chosen response was a multimillion-dollar centennial celebration. For this occasion, it was necessary to fashion a "New Liberal" and multicultural story, and that was what the organizers set out to produce. After decades of passivity regarding its image—and responding now not just to immediate internal concerns but also to the broader developments in Canadian political culture—the Force joined with public relations firms and entrepreneurs to reinvent its image, and its past.

5

Embracing Modernity, Liberalizing the Past:
The 1973 Centennial Celebrations

Canada Is Told to Shed 'Rose Marie' Image

— New York *Times* headline, November 5, 1969

In 1973 the RCMP celebrated its one-hundredth anniversary—quite an accomplishment, one might say, for an organization that was just fifty-three years old at the time. The Royal Canadian Mounted Police was officially created by an act of Parliament in November 1919, and effectively began its national role in February 1920. As Gregory Kealey has convincingly argued, one of the key elements in the creation of the new police force was the federal government's opposition to the massive labour revolt that had shaken the country at the end of the First World War—a point that the classic myth, which highlighted the Force's dealings with shady Eastern European immigrants intent on overthrowing the government, makes fully clear.

The institutional ancestors of the RCMP in the field of security and intelligence were many, but included a number of agencies: the Dominion Police, which, under the authority of the minister of justice, had functioned in collaboration with municipal and provincial forces and had also hired private detectives from U.S. agencies; the Royal North-West Mounted Police, which had begun security work in 1914 as the provincial force of Alberta and Saskatchewan; the military intelligence apparatus of the minister of militia and defence; and finally the security branch of the immigration department.

An RCMP Constable distributes flour, twine and other necessities to be donated to Hare Indian widows in Fort Good Hope, N.W.T., 1953. Ironically, the Force's philanthropic role in the North was downplayed in 1973. (National Archives of Canada, George Hunter, PA114830)

EMBRACING
MODERNITY,
LIBERALIZING
THE PAST: THE
1973 CENTENNIAL
CELEBRATIONS

110

The formation of the RCMP thus brought a measure of centralization to what had been "extremely decentralized operations."[1] This security machine would later undertake such actions as the prosecution of the Communist Party leadership in 1931 and the victimization through deportation of many supposed enemy aliens. In short, the RCMP was the child of 1919: its history makes no sense unless we understand that the federal government was attempting to find new and more powerful means to bully unco-operative workers and immigrants into line. This explanation fits in well with the popular histories written by authors such as R.C. Featherstonhaugh and Delbert Young. Kealey's Marxist interpretation of the RCMP's birth is supported by an unlikely source: Stan Horrall, head of the RCMP's historical section from 1968 to 1992, who likewise emphasizes the significance of postwar labour unrest in the creation of the new police force. "It is no exaggeration," he concludes in a 1980 article, "to say that the Royal Canadian Mounted Police is but one more offspring of the Winnipeg General Strike."[2]

How, then, could a Force created in 1919-20 celebrate its "centenary" in 1973? It could do this only by a selective process of interpreting its own history—by emphasizing only one of its institutional ancestors (the RNWMP) rather than others (such as the Dominion Police or the other security apparatuses), and by de-emphasizing the obvious fact, acknowledged by earlier writers, that the Force was born in, and evolved as part of, a systematic effort on the part of the federal government to discipline and transform unruly elements within society.

Government institutions, given the resources and authority they possess, have a distinct advantage in "naturalizing" interpretations of social reality by linking them to supposedly age-old traditions. Where these "invented traditions" begin is often the single most important decision in the construction of a historical narrative, determining much of the character of the story's framework and consequently how various "facts" are positioned within it.[3]

In this case, the birth-date of 1873 was clearly not the only one organizers might have selected. In many ways, this selection was a gross distortion, because it implied a seamless historical continuity between a police force whose primary functions had been the maintenance of order and whose territory was limited to one part of the Dominion, and the more security-oriented, Canada-wide, and sophisticated apparatus that was derived from many diverse institutions and traditions in 1919. Still, choosing 1873 as the birth-date of the Force had ready advantages: the choice linked the RCMP with relatively uncontroversial historical themes such as nation-building, western settlement, and the preservation of Canadian sovereignty, rather than with the more controversial issues raised by the repression of trade unionists, socialists, and ethnic minorities during and after the Great War of 1914-18. Even the common use of the terms "the Force" or "the Mounties" implied a narrative continuity between 1873 and 1973. Granted the power to determine where the story began, the commemorative apparatus within the RCMP could also seemingly explain exactly how the Force had contributed to Canada's inevitable progress. In some respects, once the birth-date was selected, the ensuing emphases and absences were inevitable.

In 1973 the RCMP faced a dilemma. Increasingly under public scrutiny as reports of police wrongdoing increased, it could neither fully jettison a mythical narrative that had proved successful with the public over generations nor continue with a story at odds with the federal government's emergent official doctrines. The classic story of its history was so central to its identity that any attempt to break free from that story altogether would be problematic. But what then would take its place? Obviously certain key themes of the old story—the taming of the Indians, and French-speaking "half-breeds," and docile women watched over by an imperial breed of hardy men, for example—could no longer be guaranteed a sympathetic reception in a Canada interested as never before in questions of aboriginal rights, linguistic duality, and women's equality.

The answer to the dilemma was to be the presentation of a highly selective history of RCMP achievements. The chosen strategy was to finesse awkward issues, either by reinterpreting them to cast a favourable light on the actions of the Force or by ignoring them altogether. The new story revolved around the theme of the steady, peaceful evolution of a nation through the application of Western rationality and science, within which stream the Mounted Police laid the groundwork for the liberal and tolerant Canada of the 1970s. Rather than knights defending chivalric notions of monarchy, honour, and decorum, the Mounties were to some degree reimagined as missionaries of modernity—

almost Canadian commissars of the Enlightenment, spreading reason throughout the land.

The centennial organizers used a vast array of media to promote and convey this new narrative. As well, organizers produced a variety of brief synopses of the Force's history in the various programs and leaflets advertising the centennial. This, combined with the plethora of written material in both conventional and unconventional forms (such as the wall panels in displays throughout the country), resulted in a veritable Niagara of written material telling the new story of the Force's past. Canadians could find the new history when they looked up at the centennial calendars on office walls, and when they sat down to their dinner tables they could find it once again on the centennial place mats.[4]

In addition, the Force produced a Centennial Review show that toured the country as a musical-equestrian salute to the Force, presenting its history on horseback. Organizers also upheld and supported this new version of events through the use of various commemorative projects and souvenirs that played an important role in making the narrative more appealing to the public. All these very disparate media conveyed the same story of the Force: because of the centralized control over events in 1973, they could all easily be integrated into a greater unity, a coherent narrative.

New Liberalism and National Development: The Narrative of the Centennial

The story produced and repeated throughout the centennial celebrations told a new and specific story that differed greatly from the classic tale. Having obtained the Northwest Territories from the Hudson's Bay Company, the nascent Canadian nation sought to open up this area for settlement. Unfortunately, "Conditions were not conducive to orderly settlement." American whiskey traders, Fenian raiders, and the smallpox epidemic all conspired to threaten the peaceful growth of the Canadian nation. Established to knit the

EMBRACING
MODERNITY,
LIBERALIZING
THE PAST: THE
1973 CENTENNIAL
CELEBRATIONS

112

West into Confederation, the Force's chief aim was to win the confidence of the Native peoples. Scrupulously avoiding "strong-arm methods," the Force gained the respect of the Natives peoples, and "Native chiefs visited the Force, first in curiosity, afterwards in full confidence of Canada's intentions."[5] Often, the new narrative said, all that the Mounties had to do to gain this respect was to arrive in their scarlet and gold. When, for example, the Force arrived near Fort Carlton, in what is now Saskatchewan, "French half-breeds" were contemplating a separate government: the Mounties' appearance "at the scene of the threatened disaffection at once made apparent the authority of the crown."[6]

With positive Native-White relations ensured, the Force turned its efforts towards helping settlers. The Force carried out a multitude of duties not normally identified with a police force and did so consistently and with determination. Whether monitoring settlement on the Prairies or in the Yukon, the Force ensured that order and the rule of law prevailed.

Throughout its history, the new story argued, the Force had always been involved in protecting Canadian (not Imperial) sovereignty. This was particularly true of the Force's duties in the Far North. Through almost superhuman determination, the members of the Force completed Arctic patrols, mapping out the land and battling the elements in sub-zero weather—all to bring *Canadian* law to the North. Whatever their duties and wherever they were stationed, members of the Force made use of the most up-to-date technology. Far from being a romantic relic of the past, the Force was always open to new ideas and new technology in its attempt to enforce the law. This was as true of the early days as it was of the present Force.

This 1973 revision of the Mountie story was, in its avoidance of jarring ethnic generalities, a more tolerant and inclusive narrative than the classic version. Whereas the classic Mountie was a lone officer of the law enforcing order so that possessive individualism might triumph, the new Mountie was a New Liberal upholding a more general, community-generated agenda and owing allegiance to the wider organic community of "Canada." Here the organizers traded in the mythology of classical laissez-faire liberalism in favour of a new mythology that stressed a kinder, gentler liberalism. This New Liberalism lauded social and economic intervention by the government in an attempt to maintain agreed-upon community standards.

Throughout the new narrative, the police were always referred to as "the Force," a seemingly innocuous title (and one commonly used by its members). However, "the Force" carried with it connotations of dynamism, progress, confidence, and, above all, continuity—and a continuity much more manufactured than actual. This label was a way to unite the histories of the North-West Mounted Police and the Royal Canadian Mounted Police, to minimize the division between the early years and the present day.

The organizers of the centennial presented the Force as the key element ensuring that the country's development had taken a necessary and relatively smooth road to its present happy condition. Any problems encountered along the way were dealt with efficiently by the men in scarlet and, as a result, progress was achieved. Indeed, in the 1970s, progress was still being achieved and, in accordance with its efficient and orderly tradition, the Force was still playing a key role by carrying out the same duties it had fulfilled in the past. Here was a romanticized story of Canadian nation-building, and while it may have ignored the tragedies undergone by the Native peoples on the prairies or the great complexities involved in policing a country the size of Canada, it did sustain the desired image of continuity, efficiency, and coherence.

Another characteristic of the new history was its concentration on the early years of the Force at the expense of those particularly complex decades from 1910 to 1950, a period that might be termed the "four missing decades" of the RCMP's new history. As well, in order to contribute to a continuous national narrative, the official history of the RCMP in 1973 needed to assert what was patently untrue: that the RCMP had always sustained a vision of "Canada" as a bilingual, multicultural, liberal-democratic state.

To demonstrate the continuity of this vision, the RCMP required an image of itself as an efficient and progressive organization dedicated to technological advancement and a pluralist society. The new narrative involved all types of people. For the most part the RCMP functionaries now avoided the tendency, characteristic of the classic RCMP story, to turn Francophones, Indians, Ameri-

EMBRACING
MODERNITY,
LIBERALIZING
THE PAST: THE
1973 CENTENNIAL
CELEBRATIONS

114

cans, and immigrants into the enemy. In the new story, progress was achieved through the actions of the Force and continued to be ensured through the use of the latest technology in the Force's continuing quest to "uphold the right"— the "right" having been reconceptualized in the light of science, modernity, and late twentieth-century Canadian multicultural and bilingual nationalism.

There was nothing accidental about this emphasis on a continuous national police history. In devising the storyline for the RCMP exhibit in Toronto, for example, consultants agreed with the Force that, as in other representations of the narrative, "In general, history would not be separated from the present but the continuum of action with different means would be stressed."[7] Organizers were intent on "counterpointing" the RCMP's historical role with its present duties in a strategy of emphasizing continuities. For example, a report on the Toronto exhibit by Dudas, Kuypers, Adamson Ltd. promised to relate "a historical report on whiskey traders in the West to a contemporary report on dope peddlers in cities."[8] The organizers, then, directly associated the present duties of the Force with those of the past, thus both "traditionalizing" its current duties and amplifying the present resonance of past accomplishments.

A letter to Superintendent Saul from Folio Creative, one of the firms hired to advise the Force, provides a revealing look at the construction of the new narrative. The letter alludes to the "spark" of excitement that had emerged when planners discussed the narrative at a recent meeting:

This "spark" again flared up in chatting with the RCMP Historian, Mr. Horrall, and yourself when we were in his office—especially when we started trying to land on the highlights from history that would be meaningful to the Centennial Show. He talked about the settlement of the West, the coming of the railroad, the police involvement with the Gold Rush, the move East and North to the Canadian Arctic, and always as a major theme, the importance of Canadian sovereignty, of keeping this vast territory Canadian.[9]

The shape of this narrative of nationalism and enlightenment largely determined which historical events and patterns would figure within the story. Still,

the narrative was by no means entirely fictional. In some ways the Force did have a positive record to build on, particularly when contrasted with experiences south of the border (a characteristic that the Canadian contributors to the classic myth often played up). The North-West Mounted Police did play a role in protecting Indians from whiskey peddlers, and it did arrive out west before most settlers had come—thus decreasing the opportunity for lawlessness. The centennial narrative represented several events in ways that most "experts" would agree with; it omitted others, apparently because they did not fit the proposed new history. The organizers constructed the RCMP's 1973 narrative in such a way that facts and legends were intertwined. The new history of the Force was selective more than obviously wrong: organizers reinvented a liberal, enlightened past for the RCMP by excluding contrary evidence, as a consideration of four key themes of RCMP history will show.

"Gallant attack on Big Bear's band by a handful of Mounted Police under Inspector Steele and Squadron Sergt.-Major Fury" was the caption for this lithograph in an 1885 edition of the *Illustrated War News*. The story of Big Bear's treachery survived largely intact when supporters of the Force renovated its history in 1973. (Glenbow Archives, Calgary, Alberta, NA-1353-33)

Native-White Relations

The Force based its reputation primarily on its role in settling the west; the most potentially controversial aspect of this process in 1973 involved the resulting effects on the Aboriginal population. The centennial narrative was deftly structured to emphasize only one side of the Force's relationship with the Native peoples. The narrative portrayed the Force as the protector of the Native peoples, indeed as *the* reason why unruly settlers did not destroy the Aboriginal population altogether. It ignored, of course, the role the police played in ushering in a century-long era of stagnation and destitution for Native peoples on reserves by apprehending "any people found off the reserves without passes" and returning them to their reserve.[10]

To demonstrate the benevolent relationship that the Force had maintained with the Native peoples, the new narrative relied upon early Aboriginal reaction to the Force. Take, for instance, this excerpt from a wall panel at the Toronto exhibit:

From the beginning, one of the main roles of the RCMP was to be the visible presence of Law and Government across the nation "regardless of how remote the region." In the Wes[t], this stopped whiskey trading and raids on Indian lands. "If the Police had not come, where would we all be now[?]" asked Crowfoot . . . Chief of the Blackfoot Confederacy when he helped to bring 50,000 square miles of Indian land peacefully into Canada in 1874 under treaty number 7.[11]

EMBRACING

MODERNITY,

LIBERALIZING

THE PAST: THE

1973 CENTENNIAL

CELEBRATIONS

118

The wall panel makes no mention of Native reaction to the Force's role in bringing about Western settlement once the reserve system had exacted its toll. Instead, the Force took efforts to make the most of Native allies like Crowfoot. Quite deliberately, the narrative selected Crowfoot as the only Native to be given prominence; an official memo even advised that he "should be represented in place of any other Indian Chiefs from our historical association with the Indian Tribes."[12] Crowfoot undoubtedly praised the Mounted Police for proscribing the whiskey trade. His relationship with the legendary James F. Macleod may indeed have been based on trust and friendship, elevating him to the status of the sole Indian in the RCMP-Native relationship. But implying that such relations of trust and friendship were the long-standing general norm represented a tactic that was more convenient than accurate. In the 1973 RCMP narrative, Crowfoot takes on the elevated stature of an enthusiastic ally, a role that is difficult to reconcile with historian Henry Klassen's analysis of the chief's actual dealings with the RCMP: "Crowfoot's trust always embraced a few honourable policemen like James F. Macleod and Cecil Denny, but it was extended to the Force in a general sense only as long as he saw no police injustice to Indians. When such injustice occurred he quickly lost a great deal of faith in the Force and was as suspicious of most policemen as he was of many other whites."[13]

This more complicated view of Crowfoot was not useful to, and indeed subverted, the revised history of the Force. No longer singled out as the enemy, Native peoples were symbolically welcomed into the new history—but only as cheerleaders, never as tenacious critics. Their presence reassured the audience that past conflicts were little more than the growing pains of a maturing Canadian nation.

In several places significant liberties were taken with the basic issue of why the North-West Mounted Police had been created in the first place. A slide show designed by Mosaic Films for the Force's mobile exhibit entitled "A Century In Scarlet" offered the following proclamation:

> In May, 1873, 22 Canadian Indians were massacred by whites from Montana.
>
> Action was imperative. On August 30th, an Order-in-Council created the North West Mounted Police. . . .
>
> One hundred years ago, a few dedicated men brought law and order to Canada's North West. As "Button Chief" of the Blood Indian tribe put it: "Before the arrival of the North West Mounted Police, when I laid my head down at night, every sound frightened me . . . now I can sleep and I am not afraid." The policeman's job today is essentially unchanged, though far more difficult.[14]

Ignoring the important condition that these Indians were "Canadian" only to the extent that they were possessions rather than citizens (they lacked the right to vote, along with many other civil liberties, until 1960), the film led the audience to believe that the Force was created more to protect Natives from unruly settlers than to protect the Dominion's sovereignty from Americans. Moreover, the narrative deftly asserted an unlikely continuity between this accomplishment and the Force's present-day operations.

The commemorative place mat issued for the centennial shifted the blame for Western disorders towards the Indians, and attributed the creation of the Force to the need to deal with "Indian unrest" and to "protect settlers."[15] While these two versions were contradictory, they both fit easily into the narrative. The Force was necessary to clean up the West, and whether that duty involved protecting Indians from the whites or Canadian society from Indian unrest, the result was the West's smooth, orderly transition into civilization. Even if the Native peoples were to blame for the initial unrest, the lesson to be learned was

that with the aid of the Force, even Indians had come to accept the forward march of progress.

It is particularly interesting to note how the new story addressed the Northwest Rebellion of 1885. The officially sanctioned Centennial Calendar for 1973 offers a fascinating example of how an event so potentially disruptive to the creation of an enlightened, nation-building narrative was instead incorporated neatly into the story of progress. The calendar's depiction of "The Riel Rebellion" makes a villain of Big Bear, chief of the Plains Cree, for perpetrating the "infamous Frog Lake Massacre" (a conflict that, it has been suggested, had little to do with the rebellion).[16] Moreover, the grossly inaccurate claim that Big Bear precipitated the massacre explains why no mention is given to Big Bear's well-documented attempts to produce a peaceful compromise with the government, or of his earlier continuing efforts to keep his people from rebelling. Evidence of a federal government rebuffing peace initiatives on behalf of the Native population while escalating armed conflict did not make for good copy in the 1970s. The only reason given for the uprising was the rather vague assertion that "Indian and Metis resentment boiled over in the North West in 1885." Most disturbing of all was the picture that accompanied this description. In the illustration the subject position of the viewer (the position from which the picture is interpreted) is that of the besieged NWMP men behind the barriers as the "enemy" approaches.

Viewers are clearly supposed to imagine themselves situated behind the barriers with the Mounties, in a purely defensive posture. Moreover, whereas the Mounties are humanized in the illustration as men with well-detailed faces, most of the Métis enemy are faceless. The new RCMP narrative was, then, handling a delicate situation as best it could, by presenting valiant Mounties in a purely defensive posture. The potentially controversial role of the Force in the rebellion disappears, and the rebellion becomes just another in a long list of examples of the Force's contribution to the building of the Canadian nation. It takes its place with other events that show the Force's role as one of quiet, polite assistance to settlers, understanding to Native peoples, and humane self-defence when necessary.

According to the new narrative of 1973, two key lessons were to be learned from the Northwest Rebellion. First, instead of being a complicated event resulting from the federal government's policies in the West, and from Métis and Native demands, the rebellion was simply another example of how the Force maintained order in Canada. Second, as the discussion surrounding the storyline for the Toronto exhibit revealed, a great deal of similarity existed between the "cooperative execution of responsibilities by the Militia and the RCMP in the second Riel rebellion and the contemporary divisions of responsibility between the RCMP, the Ontario Provincial Police and the Toronto Municipal Police."[17] The Northwest Rebellion was, then, an example of federalism in action: yet another instance of the new narrative putting a positive spin on the potentially sensitive topic of Native-white relations.

Settling the West: A Tradition of Service

EMBRACING
MODERNITY,
LIBERALIZING
THE PAST: THE
1973 CENTENNIAL
CELEBRATIONS

122

Central to any history of the Force is the orderly settlement of the West. The new narrative portrayed the Great March West as an arduous trek that, despite its difficulties, resulted in a reinvigorated body whose orderly and calm aid to newcomers was invaluable for the newly created nation. To demonstrate the self-abnegation of the Force, the centennial history related the story of one Constable Conradi. This Conradi, the story went, was told that a family with ten children was being threatened by an approaching fire, but that they "were too far away to be reached in time." Still, he decided that it was his duty to try to help them, and he "galloped off." Reaching the house, "Conradi ran through the flames, grabbed the two youngest children and led them all to safety. His hair was singed, his clothing scorched and his hands and arms badly burned. His horse was so badly injured it had to be shot the next morning. For his pluck and endurance he was promoted to Corporal."[18]

It was with such "pluck" that the Force apparently carried out all of its obligations. A similar message was printed on one of the wall panels that offered visitors to the Toronto exhibit this précis of the Force's history from former Commissioner G.B. McClellan: "Common and Uncommon men mustered and annealed into one Force who, when called upon to do the impossible, did just that."[19] Apart from the heroism of individual officers in carrying out their duty to the collective, the power of the individual Mountie and the potential for the abuse of this power, so much a theme of classic Mountie literature, were characteristically omitted as a topic in the New Liberal world of the 1970s. An excerpt from Commissioner Maurice Nadon's May 23, 1974 speech at the Officer's Mess Dinner in Ottawa suggests why. "The whole thing," Nadon said, referring to the Mountie's individual authority, "was enough to give a civil rights activist a seizure. . . . The man on the spot had to act on his own without reference to higher authority for guidance. By the time instructions arrived the time of action was long past."[20]

With one "Force" now the star of the narrative, the settlement of the West thus seemed orderly and inevitable, carried out by a united group of men who were happy to do their duty and underwent tremendous hardships in doing so. Too great an emphasis on the lone Mountie, such an important element in the classic Mountie fiction, would offend New Liberal sensibilities in the 1970s.

However satisfying this 1973 vision of the Force as humble servant of the settler may be, it pays to recall how partial and selective a rendition of the record it was. Several scholars examining the Force have demonstrated the complexity of western settlement during those early years. E.C. Morgan, writing in 1974 about the internal problems that plagued the Force in its first decade, argued that the problems faced during the Great March seem to have been perpetuated and exacerbated by the Force's own ineptitude. For example, a Medical Board held in 1874 at Fort Garry found that "two men recruited in the previous year were blind in the right eye, five suffered from acute heart disease . . . one from tuberculosis . . . and one from a fracture of the upper part of a leg—all of which conditions existed previous to enlistment."[21] Such conditions suggest that the adversity faced by the Force was in part attributable to its own inefficiency in recruiting appropriate men.

Even more startling is Morgan's assertion that by December 1875, only two years after the Force's official inception, "more than half of the approximately 150 men recruited in the fall of 1873 had already left the service," because of the "inadequacy of medical examinations," poor training, a lengthy delay in receiving their pay, and the "effects of isolation and other hardships."[22] These hardships had their repercussions on the behaviour of the Mounted Police on the Prairies. The Force was subject to severe public criticism during the 1870s for apparent improper conduct. In 1878 Lieutenant-Governor Laird was moved to address the following message to Commissioner Macleod: "I fear from what reports are brought me, that some of your officers at Fort Walsh are making rather free with the women around there. It is to be hoped that the good name of the Force will not be hurt through too open indulgence of that kind. And I sincerely hope that Indian women will not be treated in a way that hereafter may give trouble."[23]

This sort of story was not included in the official narrative, for obvious reasons. The Force had no interest in displaying its past shortcomings and inadequacies; and to doubt its central and beneficent role in the West would have been to doubt the core notion of the orderly, inevitable, efficient growth of the Force itself. It was far better to assert that the settlers were assisted, and that Canada therefore took shape.

Having established the clean reputation of the Force in those early years, the new narrative slyly hinted that those characteristics were inherent attributes:

> In the hundred years since its establishment, the Force has had to change
> with the times. One thing that has not changed is its tradition of service to
> the community all across Canada. Many times the Force has been called
> upon to do things that most people would never associate with the work of
> a police Force. The Force has delivered mail in the Yukon, inoculated native
> peoples in remote areas to prevent epidemics of smallpox, protected animals
> and migratory birds, provided instruction in water safety and performed
> many various other services to people.[24]

This "service to the community" very much reflected the vocabulary of New Liberalism. It transported visions of a caring welfare state back to the early days of the Force. The statement combined a positive sense of history as progress with a glowing enthusiasm for technology: this continuous national history culminated in the gleaming machines of modernity, which arrived at no cost to the caring community they served.

Multiculturalism resonated in this new story of western settlement, a story emphasizing the Force's duties to the community. The narrative conceded that some difficulties had arisen because of language barriers and that "some" of the immigrants "had religious beliefs which posed special problems for the Force." Nonetheless, the Force's *Pictorial History* describes even the Doukhobors (so maligned in Delbert Young's book just five years earlier) as "excellent farmers."[25]

EMBRACING
MODERNITY,
LIBERALIZING
THE PAST: THE
1973 CENTENNIAL
CELEBRATIONS

124

Once again, this version was selective. For instance, an insightful article by Carl Betke scrutinizes the vast array of duties performed by the Force. For Betke, the historical record demonstrates that the Mounted Police of those early days often expressed disparaging views of nineteenth-century immigrants. While Force members tended to measure the worth of individual settlers by their eventual economic success, they subjected Ukrainian immigrants in particular to a double standard.[26] Ukrainian, Jewish, and even French settlers were targets of the Force's intolerance. Inspector D'Arcy Strickland, for example, referred to French settlers living near Duck Lake in the 1890s as "a very undesirable class of people."[27] The Force gave aid to some settlers, but not all to the same extent. Officers discriminated against some and helped others—contrary to the official vision of Canada as "multicultural within a bilingual framework."

Betke also found that "classical liberal" assumptions regarding aid greatly influenced the activities of the Force. In 1888 Superintendent A.B. Perry warned, "Free issue of rations must, of course, be made, to prevent actual starvation, but where the Government thus acts in a paternal manner great care must be exercised to prevent the recipient from deeming as a right what is given in pity."[28] The ideas of a deserving and undeserving poor and of poverty as an individual problem were commonplace in Victorian institutions, but that laissez-faire liberalism of earlier times was starkly incompatible with the Force's New Liberal narrative of steady, orderly progress leading to a pluralistic and benevolent nation.

The new history portrayed the vast array of duties carried out by the Force as the key to a smooth progression for the West, and did not question whether or not the Force willingly carried out these duties. As it happened, members of the Force often expressed resentment about their work, and the sense of cheerful versatility truly is an "invented tradition." Among the various character sketches in the centennial literature, a missing element is a picture of Commissioner L.W. Herchmer bemoaning the Force's involvement in quarantining cattle and appearing "a trifle grumpy, for relief work superseded what he regarded as proper police work."[29] In the new narrative the faithful Mountie was required to be a happy Jack-of-all-Trades.

The North

It was the Arctic—site of a fierce struggle between humanity and nature, focus of modern Canada's preoccupation with sovereignty, and locus of highly scientific exploration—that gave the RCMP the best opportunity to relate the nineteenth century's theme of western growth to the twentieth century's liberal progress. The North was a far less divisive setting than the West. French-Canadians did not see in northern development an English-Canadian "plot" to keep the spoils for themselves, and Northern exploration was a national aim involving science and technology, also a seemingly value-free goal. The story of the *St. Roch*, the first ship to travel through the Northwest Passage and back again, highlighted the role of technology in present-day policing. A wall panel from the Toronto exhibit states:

EMBRACING
MODERNITY,
LIBERALIZING
THE PAST: THE
1973 CENTENNIAL
CELEBRATIONS

126

> In 1940-1944, RCMP Schooner "St. Roch" . . . under command of Superintendent Larsen . . . was the first to travel the North West Passage in both direction[s].
>
> Today, with its most northerly post at Grix Fiord . . . this "Purely civil, not military body with as little Gold lace and fine feathers as possible" (Macdonald) can be proud of its role in shaping the Map of Canada . . . as we know it.[30]

Ironically, this use of the *St. Roch* and its skipper, Henry Larsen, provides a wonderful example of how the truly benevolent duties undertaken by the Force in the past were left outside the narrative because they also did not fit in as easily with its New Liberal themes. Larsen was perhaps the most outspoken critic of the treatment of the Inuit by traders and by the federal government. Years before Larsen entered the picture, the RCMP had been criticizing the government for its inaction concerning the deplorable living conditions faced by the Eskimos, as they were called, and the dishonest business practices of the traders. Grise Fiord, Canada's most northerly Inuit settlement, was an artificial construct of the federal government: Inuit were moved into the area in 1953 to

Members of crew of the *St. Roch* on its record-breaking voyage, including Constable Albert Chartrand (second from right). Chartrand died en route — a tragedy explored in classic literature but unmentioned in 1973. (Glenbow Archives, Calgary, Alberta, NA-2821-3)

help establish Canada's sovereignty over the arctic islands, though ostensibly as well to alleviate poor economic conditions. By the early 1950s, Larsen, then commanding "G" Division, was speaking out against the social conditions faced by the Inuit. One result was a conference held on the subject in early 1952, which ushered in significant reforms.[31]

Larsen's own book, *The Big Ship* (1967), written partially as a response to mounting criticism directed towards the Force for the deteriorating welfare of the Inuit, indicates the incompatibility between his view of the RCMP's activities in the North and the later 1973 narrative:

> During my years in the Arctic I often felt that it really was a crime that these children of Nature couldn't have been left alone to live their lives according to the customs and rules their forefathers had followed through generations. When the white man arrived with his ideas of right and wrong he changed, by force, in a way, the lives of these innocent and gullible people,

who always did their utmost to please the white man and follow his rules, even to the point where they were the losers.[32]

While Larsen's words do not constitute a damning critique of the Force, they do conflict with the logic of the RCMP's 1973 narrative, which insisted upon the identity of the Force and the nation as well as the technological benefits closely associated with modernity. The logic of the narrative did not always allow the RCMP to develop as fully as it might have done the positive relationship it had sometimes enjoyed with the Inuit. Rather than remembering conflict with Ottawa over abuses of the Inuit—obviously an unlikely theme for a federally funded commemoration—organizers chose to focus on the role of technology in capturing Arctic criminals. The most celebrated example was "The Mad Trapper of Rat River," whose pursuit marked the "first time in its history the RCMP called on an aircraft to assist in a manhunt."[33]

EMBRACING
MODERNITY,
LIBERALIZING
THE PAST: THE
1973 CENTENNIAL
CELEBRATIONS

128

Labour

If any topic was striking in its near absence from the centennial history, it was the role of the Force in labour disputes. In the 256-page pictorial history, the Winnipeg General Strike is granted a single paragraph of text and three captioned photographs, which show the police responding to three of their comrades being knocked off their horses.[34] The book did not mention other labour conflicts, at Estevan and Lethbridge, for example. In an article published just seven years after the centennial, Stan Horrall—the main authority for the 1973 volume—presents a rather damning critique of the federal government's failure to adhere to the Force's advice concerning the events in Winnipeg. Although the Mounted Police had informed Ottawa that the strike was not the beginning of a revolution, Horrall surmised that the federal government was greatly influenced by the idea of the "red scare," and he lamented that the Force's point of view had "little impact in Ottawa."[35] This later critique would obviously have been unwelcome in the 1973 narrative, predicated as it was on pluralism and progress.

Certainly the violence involved in labour disputes did not fit well with the "orderly" narrative now under construction. In addition, in the case of the Winnipeg General Strike, it was hardly likely that the Force would feel comfortable shifting the blame onto the federal government. Internal strife did not fit in well with the ideas of progress, harmony, and continuity as stressed by the Force's new history. The Winnipeg General Strike, a common feature of both the classic story and the left-wing critique, received little attention in 1973.

Strikes are messy, complicated, and often highly controversial events. As such, they do not lend themselves to a linear story of harmony and progress— even when the evidence suggests that the members of the Royal North-West Mounted Police were not unthinking goons who rejoiced at the thought of doing battle with the strikers.

In his examination of RNWMP involvement in the 1906 Lethbridge coal strike, for example, William M. Baker illustrates the complex and tense relations between the strikers and the Force. While riots did occur, they were minor conflicts and the exception rather than the rule over the course of the strike. Instead, the dominant characteristic of the strike seems to have been a cautious game of negotiation and public positioning in which the two sides were occasionally able to overcome their biases and their shared feelings of distrust.[36]

Steve Hewitt finds a similar scenario in his investigation of the 1931 Estevan strike and riot. Many of the officers involved in policing the strike "attempted to be balanced in their assessment of the reasons behind the strike." Moreover, some officers "openly sympathized with the striking miners despite their own class and ethnic prejudices." In the end, however, these men "followed the orders of their superiors, a group that strongly espoused the anti-communist rhetoric of the RCMP's political master, the Conservative government of R.B. Bennett."[37] Hewitt's findings call into question the view (prevalent in both the classic and left-wing histories) of the RCMP as a monolithic organization.

That monolithic view of the Force is, of course, easier to work with—and the Force that appears in the 1973 centennial narrative is no less unified and simplistic than the earlier versions. As such it remains a manageable protagonist for the organizers' chosen tale of progress. Strikes, and other events in which the Force might appear in some way divided, are no less damaging to a "continuous national history" when they illustrate this complexity, than they are when they show the RCMP in a bad light. Messy history is not reassuring history, and because of that shortcoming it is not very marketable either.

A Calendar of Events

EMBRACING
MODERNITY,
LIBERALIZING
THE PAST: THE
1973 CENTENNIAL
CELEBRATIONS

130

The RCMP Centennial Calendar provides a succinct example containing all four themes (Native-white relations, Western settlement, the North, and labour). The calendar, produced by the Regina Chamber of Commerce, had the full backing of the Force. As an organization experienced in the arts of promotion, the Chamber of Commerce presumably had no difficulty in manufacturing an acceptable synopsis of the Force's past.

The calendar outlines the settlement of the West and succinctly describes the Force as "The Settler's Friend," saluting it for the variety of tasks it carried out in aid of immigrants from around the world. A tribute to the *St. Roch* and a description of the use of planes to track criminals in the Arctic offer suitable connections to the Force's activities in the 1970s. Finally, the calendar offers romantic depictions of the police on horseback performing "the charge" for the Musical Ride (combined with the convenient omission of the Force's role in quelling labour unrest, including its role in putting down a major riot in Regina in 1935, right on the Chamber of Commerce's doorstep.) The effect allows for the potentially intimidating picture of a mounted Force to remain a picturesque and benign tourist attraction.

Again this selective vision, combined with the preponderance of RCMP members appearing in review-order uniform whatever the setting, suggested a continuity between the Force of yesterday and the 1970s. While each portrait on the calendar was capable of standing by itself and projecting a single image to its audience, taken together the images, along with a brief caption of text, produced exactly the narrative desired by the Force and the private companies involved in the centennial.[38]

Whatever form the written narrative took—calendar, pictorial history, wall panel, or place mat—it never deviated far from
the new official story of progress, harmony, and continuity. Yet
the RCMP, long aware of the power of public performances
(after all, the public had been requesting its presence at so
many of these over the years), clearly sensed the need to go beyond traditional forms and reach out to the public in less conventional ways.
Hiring outside advertising and entertainment experts was one way of keeping
up with the necessities of creating demand in an increasingly competitive entertainment market.

As a result, the centennial organizers were not content to leave history in written form. Attempting to appeal to as many people as possible, organizers sent the narrative touring the country on film, in motor homes, on horseback, even on pop cans. All of these projects helped to sustain the new narrative of the Force's history while reaching out to new audiences and engaging them directly. The most involved of these attempts was the Centennial Review, a scripted re-enactment of the Force's past.

EMBRACING
MODERNITY,
LIBERALIZING
THE PAST: THE
1973 CENTENNIAL
CELEBRATIONS

132

Re-enacting the Past: The Centennial Review

One of the most spectacular presentations involved in the centennial celebrations was the Centennial Review. Through detailed choreography the RCMP was able to take the complex topic of Canada's westward expansion and reinterpret it to produce a "living," accessible version of the Force's new image. As an insert in the souvenir program explained, this event combined music, an equestrian performance, and other demonstrations in an attempt to "illustrate the history of the RCMP as well as its contemporary image through the following format."

Overture
The March West
The Signing of the Great Blackfoot Treaty (No. 7)
The RCMP Band in Concert
The RCMP Choral Group

INTERMISSION

The Eight Horse Precision Jumping Team
The Drill Team
The RCMP Service Dogs
Mounted Arms Competition
Physical Training and Self-Defence
The RCMP Musical Ride
Finale[39]

In 1973 various entertainment groups and businesses urged customers to let themselves go, and purchase a piece of the past by buying a ticket to the RCMP Centennial Review. (Reprinted by permission of Northlands Park)

As with many centennial films and expositions, this project was contracted out to a private firm. Randy Avery, of the Calgary Young Canadians and the Force's "entertainment consultant," was the writer-director, and the concept originated with him —although Saul had long been looking for a way to combine the Musical Ride and the RCMP Band to produce a spectacle capable of capturing and retaining the public's attention.[40]

The performance began "with a re-enactment of the original March West with a musical background, the cast entering the arena through the proscenium constructed in the form of a Fort." The great marchers, as we shall see, were a motley crew of types and nationalities. After the trek "came a re-enactment of the signing of Treaty No. 7 by Chief Crowfoot." A choral group then sang "a medley of provincial songs" and concluded the first half of the show with a rendition of Avery's "Ride A Black Horse." The second half of the show "began with eight mounted men in Review Order in a precision jumping exhibition" and "was followed by a dog routine." Next, "three mounted men in period uniform" appeared and participated "in a timed mounted arms competition using sword, revolver and lance over a prescribed obstacle course." After a display of gymnastics and self-defence tactics, "The second half concluded with the Musical Ride which embodied a finale involving all members of the Review . . . culminating in a march out the Fort gates to the strains of the Regimental March."[41]

At the end of each performance, Saul would read a dedication:

On the occasion of its 100th anniversary the Force reflects upon the deeds of its many members who dedicated their lives unselfishly to the cause of justice. . . . Tho time does not permit recounting the heroic acts of later members it is sufficient to say that *all* members, *past and present are faithfully*

represented by the true Canadian heroes who emerged from the first force
French—Macleod—Steel[e]—Walsh—Potts . . . Canada today is a thriv-
ing, growing country! . . . Young! Vital! determined! and tho we pause mo-
mentarily to honor the past . . . The RCMP now turns with eyes set to the
future—God willing we shall do our best![42]

EMBRACING

MODERNITY,

LIBERALIZING

THE PAST: THE

1973 CENTENNIAL

CELEBRATIONS

134

The review epitomized the new narrative. How better to convey a sense of
the RCMP as a force of orderly progress than to re-enact the moment of birth as a
carefully scripted pageant, free of the hesitations, demoralization, and ill health
of so many of the actual recruits? There was also no trace of those damsels in distress who had once been so prevalent in the classic myth. Instead one found success stories of the March West and the signing of the Great Blackfoot Treaty.
Conveniently absent was any mention of the Northwest Rebellion. By controlling the content of the review and keeping closely to a script, Avery and Saul not
surprisingly produced a tidy, conflict-free story of order and success.

While it is perhaps impossible to measure the impact that the individual
actors had on the people who arrived in droves to view their show, it is interesting to note how the characters they played reflected the original march. The
show described the Force of 1873 as "A Mixture of Many Races,"[43] and a brief
look at Avery's character sketches suggests a rather eclectic group of men united
in their allegiance to each other. Here were some of the "great marchers":

#5. Metis Scout—very close [sic] mouth, doesn't particularly like Indians,
doesn't trust them . . .
s13. A Czechoslovakian immigrant trying to learn the English language,
worked as a labourer 6 months before joining the Force . . .
s.16. Half-breed scout—a loner, does as he's told but takes his time . . .
s.17. Happy-go-lucky Irishman—loves to sing and dance, great man to be
on your side in a fight.[44]

The ethnic stereotyping here is striking: the half-breed scout is lethargic,
and the Irishman is gregarious and outgoing; yet neither is vicious or threaten-

ing. Unlike the classic story of the Force, in this new narrative there is no "other" turned into the enemy. Eastern Europeans were no longer the greasy, yellow-toothed villains of classic Mountie fiction during the Cold War. In a remarkable turnaround, some of them were (at least potentially) original Mounties. How better to demonstrate the theme of continuity modified by change than by using such a display to advertise the Force's new (but allegedly traditional) openness to all Canadians, regardless of race, religion, or language?

Only the Czechoslovakian, having recently immigrated to Canada, fails to fit a stereotype—though perhaps the imagined Czechoslovakian was too afflicted with a sense of his unreality to develop a secure sense of his ethnic essence. Czechoslovakia did not exist in 1874. The inclusion of this character most likely owed more to the events of the Prague Spring of 1968 and the federal policy of multiculturalism than to any Eastern European representation in the original Force. Of the 245 recruits in 1873, a plurality (115) came from Ontario, while the United Kingdom contributed nearly twice as many (65) as Quebec (34). According to historian R.C. Macleod, the "typical officer of the period . . . was Canadian-born, drawn from the governing elite of eastern Canada." While "the police found it useful to have a few French-speaking officers to cope with Metis communities . . . three or four French-Canadian officers sufficed for these purposes and those in charge of the police seem to have been reluctant to include any more."[45]

Not only did the review result in a kinder, gentler March West, with none of the Force's actual inefficiencies inhibiting its progress, but it also managed to glorify Treaty No. 7 without having to deal with such unsavoury topics as the role played by the Force in Indian Commissioner Edgar Dewdney's attempt to starve and force the Plains Cree into submission shortly after the signing of the treaty. Although this, too, was a complex event. The Force was not entirely compliant in Dewdney's campaign. Commissioner Irvine, for instance, eventually disobeyed the starvation policy to, in his view, prevent what would have been certain hostilities.[46]

The review presented Treaty No. 7 itself as a voluntary option entered into by the Indians with no mention given of their military inferiority vis-à-vis the Empire, the threat of starvation, or Ottawa's willingness to use such hardship as a lever to force their compliance. On the contrary, said the announcer: "The Indians were well treated by the Mounties. And so in early 1877, The Sarcee, Blood and Blackfoot Tribes met with Lieutenant Govenor [sic] Laird and Assistant Commissioner Macleod for the signing of Treaty No. 7." Further, the resulting destitution experienced by the Indians was not the result of treaties, but could be blamed on "evil spirits." It was left to an RCMP officer playing Crowfoot to pay a lasting tribute to the Mounties on behalf of Canada's Native people:

As the feathers of a bird
Protect the bird in winter
So the redcoat protects the redskin man
If the Force had not arrived
Many would not be alive
At the hands of evil men
Tho the future generations may have sorrow
Tho evil spirits may destroy our plan
Let it be told that on this day
A white man bold
And Indian Brave
Shook hands as brothers
Man to Man[47]

The white man and Indian brave shaking hands as brothers recalls Benedict Anderson's image of William and Harold meeting as brothers at Hastings in 1066. Conflict and distrust melt into air, to be replaced by a "reassurance of fratricide" and the message that Mountie and Native were equal partners in the building of a nation.

As for other instances of conflict between the Force and large groups of people, they were simply excluded. As with the 1973 narrative in general, the review conveniently overlooked the topic of labour unrest. While the equestrian show demonstrated manoeuvres such as the "Star" and the "Charge," one formation significantly not on display was the "Flying Wedge"—the formation used

EMBRACING
MODERNITY,
LIBERALIZING
THE PAST: THE
1973 CENTENNIAL
CELEBRATIONS

136

to intimidate strikers in disturbances such as those in Estevan and Winnipeg.

Finally, for fear that the audience might think the Force anachronistic, the success of the early years was deftly connected to a physically fit, and technologically developed, present-day Force through the presentation of modern police weapons, mounted arms displays, training methods, and police dogs. The strength and physical prowess prominently on display reflected a transition in ideal masculinity. Chivalry and men of slight build were out; muscular builds and men of action were in. Aggressiveness and physical force had thus surpassed Victorian ideals of manhood.[48] To solidify the continuity of past and present, the Centennial Review concluded with the seemingly timeless Musical Ride, first performed publicly in 1904.[49] The Ride, combined with Saul's dedication, closed the performance with a reassuring sense of the continuing great unbroken tradition of the Force and the Canadian nation.

Audiences greeted the show with ovations wherever it was performed. Newspaper reporters praised its Canadian production and content.[50] Bryan Hay of the Victoria *Daily Times* labelled the show "magnificent," and went on: "The thundering horses, the flashing lances, the glitter of polished metal and leather, they all help to stir the spirits and stimulate the senses and burst a little with the patriotic pride for which we so often laugh at our cousins to the South of us."[51]

To encourage the public to attend the show, Hay's colleague at the *Daily Times*, Erith Smith, summarized the show's itinerary and offered as well some of the more optimistic interpretations of the Force's past. He described Treaty No. 7 as "a treaty that sealed the respect with which the red-coated force was regarded by all Indians in Canada."[52] The Edmonton *Journal* called the show a "once-in-a-lifetime spectacle," and Edmontonians responded by lining up for hours for a chance to attend.[53]

Exhibitions

Organizers also set up exhibitions in major cities across the country. These exhibits told the Force's story through bilingual wall panels and stressed its

current roles through "hands-on" exhibits of technology used in crime detection. At the Toronto exhibit in the Ontario Science Centre, visitors were encouraged to take home a souvenir of technologically advanced crime detection in the form of a computer printout, part of which read:

> The members of the Royal Canadian Mounted Police are proud to be playing such a major role in the development and operation of the [Canadian Police Information Centre] system. In 1973, our Centennial year, we are especially pleased that we can help in providing a law-enforcement service on behalf of all Canadians that truly reflects the computer age.
>
> Please accept this message as a souvenir of our exhibit at the Ontario Science Centre.[54]

However, as another wall panel indicated, even in the Science Centre there was never a complete break with the early years. The RCMP did use "analysis by X-Ray diffraction, infrared spectrometry, and atomic absorption techniques. But today, as in 1900, detail, scrutiny and intelligent observation on the spot remains the basis of all police investigations."[55]

The "Flare Square" exhibit in Calgary was also loyal to the themes of the new narrative. This site of three and a half acres on the Calgary Stampede grounds was entitled "Flare Square Salutes A 'Century in Scarlet' of the RCMP." The organizers divided the exhibit into distinct areas dealing with the "Historical," "Contemporary," "Arctic," and "Veterans" aspects of the Force. They also set down an "action" area, which offered displays of "Physical Training" as well as a "Mounted Arms Equestrian Show."[56] The Ottawa, Vancouver, and Winnipeg exhibits provided visitors with a chance to explore the Force's past and present under a futuristic geodesic "Canadome." As one official informed a Canadian Press reporter, these exhibits all told similar stories: "They illustrate the history of the force, its contribution to the growth and development of Canada and its role in society today."[57]

Updating the Force's image went so far as to include music calculated to appeal to an audience younger than the one that usually attended Musical Ride and police demonstrations. Organizers pulled together a rock group to accompany the review as it crossed the country, and in an attempt to modernize the regular band's performance, Bramwell Smith, the music director, made a trip to Las Vegas to learn about the latest in the way of entertainment. Smith's report back to Saul suggests that his trip was highly educational. Most of the shows he saw were, he said, "relying upon totally unacceptable humour segued into a sea of bare breasted women," and he enclosed a brochure to illustrate his point. "From the production standpoint, several lighting ideas might be considered for incorporation in the Review."[58]

If Smith found his trip revealing in one respect and enlightening in another, in general the turn to rock 'n' roll helped put a more modern face on the Force, as it attempted to escape the burdens of "Rose Marie" and reach out to a young audience lacking in complete enthusiasm for police forces and presumably with little interest in the Force's history.

In a more direct attempt to involve the public—and in particular the young baby boom generation—the Toronto exhibit planned to use "Waldo the talking police car." The car would produce "pretend" tickets that would be given to those who for some reason were moved to talk to cars.[59] A similar project was used in Calgary at the "Flare Square" exhibition site. Here, each person attending got a passport complete with a message from the commissioner and a place for the person's thumb-print.[60] Waldo and the passport were both attempts to imprint upon the public the modern image of the friendly Force—an organization that, in revering tradition, also fully accepted the most advanced technology.

Projects Approved and Declined

As the gimmick of "Waldo the talking police car" indicates, almost anything associated with the Force could be used to influence the public's perception of the narrative. Still, the centennial planners pondered not only the potential but also the danger of such popularization through mass culture. As a result, they

EMBRACING
MODERNITY,
LIBERALIZING
THE PAST: THE
1973 CENTENNIAL
CELEBRATIONS

140

thoroughly vetted any commercial projects or souvenirs on RCMP themes designed and marketed by private interests. One concern was that the products "depict appropriate symbols" of the Force's past: "Fort Whoop-up, Fort Calgary, Fort Edmonton, Commissioner Macleod, Jerry Potts, etc."[61] Another concern was that the company or individual involved enjoy "a good reputation in their retailing."[62] Overall, Commissioner Higgitt stated, "As long as the articles have been accurate and in good taste, we have been honoured to cooperate in these ventures to provide suitable centennial mementoes."[63]

The Advisory Committee declined some articles simply because they were not part of the new RCMP story and, in fact, offered a competing image of the Force's history. This was certainly the case with the proposals from Smith and Wesson for a commemorative RCMP hand gun and from Winchester for a commemorative rifle. Both "souvenirs" conflicted with the Canadian myth of an orderly West.[64] The narrative of the Centennial Review read by the public-address announcer stated this facet emphatically: "These red coated men of one hundred years ago, brought peace to an unpeaceful country, and without one shot being fired during the first eleven years." The Force's manner of dealing with the various proposals concerning alcohol was more complex. Presumably worried about any connection with drinking and driving, and anxious to defend its mythic role as scourge of the whiskey trader, the Advisory Committee refused to be associated with a calendar sponsored by Labatts Breweries.[65] The committee permitted the production of commemorative drinking glasses and coasters, but limited their distribution to members of the Force.[66]

More innocuous items seemed to gain the Force's favour. Souvenir sugar packets with images of the Force on them were approved, according to one inspector, because of their "good taste (pardon the pun) in the choice of photographs."[67] Items such as Mountie-themed potato chips and aluminum cans were vetoed because of the fear that they would be left strewn about the country and the RCMP would then be associated with littering. Somewhat inconsistently, however, the Advisory Committee did accept a proposal by Charles Wilson Ltd. to produce pop cartons, on condition that the manufacturer strike the phrase "Here comes the Fizz" from the product.[68]

DIVINE SERVICE IN CAMP ON SUNDAYS.

This Henri Julien sketch of the Great March West, entitled "Divine Service in Camp on Sundays," was reprinted in the 1973 RCMP Centennial souvenir program. Rather than emphasizing the Christian motives behind the colonizing of the Canadian west, the 1973 caption asserted that "members of the Force have always enjoyed singing." (Glenbow Archives, Calgary, Alberta, NA-361-7)

More centrally related to the RCMP's preferred role was its approval of a submission from the Canadian Bible Society, which requested that photographs of the Force appear on "Scripture Selections." The following excerpts from these "Selections" suggest why the RCMP might have readily agreed to this somewhat unliberal collaboration of Church and State.

> Everyone must obey the state authorities; for no authority exists without God's permission, and the existing authorities have been put there by God. . . .
>
> This is also the reason that you pay taxes; for the authorities are working for God when they fulfill their duties. Pay, then, what you owe them; pay them your personal and property taxes and show respect and honor for them all. . . .
>
> Be in debt to no one—the only debt you should have is to love one another.[69]

Religion and the Mountie myth had been brought together earlier in the century by Ralph Connor; the linking of the Force and religion in 1973 suggests that, much as the RCMP was keen to renovate its narrative in keeping with the social realities of postwar Canada, it was engaged in editing out only certain elements of the classic narrative, and not abandoning it altogether.

Indeed, the commissioner himself co-operated with the National Arts Centre, Ottawa, in its attempt to obtain the rights to the opera version of *Rose Marie*.[70] The centennial's connection with the royal visits of Queen Elizabeth and Prince Philip also indicated that the Force could not (and would not) break completely with its classic image. Renovation of the myth—the blurring or removal of its obviously controversial antilabour, anti-Native, anti-French-Canadian and antifemale overtones—did not mean losing the romance of the RCMP. The centennial celebrations in 1973 were clearly an attempt to have both the comforts of the old and the excitement of the new.

Anxious to avoid restricting the narrative to its written form, organizers had produced a wide array of projects, "live" exhibitions, and souvenirs in an attempt to maximize their audience and take full advantage of the wide dissemination possible through the commodification of the new image. The RCMP had responded well to the challenges of the increasingly competitive entertainment market. After much fanfare and effort, the centennial celebrations eventually came to a close. It was then time to tally up the reviews and see if the Force had been successful in renovating its history and staving off embarrassing critiques. The public response suggested that it had.

6

Upholding the Image, Maintaining the Rights: The Mountie Enters the World of Postmodernity, 1973-97

The beautiful lull,
the dangerous tug
we get to feel small
from high up above
and after a glimpse
over the top
the rest of the world
becomes a giftshop.

— *The Tragically Hip, 1996*

Goofy, or not? The RCMP's deal with Disney was a hotly debated topic in the summer of 1995 and after. With his renovation consolidated by the 1973 RCMP Centennial, the Mountie image was a safe acquisition for Disney. (Aislin—*The Gazette*)

The most bizarre political decision of this decade may be the Chrétien government's sale of licensing rights for properties associated with the RCMP to the Disney Corporation, America's most powerful cultural institution. The Disney Decision was avoidable. But, for better or for worse, new technology ranging from "Death Star" satellite broadcasting to the Internet makes it virtually impossible to regulate what Canadians watch and interact with. The wall has been breached, and the world is spilling in.

— Angus Reid, *Shakedown: How the New Economy Is Changing Our Lives*, 1996

UPHOLDING
THE IMAGE,
MAINTAINING
THE RIGHTS:
THE MOUNTIE
ENTERS THE
WORLD OF
POSTMODERNITY,
1973-97

146

One of the most popular rides at Disneyland is one of the oldest. "It's a Small World" is a peaceful journey through a sparkling blue castle in which parents and children can sit comfortably together in tightly controlled boats and view dolls representing many of the world's nations. As your boat enters the castle, the first doll that greets you is a Mountie. It is—so far as I could tell—the only representative in that small world of Canada.

Regaled in his scarlet tunic and stetson hat, the Mountie smiles a buck-toothed smile at guests, welcoming them to a land of peace, harmony, and goodwill. A brightly coloured raven rests upon his hat. The bird is clearly there to represent Canada's Aboriginal population. Its presence on the Mountie's head, and the Mountie's carefree and nonchalant expression, suggest an absence of tension and conflict between the two characters. Disneyland's Mountie is clearly a product of the renovation that was consolidated in the 1973 Centennial. As you drift past these two figures, you begin to hear the song that is "sung" melodically by the Mountie and other characters inside the castle. It seems fitting that in a world increasingly connected by satellites and fibre-optic cables, at the heart of Disney's empire a chorus of toy children reminds us melodically, *it really is a small world after all.*

We tend to remember the year 1973 for a variety of events. The U.S. withdrawal from Vietnam, the Watergate scandal, and the Arab-Israeli War are among the most easily recalled. The year was also a watershed in terms of economic globalization and dislocation. The early 1970s marked the end of the economic boom of the postwar period. It was also a time in which the West entered a new economic and cultural era. The days of the "Fordist" compromise in which state regulation worked to maintain a balance between industrial production and public consumption were drawing to a close. What was soon to emerge was a much more global, far less regulated system of exchange. Benjamin Barber has aptly summarized this new system in a single word: McWorld.

McWorld, Barber argues, "forges global markets rooted in consumption and profit, leaving to an untrustworthy, if not altogether fictitious invisible hand issues of public interest and common good." It is, he continues, "a product of popular culture driven by expansionist commerce," and "Its template is

American, its form style. Its goods are as much images as matériel, an aesthetic as well as a product line. It is about culture as commodity, apparel as ideology."[1]

This transition from an industrial to a postindustrial world has been marked by the rise in power of the service and entertainment industries. In suggesting what this means in the U.S. context, Barber is less than optimistic:

> In the nineteenth century, the great monopolies in oil, steel, coal, and the railways were finally dismantled by vigorous government anti-trust regulation. But Michael Eisner is no Rockefeller and Bill Gates is no Vanderbilt and Steven Spielberg is no Carnegie. Eisner, Gates, and Spielberg are far more powerful, for theirs is a power not over oil, steel, and railroads—mere muscles of our modern industrial bodies—but over pictures, information, and ideas—the very sinews of our postmodern soul.[2]

The present-day Mountie and raven at the entrance of the "It's a Small World" ride at Disneyland, California. The RCMP's licensing agreement with the ubiquitous Magic Kingdom demonstrated for many that, in an era of global marketing, it really is "a small world after all." (Author's photo)

Canada, and the image of the Mountie, were not immune to this transition. Where once industrial companies like Monsanto Chemicals led the way in soliciting photos of the Mountie for their catalogues and newsletters, the 1970s and 1980s saw service industries (and tourism in particular) come to the fore. In the early stages of this transition, the federal government actively assisted Canada's service industries in using the Mountie image. Yet by the 1990s the momentum of McWorld had clearly won out. If, as Barber argues, "the table for McWorld has been set by Hollywood" and the entertainment industry, it comes as no surprise that in an age when governments are abandoning their once-crucial regulatory duties, and economic and cultural power is becoming increasingly concentrated through multinational mergers, Disney should emerge as the heir to the Mountie image and inherit the responsibility for upholding the image and a healthy portion of the profits to boot.[3] The 1973 centennial played a key role in preparing the mythic Mountie for his postmodern duties.

As all such things must, the centennial celebrations did come to an end, but they had a lasting impact upon the Force's image. Representations of the RCMP in its own publications, in popular literature, children's activity books, and even on television programs were now greatly informed by the new narrative of 1973.

UPHOLDING
THE IMAGE,
MAINTAINING
THE RIGHTS:
THE MOUNTIE
ENTERS THE
WORLD OF
POSTMODERNITY,
1973-97

148

In this way a new Mountie tradition was consolidated and, as a result, so too was a new version of English-Canadian public memory. The historical tensions in Canada's past were slowly being overcome. This new conflict-free version of Canada's past offered renewed marketing potential, which was eventually seized upon by one of the world's largest entertainment conglomerates. The mythic Mountie was becoming disconnected from the Force's complicated and tangible past. The image of the Mountie was becoming a sort of free-floating image, purged of its classic baggage.

Even before the centennial ended, letters poured into RCMP headquarters paying tribute to the Force. Public reaction to the centennial suggests that the new and improved history of the RCMP was well-received. With the celebrations behind it, the Force again turned its energies towards the day-to-day administrative activities necessary to respond to public demand for its image. As usual many requests came from the private sector, but the 1970s and 1980s saw a new twist: the federal government actively employed the image of its police force to "sell" the country around the world. By 1995, having already contracted out the renovation of its history in 1973, the Force eventually contracted out the day-to-day administrative responsibilities necessary to police its image. Herein lay the origins of the infamous Disney deal.

Dear Mounties: Public Reaction to the 1973 Centennial

Throughout the 1970s, revelations continued to emerge about RCMP illegalities. In 1974 former Constable Robert Samson was charged in connection with a bomb explosion, and by 1977 RCMP woes were a regular feature in newspaper editorials.[4] Yet when the federal Conservatives attempted to take the government to task for the RCMP's misdeeds, they faced an angry backlash from a public offended that the Tories would attack the Force.[5]

In January 1978, after years of startling exposés about RCMP wrongdoing, a public opinion poll asked Canadians if they thought the RCMP had "too much power and authority, or not enough." One-third of respondents indicated that

Centennial salute

The tension between women's greater public autonomy, and their exclusion from the Force, is captured by this 1973 cartoon from the Ottawa *Citizen*. (Reprinted with permission of Rusins Kaufmanis)

they felt the Force had too little power, while 41 per cent said the police had "about the right level of power and authority." A scant 19 per cent said that the Force's power was excessive.[6] Apparently, the RCMP's various escapades, uncovered and thoroughly documented in the 1970s, did not result in the Canadian people losing faith in their famous police force.

This public support has been attributed, in part, to the classic mythology of the Mountie.[7] However, given the shifting social mores of the 1960s and 1970s, it would seem that the handling of RCMP history in the 1970s, and the organizers' willingness to reinvent the institution's traditions during the centennial, were equally responsible for the continued grip on the loyalty of most Canadians. Just as important, though, in reworking the national memory was the *willingness* of the public to accept a new version of its country's past. The new story of the RCMP was not a saga of British imperial expansion, but of Canadian nation-building, with the Force front and centre in a tale of progress. Native peoples were no longer vilified; they were allies. The gender stereotypes of the debonair yet able Mountie and the fawning, helpless damsel in distress, so prevalent in the classic myth, were nowhere to be seen in 1973.

The Force itself was also beginning to respond to the changing place of women, Native peoples, and French-Canadians in Canadian society. In September 1970 the Force undertook a study "to determine the areas in which the Force could use the services of women." Outside pressure helped push the initiative along. B.C. Attorney General Alex Macdonald suggested publicly that women should be hired by the Force for traffic patrol. The RCMP was at first cool to this suggestion, though organizations such as the National Council of Women were now pushing it to accept female applicants for regular positions.[8] By October of the Force's centennial year Commissioner Higgitt was informing the solicitor general that "while we have recognized the principle that there is room for female police officers, we have yet to define the specific role to be played."

In December the Force opted to hire women as "Special Constables," and on September 23, 1974, the first female recruits were admitted to the Force's training centre in Regina.[9] Media reaction was generally positive and ascribed

Uluschak EDMONTON JOURNAL

Some observers appeared dubious of the message Canada was sending to the Queen when she visited Canada to honour the Force. (Reprinted courtesy of National Archives of Canada and Edd Uluschak)

this change in policy to both the recent Royal Commission on the Status of Women as well as to broader changes within society.[10] As Victoria *Daily Times* reporter Derek Sidenius commented rather optimistically, "One of the last vestiges of the male chauvinist's world [had] crumbled," though the threat of a legal challenge was necessary to convince the RCMP to allow women onto its auxiliary force.[11]

In the mid-1970s the RCMP also made an effort to better integrate the Aboriginal population into the Force. In 1971 an experimental program created positions for eleven "Special Native Constables" to act as liaisons between the Force and Native people on reserves.[12] By 1976 a Special Natives Constables program was fully in effect, training Aboriginal members of the Force to move into these liaison positions.[13] Also, despite public grumbling throughout the decade, the Force pushed on with its bilingualism policy.

In 1973 Canada's westward expansion had become not just another example of the British Empire civilizing the world, but a multicultural and bilingual March West that would pave the way for the tolerant and pluralistic Canada of today. Corporal Cameron and Dale of the Mounted, icons of rugged individualism, yielded pride of place as heroes to James Macleod and James Walsh, down-to-earth proponents of order and procedure. Yet however new the multiculturalism of the Force and its technologies of order, the public narrative of 1973 conveyed a reassuring and consistent message: Canada's Mounted Police were on duty to protect the public and secure the "good life" they had done so much to establish.

Canada's Mounted Police were also on duty to protect the Queen when she arrived to pay tribute to them during their centennial year. The Queen stressed the "unifying" role that she hoped to play in Canada. Doug Small of Canadian Press reported, "Past debates over the usefulness of the monarchy . . . appeared to give way to an attitude of quiet acceptance." A "holiday spirit" prevailed during the Queen's visit to Regina, and the *Leader Post* termed the visit "more successful than expected."[14] Not even a Métis boycott of the festivities (to protest RCMP oppression of Native peoples) or Chief David Ahenakew's public admonishments to her majesty to help alleviate Native poverty spoiled the fun.[15] The Queen's remarks on Native issues were approved in advance by the federal government—a fitting comment on the place of the monarchy in Canadian society at the time.[16]

In general the centennial program seemed to have run smoothly, facing few, if any, major problems. Although there were two empty bomb threats, on the public relations front the centennial appeared to be a shining success. Even violent clashes on Parliament Hill between Mounties and striking railway workers in August and the Native Youth Association in October could not overshadow the celebrations.[17] The evidence suggests that most of the public fully supported the commemoration, and that the shows and exhibits were well-attended. In Vancouver the attendance figures for the RCMP exhibit indicated

UPHOLDING

THE IMAGE,

MAINTAINING

THE RIGHTS:

THE MOUNTIE

ENTERS THE

WORLD OF

POSTMODERNITY,

1973-97

152

that over sixty thousand people had visited during the month of July alone. When the Centennial Review made its way out west, attendance figures for Vancouver and Kelowna combined to exceed forty thousand. The exhibit at the Ontario Science Centre in Toronto was so well-attended that in early July organizers were estimating that over half a million people would visit before the exhibit closed.[18] In addition the Force received a vast amount of mail from the public, and schools in particular, requesting written centennial material.

As we have seen, such requests for information were not answered with a balanced presentation of the Force's history. Official histories generally present official viewpoints. In this case, however, the institution had the unusual ability to reach millions of Canadians and present a version of events that took on the aura of an authoritative and official history. Journalistic tributes to the Force seemed willing to endorse the new story of the RCMP. Newspapers and magazines as varied as the Vancouver *Province*, the *Atlantic Advocate*, and Canadian Mortgage and Housing Corporation's magazine *North* all produced synopses of the Force's history that strayed little from the 1973 narrative.[19]

Attendance figures and newspaper coverage, of course, do not tell us the whole story about the centennial's impact on the general population. A more vivid sense of what the centennial—and the Mounties—meant to Canadians can be discerned by employing an old RCMP trick: reading people's mail. Hundreds of letters were sent to RCMP headquarters in response to the activities of the celebrations. Most of these were extremely laudatory. At first glance they appear simply as fitting tributes from an adoring public that enjoyed the celebrations, particularly the spectacle of the Force's Centennial Review as it toured the country. Closer analysis suggests, however, that many of the themes and messages of the centennial narrative were taken deeply to heart by those who penned the letters, particularly the ones from Western Canada.

The most frequent topic of correspondence was the Centennial Review. Janet Timm and Annette Jaenen described the patriotic pride they felt in viewing the show in Winnipeg: "Words could never express the pride and patriotic feeling the Review creates in the audience. It makes people realize that we of Canada have the world's best police force. . . . May you have another wonderful

100 years!"[20] A letter from another Manitoban suggested that renovating the classic myth had not meant a decline in the Force's popularity with the young men of the nation. He exhorted his fellow Canadians to stand behind the Force:

> Every Canadian has not only the right but the duty to be proud of the RCMP and their colourful history.
>
> They say that every boy in the United States dreams of growing up and becoming President. If every boy in Canada could see your show I'm sure their dreams would be to become a member of the famed and respected Royal Canadian Mounted Police.[21]

Once again, here was the ever-present comparison with the United States, and with it an expression of Canadian patriotism. For his part, David Hankinson of CKXL News in Calgary admitted that the finale of the review brought "a lump to my throat and tears to my eyes." He added that he had overheard a staff member declare, "If they'd raised an old sock in place of the Canadian flag when that horse and rider came on stage, I would have saluted it."[22]

A CFRN radio and television editorial broadcast in Edmonton demonstrated the ascendancy of the new Canadian nationalism and the Force's centrality to it. In doing so it reaffirmed the Force's connection with liberal-democratic ideals while suggesting the Force was distinctly Canadian:

> Let's show the world what we have just as various countries have shown us their best be it the Moscow Circus or Peking Opera to the National Ballet, the Stuttgart Symphony or the British changing of the Guard.
>
> The RCMP musical ride and band is the most unique show in the world bar none. . . .
>
> People behind the Iron and Bamboo curtains, as well as other nations, have shown us their fare. Now let's show them [ours].[23]

The Cold War rhetoric here underlines the fact that audience members were never entirely restricted to just one way of responding to the new story of

UPHOLDING
THE IMAGE,
MAINTAINING
THE RIGHTS:
THE MOUNTIE
ENTERS THE
WORLD OF
POSTMODERNITY,
1973-97

154

the Force. Despite organizers' attempts to minimize the Cold War connota-tions of the Force's duties, for some the Force would remain a symbol of West-ern superiority. But the fact that the editorial chose to differentiate the Canadian celebration from the "British changing of the Guard" suggests that one element of the centennial—the shedding of the British and imperialist bag-gage in favour of a decidedly Canadian persona for the Force—was generally accepted by the audience.

Most audience members were content to thank the Force for rekindling a sense of pride in their country—and giving them a vivid sense of its history. One woman revealingly thanked the Force for "giving me something to believe in." She shared the Force's vision of itself: a past "colourful and . . . steeped in traditions" combined with "a bright and hopeful future." She closed her letter: "Wish I could thank every member, past and present, for showing me what it means to be a Canadian."[24] These sentiments were held by those who had *become* Canadians as well. Joan Lloyd of Chatham, Ontario declared, "I am a Canadian by choice rather than by birth but I felt as proud of Canada last evening, as I ever did watching similar-type events in my native land." She reported that her "children have talked of nothing else today, and I am sure this has brought them a good part of their Canadian Heritage."[25] This was a spirit of community that seemingly welcomed new members.

Often letters equated the RCMP with the nation itself. John Holdstock, an administrator at Queen Alexandra Hospital for Sick Children in Victoria, declared that the "history of the Royal Canadian Mounted Police is indeed really the history of Canada and the fact that you can involve yourselves so deeply with the community in addition to maintaining law and order deserves the highest commendation."[26] Others indicated that the narrative had success-fully communicated the notion of a liberal, progressive order. Having watched the review, the Pigott family of Ottawa was united in its praise of "the visual story of the thread of order that ties this nation together."

Going home that day, the 82-year old grandfather said, "I feel a better Canadian," the 11-year old, daughter, danced through the corridor singing snatches of the song, and the parents of two teen-aged boys felt a sense of gratitude that their sons could see the spirit of purpose and discipline in the young men's eyes.[27]

The centennial's appeal to children would continue to serve the Force well. The Force received many requests from schools and clubs for educational material about the Force. One teacher from Regina sought a film of the review to show her students.[28] The centennial celebrations had delighted thousands of children in 1973 and, preserved on film and presented in schools, it would do so for years to come.

Evident in all of these letters is the centrality of the Force to the imagined community called Canada. That this centrality has been preserved for over one hundred years owes much to the power of tradition and the organizers' intelligent capacity to renovate it. The Force, it seems, had been successful in its objective: at a time when many elements in society were increasingly questioning authority, the Force had dramatically remade its image without forfeiting the benefits of its romantic tradition.

The glowing reviews did come at a cost, however. Some observers remained uncomfortable with the RCMP's new image. Some opposed the bilingualism practised in the centennial. One Ontarian who went to the Centennial Review in Ottawa, for instance, objected to having to listen to the opening remarks in French. "When the show is performed in Quebec naturally the language should be French," the critic reasoned, "but in the rest of Canada let us be proud of our language and our race."[29] Others objected to the Force's apparent decision to distance itself from the monarchy. R.H. Reid, on behalf of the Dominion of Canada English Speaking Association, lamented that the review did not include "God Save the Queen." Mrs. Nettie Leaman of Moncton offered a similar lament, complaining that "everything involving Royalty appears to be slipping from us."[30]

Others objected to the Force's attempt to appeal to a younger generation. Mrs. C. King, of Maple Ridge, B.C., thought that the tone of the review had been lowered "by subjecting the audience to a programme completely devoted

UPHOLDING
THE IMAGE,
MAINTAINING
THE RIGHTS:
THE MOUNTIE
ENTERS THE
WORLD OF
POSTMODERNITY,
1973-97

156

to 'pop' music." Upset by this "attempt to show the younger generation that the Force is 'with it,'" she told the commissioner, "Military bands of the stature of the RCMP . . . don't require to be 'sold' to an audience by shabby 'show biz' methods." She concluded by reminding him, "The band is a fine collection of musicians, with a long tradition, a tradition that seems to have been thrown to the winds."[31] Mrs. King was not alone in her opinion. Bernard and Brigitte Doughton criticized the Force for its attempt to "pander to the youth of our world" and for giving in to a culture that no longer revered "discipline, manners and martial aims." They told the commissioner that the Force was "and always will be a part of the evolving scene in Canada, but as a permanent feature I should think you could be above current fadism."[32] Here centennial organizers had simply been following what was sound business practice at the time: they were conscious of the importance of tailoring their show to the demographic bulge that was the baby boomers.[33]

Another observer, though disappointed with the Force's musical attempt to broaden its appeal, was ready to "admit that an old-fashioned Military Band concert under the direction of one of our old Bandmasters would probably not have brought half Saturday night's audience across the street to attend." Commissioner Higgitt's measured response to this observation alluded to the political dilemma the Force faced: "The performance has to be geared to such a broad cross-section of audiences that we have found it almost impossible to satisfy every taste." He hoped the Force had "struck a reasonable balance between the traditional and the modern," a comment that typified the organizers' general approach in 1973.[34]

Judging by the RCMP files, these sorts of complaints were in the minority. If they had been published, they might have elicited a response along the lines of a letter replying to a Vancouver *Province* article critical of the review. The "drivel" written by reporter Jenni Read, the two letter-writers protested, was a "gross insult to all Canadians" and "reek[ed] of a lack of national pride." After all, "the production from start to finish was entirely Canadian," including "the music, the performers and the history on which the pageant was based." The only solace, they said, was "that in the final tribute paid by those of us in atten-

dance we were able to collectively refute her review. With the Coliseum in semi-darkness, illuminated by 12,000 flickering match lights, the words of O Canada resounded throughout in a tremendous exhibition of pride and respect for Canada and for our unique institution, the RCMP"[35] Radio station CFRN in Edmonton issued a similar call to arms in trumpeting the uniqueness of the RCMP as a source of spectacle in the world, although the broadcaster's grammar—"Let's show them something they have never seen nor ever will"—was wobbly.[36] But this stumbling summons carried a grain of truth: showing them something without them really seeing it was exactly what the Force had done in 1973. The Mountie, that most visible of symbols, had been reinvented with very little public notice, yet as part of a mass public spectacle. This overhaul of tradition was smoothly executed, and its successful outcome must account for some of the Force's remarkably enduring popularity.

Selling Canada

In July 1979 yet another letter arrived at RCMP headquarters. It carried a request from The Pentecostal Churches of Canada for two Mounties in uniform to march in a flag parade at the Twelfth Pentecostal World Conference in Vancouver in October. In the letter, Rev. James Montgomery opined, "Around the world the Royal Canadian Mounted Police are the greatest emblem of Canada."[37]

That letter and others like it suggest that the Mountie remained central to English-Canadian political culture, even though that political culture had recently undergone a dramatic transformation. The Mountie also remained crucial to "selling Canada" to the rest of the world. Now, more than ever, and with federal government support, Canada employed the Mountie, and police officers directly, in its attempts to compete for international tourist dollars in both the established markets of the Commonwealth and the United States, and the emerging markets of Southeast Asia. Whereas plans for the centennial had been ratified by government bureaucrats for the dual purpose of improving the

Force's public relations and increasing tourist traffic within Canada, by the later 1970s and into the 1980s only the latter rationale remained.

An appendix to a Canadian Government Office of Tourism catalogue, "Federal Government Programs Relevant to Tourism Development," alluded to the importance of the RCMP to Canadian tourism. The appendix was included in a letter to Commissioner Maurice Nadon in 1975, when a request was made for the commissioner's co-operation in completing an attached questionnaire. The RCMP appeared under the heading of "Federal Tourism-Related Activities, with a four-point description of its contribution to the tourism effort. First, the item stated matter of factly that the "'Mounties' probably remain Canada's leading visitor attraction." Second, the Force's own entertainment performances—the Musical Ride and the Band—also played a key role in attracting visitors. Third, the Force's museum in Regina was "a leading visitor attraction in that city." Finally, the RCMP's role as a police force also contributed to Canada's tourism effort, because "in every province and territory except Ontario and Quebec, the RCMP enforces law and security on behalf of the tourist."[38]

But the Mounties were not simply a domestic tourist attraction. They could be exported too. When the Commonwealth Games were held in Brisbane, Australia, in 1982, organizers of the Warana Parade sought six Mounties to participate in their parade, though they wanted the Canadian government to foot much of the bill. The Department of External Affairs indicated that it would be willing to cover these costs, but wished to have the members of the Force more "involved" so as to "MAXIMIZE THE AMT OF FLAG SHOWING PER TRAVEL DLR." All that was left for the Force to do, in the words of the author of an investigation report, was to wait for an "official request for six members, who know back side of front [sic] when approaching a horse."[39] When the time came, the official request from External Affairs added a twist. "A contingent of six RCMP members has been invited," wrote D.C. Arnould, director of External Information Programs Division, to the commissioner. "It would be a definite asset if one or two of these were women."[40] Women had been purged from the Mountie story in 1973. When they had entered the Force as police officers in

UPHOLDING
THE IMAGE,
MAINTAINING
THE RIGHTS:
THE MOUNTIE
ENTERS THE
WORLD OF
POSTMODERNITY,
1973-97

158

1974, they quickly found themselves appearing on the public relations stage.

Yet old images take time to fade away. When a female Mountie first appeared on ceremonial duty at Canada House in London, she had a difficult time convincing passersby that she was a real member of the Force. The onlookers were adamant that she must be a model clad in the Mountie uniform.[41] Occasionally the tensions between the classic image and the newly renovated Mountie image caused tension within the Force itself. According to journalist Paul Palango, by the early 1990s, "Many Mounties worried that public relations were becoming more important than real police work." The epitome of this obsession with public relations was, according to Palango, "an heroic portrait hanging in the foyer of the RCMP 'D' Division headquarters in Winnipeg. It depicts four Mounties in uniform: a black man, a native man, a white woman, and an Asian woman. The painting is a calculated lie."[42] The majority of the public, however, did not need to search out the scarlet-clad Mounties in London, England, or in the foyer of an RCMP detachment. Often the Mounties were brought directly into their living rooms.

Sometimes Mounties were not asked to travel very far at all to represent Canada internationally. In 1980, with his baseball team in pennant contention, the Montreal Expos' Roger D. Landry, vice-president, marketing and public affairs, wrote to Commissioner R.H. Simmonds seeking a Mountie presence at Olympic Stadium for an upcoming appearance by the Montreal Expos in the League Championship and World Series: "We will want to show, not only to Canadians from coast to coast, but also to 100 million plus international viewers, our Canadian color [sic] and certainly our best image." The best vehicle for doing this, he argued, was the RCMP:

> Without a doubt, no organization can better represent the Canadian image than the police force you direct and, on behalf of the Montreal Expos Baseball Club as well as all Canadians, I wish to invite you to participate in two possible pre-game shows on October 8 and October 15 for both the League Championship and World Series games that could take place in Montreal.[43]

UPHOLDING
THE IMAGE,
MAINTAINING
THE RIGHTS:
THE MOUNTIE
ENTERS THE
WORLD OF
POSTMODERNITY,
1973-97

160

Landry stated that Solicitor General Robert Kaplan had been informed, but that he realized the final decision rested with the commissioner. The Commissioner was quite willing to approve the plan.[44] Unfortunately, the Expos finished the season one game back of the Phillies in the National League East and missed out on the postseason games.

In the early 1980s international Mountie appearances were on the rise. In early December 1982, at the World Travel Market exhibition in London, England, the Canadian Government Office of Tourism organized a "major Canada presence." A request from Margaret Bleach of the federal government's Tourism Development Branch outlined the reasons for seeking two Mounties to appear at the market, held annually in London since 1980: "The presence of the RCMP Officers has been requested by the industry in both the United Kingdom and Canada as a means of drawing attention to the Canadian presence at WTM. The RCMP is the most readily recognizable symbol for Canada internationally. The presence of these officers provides tremendous opportunities for further media exposure."[45] One of the officers involved reported that he felt this opportunity "was a positive P.R. venture for the Force and Canadian Government" and recommended that the Force "should consider participating again, if asked."[46]

In January 1983 a letter arrived on Supt. John Bentham's desk from the Canadian tourism office requesting two RCMP officers in full uniform to participate in a two-week promotional campaign in Southeast Asia. This program, Bentham was informed, "will position Canada as a viable travel destination in this new market area." It would also promote Cathay Pacific's new service between Hong Kong and Vancouver. The office wanted the RCMP officers for their "very positive worldwide image," which, it said, would "assist our efforts to assist media exposure for Canada."[47] In what by now seems to have been a routine operation, the necessary approval was obtained. On February 1, Commissioner Simmonds sent a letter requesting approval to Solicitor General Kaplan. Simmonds wrote, "Notwithstanding what will likely be prominent involvement by commercial air carriers, I view our attendance in this undertaking as support for a Canadian Government initiative which prompts me to seek

One hundred and twenty-five years after the original Force embarked on its Great March West, travellers driving across the Prairies can opt to follow the Red Coat Trail and trace the Force's route. (Author's photo)

your approval." All costs were to be borne by the Office of Tourism.[48] Solicitor General Kaplan's positive reply arrived in the commissioner's office on February 24. With ministerial approval obtained, Bentham sent a memorandum to the commissioner suggesting his recipe for adhering to regional and linguistic representation for this event.

As a result, Cpl. J.R.E.S. Carrière and Cpl. Tom Hansen were off to Hong Kong, Manila, Djakarta, Singapore, Kuala Lumpur, and Bangkok. In the mornings they attended media interviews dressed in the Force's famous review order and spent the afternoons at the trade seminar, where, they said, "We would greet the travel agents, and be available for interviews and photo sessions by the media." They even helped distribute door prizes. In Hong Kong the two Mounties appeared on a morning television show that boasted a viewing audience of two million. In Bangkok they were photographed "mounted bare back on elephants."[49] A June 24 letter from Mel MacDonald of the Office of Tourism indicated that the venture had been a success in its eyes as well. MacDonald insisted that the two corporals had been "very valuable members of our team working long, hard and mostly hot hours in the interest of promoting Canada as a tourism destination." The "tremendous media coverage on Canada," MacDonald offered, was due in part to the presence of the two corporals: "As you know, the world-wide recognition of the RCMP opens many promotional opportunities, particularly with the media."[50]

One such promotional opportunity was the 1980 Festival Canada celebration at Disneyland, when four Mounties joined Anne Murray and members of the Buffalo Child Society Dancers in providing the necessary Canadian content for the festivities. D.R. Turner, the manager of the Canadian Government Office of Tourism, was ecstatic with the results. Disneyland, he said, assumed "the total responsibility for the two days, doing an exemplary job in presenting Canadian culture, peoples and destinations." Linking Canada's name with Disneyland, he concluded, "can only be beneficial."[51]

RCMP participation in the endeavours of what soon became renamed "Tourism Canada" was not something that the Force entered into lightly. Nor was it something that Commissioner Simmonds could wholeheartedly

UPHOLDING

THE IMAGE,

MAINTAINING

THE RIGHTS:

THE MOUNTIE

ENTERS THE

WORLD OF

POSTMODERNITY,

1973-97

162

endorse. In his now routine letter requesting approval from Solicitor General Kaplan for two uniformed Mounties to attend the World Culinary Olympics in Frankfurt, Germany, in October 1984, Commissioner Simmonds penned the following addendum: "With all we have to contend with, this really seems to be rather frivolous, but in the eyes of E.A. [External Affairs] and others it is apparently useful for Canada's image, trade and general good will."[52] Kaplan's typed response was brief and to the point. He approved the request. His penned response beneath his signature was brief as well: "Frivolous but worthwhile!"[53] Two Mounties were soon on their way to Frankfurt to do their part through tourism initiatives to counter Canada's increasing balance of payments deficit.

Given the importance of the task, it took a special type of Mountie to participate in tourism initiatives. When the Office of Tourism had wanted to place a special emphasis on "Canadian promotion in the United States" in 1978, its staff had sought Mounties to participate in a "massive Canadian presence" at the convention of the American Society of Association Executives (ASAE) in Boston. Assistant Commissioner D.J. Wright's memorandum to the "H" and "J" Divisions was specific and left no doubt as to the importance of the occasion: "You will, of course, appreciate the importance of this convention to our economy, and are each asked to provide a knowledgeable member with *at least* five (5) years service, and whose overall appearance, grooming and personality are highly suited to this task. The member may be of Cst. or NCO rank, but the qualities listed above are mandatory."[54] When the 1981 ASAE convention took place in Acapulco, Mexico, a Mr. Hamernick made it clear, according to an RCMP transit slip, that he "would prefer the member to be male because of the unmistakable image our uniform portrays."[55]

A similar rationale was used in September 1979 when T.R.G. Fletcher of the federal tourism office sought a constable to attend the 49th World Congress of the American Society of Travel Agents in Munich. The letter to Commissioner Simmonds explained that this was part of an effort being made to "improve Canada's imbalance of payments in tourism," with the Office of Tourism putting "special emphasis in the United States on promotions aimed at travel agents."[56] A little over a week later the commissioner received another letter from Fletcher, this time soliciting a constable for the Second Biannual Trade Exhibition and Conference of the Japanese Association of Travel Agents, to be held in Tokyo. The rationale was the same as in the letter of the week before, but this time the request substituted "Japan" for "the United States" as the target of an attempt to correct Canada's tourism balance of payments.[57] Mountie appearances had become part of a government strategy to decrease a balance of payments deficit. A decade or so later a funding shortfall would have the Force selling souvenirs to cover the costs of community policing.

The use of the Mountie to advertise Canada represents a transitory phase between the centennial and the infamous Disney deal of 1995. The period of the 1970s and 1980s saw the last vestiges of government intervention on a number of fronts, and the federal police force was no exception. Spurred on perhaps by the success of the centennial, the Mountie was employed by government departments for the purposes of tourism and promotion: a significant departure from the years before the centennial. The two decades after the centennial saw the emergence of Benjamin Barber's "McWorld" phenomenon, a pattern reflected as well in how the Mountie image was employed. The emergence of McWorld has been marked by an increase in the power of service industries such as tourism and entertainment. Mountie appearances at baseball games and theme parks were evidence of this. The trend has also been marked, as Cpl. Carrière's experience riding an elephant in Thailand suggests, by an increased interest on the part of Western governments and multinational corporations in the emerging economies of Southeast Asia. The table for the promotional trips had been set by the 1973 centennial. Purged of his less-marketable characteristics (imperialism, racism, sexism, and laissez-faire liberalism), the Mountie was welcomed onto the stage of international trade. In a climate in which images had come to be bought and sold as commodities, the legal restrictions of the RCMP Act were no match for the trend towards economic globalization and flexible accumulation. After all, the Canadian government was not the only party looking to profit from the Mountie image.

In the early 1950s, with the Canadian Pacific Railway long since completed, and the company's hotels renowned throughout the world, RCMP officers no longer patrolled the Alberta Rockies on horseback. They did, however, serve as powerful tourist attractions. In the 1990s, the RCMP and the CPR again joined forces, this time to promote the gallant Musical Ride. (Glenbow Archives, Calgary, Alberta, NA-2575-8)

The CPR, and Disney

A year or so before the Disney debate began its lengthy domination of editorial pages across the country, a similar—though much smaller—debate took place concerning a newly approved logo of the Canadian Pacific Railway. The new design, which boasted U.S. and Canadian flags, raised the ire of self-proclaimed Canadian nationalists. While spokespeople for the CPR explained that the logo reflected their present business position, many observers remained upset.

The wailing and posturing that would greet the Disney announcement overshadowed another marketing agreement between the RCMP and a corporate entity—that same CPR. On June 30, 1995, Commissioner Philip Murray and the Mounted Police Foundation announced that the CPR would become the first ever national sponsor of the Musical Ride. The ride had been cancelled and reinstated several times in its history, but now CPR funding would allow more Canadians than ever before to see the Ride in person.[58] If the Disney deal did not lend itself to precedent, the CPR support of the Musical Ride was a perfect match for the reinvented image of the Force, and of Canada. RCMP announcements of the deal stressed the "natural link" between the two organizations. After all, "It was the construction of the Canadian Pacific Railway that opened up the west for settlement," while "The RCMP served to ensure that the line was peacefully built."[59] An internal RCMP organ, *The Pony Express*, supported this line of thought by stating that in the past, "Members were given the responsibility of telling Native peoples what was taking place, and ensuring that their rights were protected." It concluded by asserting that the "RCMP and Canadian Pacific Limited remain partners in nation-building to this day."[60] The CPR vice-president of personnel and administration, Ken Benson, made clear the appeal of the Mounties for the business community: "We're placing our name alongside something the public—including political constituencies and our stockholders—views favourably."[61]

Purged of the conflict, racism, and complications that dominated the expansion of the West and the early years of the Force's mandate, the Mountie was an ideal acquisition for Disney. In summer 1995 newspaper headlines across Canada announced the "selling" of the Mountie image to Disney. Despite an initial flurry of laments, within a year editorials were praising the deal. What many involved in the debate seemed to miss was how the RCMP's image was now being defined solely in monetary terms. Fully in tune with the times, the Force's image remained a cash cow for businesses. The renovation of Mountie mythology, as consolidated by the centennial, meant that the Mountie was more politically and culturally acceptable and hence, more marketable.

In a January 1995 news release, Solicitor General Herb Gray announced the launching of the RCMP's product-licensing program:

The 'Mountie' is one of the most widely recognized symbols in the world. It is simultaneously representative of the RCMP and Canada. Consequently,

UPHOLDING

THE IMAGE,

MAINTAINING

THE RIGHTS:

THE MOUNTIE

ENTERS THE

WORLD OF

POSTMODERNITY,

1973-97

166

the RCMP image is found reproduced on a myriad of consumer goods . . . which are marketed internationally. Some of these products are of high quality, tastefully produced and reflect most favourably on the RCMP. Unfortunately, there are many unauthorized products in the marketplace that cannot be characterized in this manner.

He went on to outline the plan. A "comprehensive Trade Mark protection program" had been initiated. A new licensing program would generate revenues for community policing "without increased burden to the Canadian tax payer." The Mounted Police Foundation, "a non-profit, volunteer organization" made up of "prominent Canadians" would administer the program. This foundation was "committed to ensuring that the goodwill presently associated with the RCMP image is protected and continues to offer marketing opportunities to the Canadian business community."[62] Welcome to McWorld: the world is a marketplace; governments extricate themselves from commitments to spending on public goods such as policing; image is commodity.

An RCMP news release announcing the sponsorship of a scholarship for a Rosetown, Saskatchewan, Central High School student who participated in and supported "a chemical free graduation" outlined the history and purpose of the program in more detail. Incorporated in 1994, the Mounted Police Foundation (MPF) has a board of directors consisting of "prominent Canadians who volunteer their time." The 1995 agreement between the MPF and Walt Disney Company (Canada) Ltd. stipulates that "Disney Canada will give preference to Canadian companies as licensees for the production of quality consumer products bearing the RCMP image." The Force's proportion of the royalties will be used to "support community policing projects" that will in turn support services that are "not part of the normal RCMP policing service."[63]

By February 1996, with the debate having for the most part subsided, Bill Pratt, president of the Mounted Police Foundation, seemed glowingly optimistic:

As promised when we first an[n]ounced this program a year ago, it is truly a triple-win situation. The RCMP ensures that its image is better protected and respected, not only in Canada, but around the world. Canadian businesses, large and small, benefit from new opportunities created by an innovative and energetic licensing program. . . . But most importantly . . . Canadian communities win too. The funds generated by the licensing program are being turned around and funnelled into valuable community projects from coast to coast.[64]

At times, even the community projects seemed to disappear into the background, hidden behind the rhetoric of business opportunities.

"The RCMP," according to Kevin Fowler of the RCMP's Public Affairs and Information Directorate, "is a marketable commodity." The "Disney" decision has thus been couched in terms that ensured its acceptance on Bay Street. Fowler's statement is not a lament about the tacky souvenirs of years gone by, nor is it an explanation of why it is necessary to fund community policing programs through the sale of T-shirts and baseball caps. It is a statement of what is apparently important to English-Canadians in the 1990s. In outlining the role of the Mounted Police Foundation, Fowler's focus remained on financial concerns: "The Foundation is committed to ensuring that the good will presently associated with the RCMP image continues to offer strong global marketing opportunities to the commercial and industrial communities."

So much for the organic community of Canada. And so much for the Force's concern of the 1970s to overcome the adverse publicity of its legal transgressions. These were not the words of a Force concerned with its public image in the way it had been in the 1970s. This was not about updating its image, for that had already been done. By the 1990s the Force was, like any other government department, anxious to avoid the finance minister's glare. The licensing program, Fowler continued, "will offer supplementary funding without increased dependence on the taxpayer, for the services and initiatives the RCMP strives to bring to the Canadian public."[65]

This is McWorld. It is a world in which English-Canadians, their government believes, want increased policing with no increase in public expenditure. The rhetoric behind the Disney deal tells us this. Yet the Mountie image tells us something else: English-Canadians are hesitant to embrace fully the laissez-faire ideology of such a position. Hence the irony of renovating the mythic Mountie to exemplify a New Liberal vision of Canada and then continuing to celebrate this image while slowly dismantling the actual welfare state.

UPHOLDING
THE IMAGE,
MAINTAINING
THE RIGHTS:
THE MOUNTIE
ENTERS THE
WORLD OF
POSTMODERNITY,
1973-97

168

The Mountie Today

The 1973 centennial had a lasting impact upon the RCMP's own publications. For so long suspended with a 1930 version of events, the post-1973 literature now pushed all the right buttons by offering a kinder, gentler history with a narrative modelled on the 1973 story. In addition to the financial motivation behind the Disney deal, another concern had been the plethora of "inappropriate" souvenirs on the market. The Disney deal ensured that store shelves would be cleared of offending toys. As well, by the 1990s, the Mountie was back on prime-time television—the heart of McWorld's consumer culture.

In 1994 a new, handsome, square-jawed Mountie entered the hearts and minds of Canadians: Constable Benton Fraser of the television series *Due South*. During the summer of 1995 the show was being seen in forty-seven different countries. In some places, such as England, it was drawing 30 or 40 per cent of the TV audience.[66] During its first season on CBS, the program ranked in the top third of TV programming while maintaining top-ten status in Canada.[67] The show initially drew the ire of the Force for technical discrepancies, such as placing a badge on the stetson and wearing the shoulder strap on the wrong side. The Mounties were certainly annoyed with the pilot episode, which ended with the suggestion that Force members who reported illegalities on the part of their fellow members would be disciplined. But the Force turned the other cheek when the series' producers hired Edward Greenspan to challenge the legal restrictions on the use of its image as they were outlined in the RCMP Act.[68] Eventually the program won the Force's approval, apparently because it managed to keep violence to a minimum. According to Corporal Gilles Moreau, the RCMP's technical advisor to the show, "The values portrayed in the show are excellent."[69]

Fraser Benton
and Diefenbaker

Those values differed greatly from those offered up by Sergeant Preston several decades earlier. Despite referring to the Mountie as the "candy-box symbol of Canada," a *TV Guide* reporter, Paul Welsby, saw "a certain amount of truth" in the program. "Americans did found a country based on 'life, liberty and the pursuit of happiness,' while the Canadian way has always been 'peace, order and good government.'"[70] Here again was the seamless, continuous national history sought by so many proponents of a single national identity.

The show itself strikes a balance between "left" and "right." In the award-winning series pilot, Constable Fraser teams up with an Aboriginal Canadian to protect the environment from crooked cops and a disinterested government. Fraser, is also, however, an *individual* Mountie. By turning in a crooked member of the Force and not working within the organizational structure of the RCMP, he is reminiscent of the lone, strong-willed Mountie of the antimodern era. In this way he is a symbol of postmodern angst. He is a polite and dependable hero who does not rely on technology to solve crime, but acts on his own. He acts outside the institutions of the RCMP and the Chicago police, and he does so by relying not on technology, but on his senses. *Due South* is reminiscent of the classic myth in another way too: Constable Fraser's discomfort around women.

Yet Benton Fraser is very much a "new" Mountie. His Victorian sensibilities are not prescriptive; they exist to entertain us. The classic tale of the Force did not have room for Aboriginal allies. It did not feature a Mountie drawing on Native mythology in doling out advice, nor did classic Mounties take orders from female superiors (Fraser answers to RCMP Inspector Meg Thatcher). But like all mythic Mounties, Fraser is a product of his time. At a time when Quebec separatists and American consumer culture are forcing English Canada to think about its own identity, Constable Fraser's characteristics (and thus our own) are contrasted with those of his lovable yet obnoxious partner, Ray Vecchio. Vecchio's heavy-handed "American" approach is often shown up by the Mountie's calm and discerning "Canadian" judgement.

Fraser is the stereotypically polite Canadian—a facet often contrasted with the stereotype of the brash American. Unlike the 1950s CBC television sketch that pitted the ignorant, pushy U.S. tourist against the stoic and upright Mountie, *Due South* presents the Mountie as the outsider, now stationed at the Canadian Consulate in Chicago—a sly way of making the series marketable outside of Canada. As Canadians adapt more and more aspects of American political culture, this contrast is a comfortable one to rely on. Watching Constable Fraser politely give up his place in an elevator or a cab, or lending a $100 bill to a complete stranger on the streets of Chicago, is a more comforting pastime than contemplating the dismantling of the Canadian welfare state.

The "inside" jokes that dominate the show's script suggest a return to a once-prominent theme in popular histories of the Force: the differentiation of Canadians from Americans through descriptions of the Mountie's exploits. Whether they are jokes that Canadian viewers are certain no American viewer would get (naming Fraser's dog and a reporter after former Canadian prime ministers, and an Oregon terrorist group the "Fathers of Confederation") or constantly having Fraser show Vecchio the "right" way to do things, the contrast is always there. The tension was articulated nicely in the pilot episode, when, after the two cops have defended themselves against the villains, Vecchio turns to Constable Fraser and announces, "We just took out seven guys . . . One more and you qualify for American citizenship."

Due South reflects the contradictions of English Canada in the days of McWorld. English-Canadians are electing governments that promise less intervention in the economy and decreased support for social programs. Yet television shows, like recent Mountie books and souvenirs, continue to celebrate a kinder, gentler Canadian ethic. And this ethic has much more in common with the welfare state that is being dismantled than it does with the laissez-faire ideology that underlies the platforms of the elected governments.

UPHOLDING
THE IMAGE,
MAINTAINING
THE RIGHTS:
THE MOUNTIE
ENTERS THE
WORLD OF
POSTMODERNITY,
1973-97

170

Today's Mountie Marketplace

The Mountie also appears on store shelves and at souvenir stands. The Disney decision was motivated by a number of factors, and according to Staff Sergeant Ken MacLean, "anger" was one of them: "For years, the Force watched helplessly the tacky, and sometimes embarrassing products made everywhere from local basements to foreign sweatshops." According to Chief Superintendent Dawson Hovey the final straw was the recent use of the Mountie image in professional wrestling and pornography videos.[71]

The new "official" merchandise is available in four brands, as described by Dana Flavelle in *The Toronto Star*: "RCMP Elite, featuring a traditional dark-haired Mountie in a red coat; RCMP country, a more rugged blond version in outdoor gear; MacLean of the Mounties, a square jawed cartoon character for teens; and Lil Mountie for infants." These images are available on a wide variety of souvenirs, including infant pacifiers, luggage, magnets, pencil cases, key fobs, and mugs.[72] The square-jawed, rugged Mountie born of antimodern concern is now being licensed by one of the world's largest entertainment empires.

The RCMP "Elite" line features upscale clothing as well as higher priced, "quality" souvenirs. One of these souvenirs is a 1998 "Historic Calendar," published by the Postcard Factory of Markham, Ontario. A percentage of the calendar's sales support RCMP community policing programs, as do other licensed souvenirs.

The bilingual calendar boasts colourful images from the Force's past and offers a synopsis of RCMP history:

> Since its inception in 1873, Canada's famous mounted police force (known since 1920 as The Royal Canadian Mounted Police) has grown to become a national symbol. In fact, the history of the Force has become intertwined with the growth and development of Canada.
>
> In the earliest days, The North-West Mounted Police made the Great March West, establishing relationships with the native peoples, and bringing law and order to the Prairies. The Force also established posts in the North, and eventually spread the Mountie presence across the country.

Today, the red-coated Mounties, who 'always get their man,' are known around the world as a symbol of Canadian pride and tradition, with an important role in justice.

UPHOLDING
THE IMAGE,
MAINTAINING
THE RIGHTS:
THE MOUNTIE
ENTERS THE
WORLD OF
POSTMODERNITY,
1973-97

172

"Growth," "development," a special "relationship" with Native peoples, and talk of "Canadian pride": these were all important elements of the 1973 centennial, and they remain prevalent in souvenirs today.

Yet the title, "Historic Calendar," is itself a little disingenuous. For while the calendar indeed presents images of the Force's past, its selections of appropriate events suggest that the designers were more concerned with the vitality of the photographs than with the prospect of conveying even the most basic snippets of the Force's history. Most of the photographs are of "posed" officers and ceremonial occasions. Many of them include visits by members of another commodified historical symbol, the British Royal Family.

The historical highlights that appear sporadically throughout the calendar contain a series of statements that are in some cases banal and in others highly rationalized, to say the least. On February 1, 1920, we are told, the Force was "renamed"—not "created" or even "reorganized," simply "renamed." That the Force was "renamed," rather than "reorganized," was one of the key lessons of the 1973 centennial. The information that on April 1, 1935, "The Force took its first role in municipal policing" seems insignificant considering that on July 1 that same year the Force was involved in what many consider the defining moment of the Depression in Canada, the Regina riot.[73] The calendar also salutes events commemorated in 1973: the *St. Roch*, Treaty No. 7, and Macleod's first meeting with Crowfoot. In this and other souvenir products, not surprisingly style triumphs over substance—a hallmark of our postmodern world.

It is a world in which, sixty years after Jeanette Macdonald and Nelson Eddy crooned "Indian Love Call" in *Rose Marie*, their voices now re-emerge on a television commercial endorsing the Compaq Armada notebook computer. Shorn of his past, the Mountie can now appear in television shows such as *North of 60*, which boasts Native peoples as RCMP officers, and *Due South*, which purges the Mountie of his less commercial classic attributes and transports him to a more marketable U.S. setting. He can also appear in the mystery novels of B.C. writer L.R. Wright, where the RCMP protagonist is simply a police officer unhindered by the cultural baggage of the red serge uniform. Current representations are able to avoid drawing on, and being weighed down by, the once dominant classic image.

A teddy bear or a plush moose in a Mountie uniform is no longer connected with the history of the Force or of the country that the toy supposedly represents. The toy is instead a blending of two potentially threatening images now tamed by the market: a wild animal, now cuddly and cute, dressed in a uniform that has been purged of its connection to a complicated and conflict-ridden past.

7

Conclusion: Re-Mounting the Force
for the Twenty-First Century

Commerce has no memory.

— John Ralston Saul, *The Unconscious Civilization*

In 1956 Mary Ann Kletter and Lloyd Wagner, two American tourists who had recently visited New Brunswick, wrote to the provincial tourist authority despondent over not having seen a "real" Mountie on their trip. Unable to reconcile the prosaic RCMP officers they did come across with the mythic heroes they had envisioned before visiting Canada, they wrote a letter to the New Brunswick Travel Bureau: " 'One'—just one Mountie in 'red'. We drove 30,000 miles in your lovely country and have yet to see one, just one. Yes, we saw Mounties, ate with them, talked with many. Are they ever dressed as you show them in the books? They are not. There is no such animal as a Mountie dressed in full red regalia."[1]

A classic image of the Force maintaining British sovereignty in the north. This photo appeared in R.G. MacBeth's 1921 history of the force, *Policing the Plains*. (National Library of Canada, C44109)

Kletter and Wagner were wrong. Because of the mythic Mountie's remarkable ability to adapt to the political conditions of his day, all the while remaining a popular symbol of English-Canadian identity, such an animal did indeed exist, though it may indeed have been hard to see in its live, human form. One of Canada's most popular symbols is a semi-aquatic rodent, the beaver. Another famous symbol, so successfully redefined in the past thirty years, the Mounted Policeman, can best be described as a close relative of the chameleon.

Back in 1921, a year after the Royal Canadian Mounted Police was formally brought into service, R.G. MacBeth published a comprehensive yet popular

CONCLUSION:

RE-MOUNTING THE

FORCE FOR THE

TWENTY-FIRST

CENTURY

176

history of the Force, *Policing the Plains*. MacBeth wrote about "warlike" Indians and "half-breeds" who were predisposed to overexcitement.[2] He reported on the Force's efforts to maintain order amidst immigrants "who had lax ideas as to the sacredness of human life" and who were predisposed to challenge authority. He also documented the difficulties the Force faced in dealing with radical Doukhobor settlers. He credited the Force with keeping idle, unemployed men in the Yukon off the streets by jailing them, and he paid tribute to a police force that accomplished many feats despite meagre support from the federal government. Above all, MacBeth stressed the importance of the Force in bringing the *Pax Britannica* to Canadian territory.[3]

In the mid-1950s, T. Morris Longstreth offered a similar story in his book, *The Scarlet Force*. Drawing upon J.P. Turner's RCMP-commissioned history of the Force's early years as well as upon interviews with officers, Longstreth's story owed much to the classic image of the Force. The Force protected "British" territory and faced "wild" and "warlike" Indians. Though faced with desertions and at times a lack of discipline, the Force struggled on with its duties, occasionally aided by Providence in its quest to bring Order to the Plains. If the government sometimes seemed disinterested in the Force's trials and tribulations, all was not lost, for the Force had strong men like James Macleod, who had won over the hearts of the Blackfoot. And when the government ordered the Force to carry out foolish policies, like usurping Native land from the first inhabitants, the Force was not to blame. The Force could be trusted to treat the childlike Indians well and to smooth over the occasional government gaff.

Recent literature on the Force tells a different story. Postcard racks or local bookstores are unlikely to display either MacBeth's story of progress or Longstreth's narrative of RCMP determination in the face of government apathy. What we are likely to find is something like Marc Tetro's 1994 booklet on the Force, *The Royal Canadian Mounted Police*. In this outline history of the Force, Tetro describes how the Mounties helped unite "the country's west with the east" by monitoring the building of the Canadian Pacific Railway. Their job included looking after the people working on the railroad. The Mounties also gained the trust of the Native peoples on the Prairies and were there to help immigrants from around the world settle into their new homes. In the North, according to Tetro, the Inuit "helped the Mounties explore the Canadian Arctic."[4] His book is a happy story of the orderly building of a nation, and it owes much to the renovation of Mountie mythology as consolidated in the 1973 RCMP centennial celebrations. As the book's back cover boasts, it is "the story of how a brand new country came together bit by bit, into the Canada we know today."[5]

A similar perspective on the Force's history appears in Helene Dobrowolsky's 1995 book commemorating the Mounties' centennial in the Yukon. In *Law of the Yukon*, Dobrowolsky offers an interpretation very much in line with the 1973 centennial literature: the Yukon was "never a lawless frontier"; "cases such as dramatic search and rescue operations, and the hunt for a modern-day 'Mad-Trapper' hark back to an earlier era"; women and First Nations people were partners in the Mounties' law enforcement efforts.[6]

The reconstructed Mounted Police post at Fort Walsh, Saskatchewan, illustrates another way in which this new history of the Force has been consolidated and preserved. Abandoned in 1883, the fort was honoured in 1927 with a historic plaque commissioned by the Historic Sites and Monuments Board of Canada (HSMBC). The inscription on the plaque owed much to the classic image of the Force. As historian James De Jonge puts it, "Written by Professor A.S. Morton of the University of Saskatchewan, the commemorative plaque reinforced the predominant colonial perspective that the Mounted Police 'imposed Queen's Law on a fretful realm' where hunting parties of Native people 'met and fought.'"[7]

The Force rebuilt the fort in the 1940s, not as a public attraction, but as "an operational ranch . . . for breeding and raising horses for ceremonial purposes." The newly built fort was officially "an operational police detachment, albeit one with a unique character that would provide a tangible link with the force's origins." Even in reconstructing a fort for its own use, the Force opted to create a "stylized and sanitized shell of the original." De Jonge points out: "Hidden behind the romanticized image of the frontier police fort was the stark reality that this had not been an especially attractive or desirable place to live during the late 1870s. Dirt, discomfort and disease were characteristic features of the early forts, but these elements did not fit well with a popular and idealized view of the past."[8] Like other restorations of the period that *were* aimed at tourists, Fort Walsh offered "rustic park buildings harmonized with the natural surroundings," and it "evoked the virtues of a rural pre-industrial era."[9]

In the 1950s increasing numbers of tourists visited the fort despite its continuing use as a working police detachment. A frustrated RCMP considered asking heritage officials to stop promoting the fort, but relented when it was pointed out that such a request once made public might reflect badly upon the Force.[10] By the mid-1960s the Force had given in to the tourists' demands, and in 1965 the RCMP decided to "develop Fort Walsh as a tourist attraction to celebrate Canada's centennial." By 1968 control over the fort had been transferred to the National and Historic Parks Branch of the federal government.

With the celebration of the Force's centennial in 1973 it was time for one more renovation of the site. The initiative came from the RCMP itself, as an Inspector Potts, a liaison officer, suggested a monument be erected at the fort to honour the creation of the Force. Though the monument was not completed in time for the centennial, it was unveiled in 1976, complete with an inscription in English, French, Cree, and Blackfoot:

> IN 1873 THE GOVERNMENT OF SIR JOHN A MACDONALD CREATED THE NORTH WEST MOUNTED POLICE TO ASSERT CANADIAN SOVEREIGNTY AND ENFORCE CANADIAN LAW IN THE NEWLY ACQUIRED NORTH-WEST TERRITORIES. WITHIN A DECADE THIS HAD BEEN DONE, AND THE ORDERLY SETTLEMENT OF THE CANADIAN PRAIRIES BEGUN. IN THE PROCESS THE FORCE ACHIEVED AN INTERNATIONAL REPUTATION FOR EVEN-HANDED JUSTICE AND DEVOTION TO DUTY.[11]

The monument itself is a far cry from the original HSMBC plaque unveiled in 1927. Instead of the Mounties imposing the Queen's law upon the warlike Indians, the statue presents a Mountie and a Native person on horseback, both raising their hands in greeting.

Located at a reconstructed Fort Walsh, this statue was designed to mark the Force's centennial. The image of Native and Mountie greeting each other on the open plains epitomizes Benedict Anderson's notion of the "reassurance of fratricide."

(Author's photo)

CONCLUSION:
RE-MOUNTING THE
FORCE FOR THE
TWENTY-FIRST
CENTURY

180

Through whichever media (television, books, souvenirs) we view the Mountie today, he is clearly not the Mountie that first appeared in literature early in the century. Canada's northern and westward expansion contains too many conflicts to be celebrated today as they were in the past. The Force today is remembered by Marc Tetro and his readers as the stars of "the story of how a brand new country came together bit by bit, into the Canada we know today."[12] Missing from the public memory of the Force's exploits and Canada's history is the conflict that often existed between some of these "bits." Instead, what remains is a politically correct mythic figure used to sell chocolate, souvenirs, and Canada to the world. Purged of his complicated past, the Mountie has become a marketing ploy. Having retained his boyish good looks and his shiny red uniform from the classic mythology, the Mountie is no longer a symbol of British imperial expansion. He is now a safe marketing strategy. Unhindered by the Force's past role in many of the most controversial events in Canada's history, the Mountie is now consumed with the same lack of historical contemplation that greets a cup of coffee or a bag of potato chips. A police force that once refused to endorse any commercial products now agrees to a request to have six Mounties appear at the New York Stock Exchange to drum up support for shares in the Alberta Energy Company.[13]

Motivations and Messages

It was the 1973 centennial and the renovation of the Mountie's image that cleared the way for this separation of the Mountie from its historical roots. Updated in the early 1970s to conform to English-Canada's changing political culture, the Mountie image escaped what had become its less attractive characteristics: imperialism, sexism, racism, and a variety of duties in which force was used upon members of the Canadian population.

To argue that the relationship between the 1973 centennial and the present postmodern Mountie is a simple case of cause and effect would be ludicrous. History is not that straightforward. There were, after all, positive revisionist histories about the Force being authored as early as the 1940s; and by the 1960s some of the themes that would dominate the centennial were beginning to make their way into elementary school curriculums.[14] But what the centennial does show, in a concentrated way, is the set of motivations involved in the renovation of the Mountie image, as well as some of the internal inconsistencies present in an effort that is symptomatic of the selective amnesia of modern nationalism.

A 1975 letter from Force historian Stan Horrall to a retired assistant commissioner offers insights into the political culture of the time in which the Mountie's metamorphosis occurred. The two were exchanging thoughts on the history of the RCMP badge. Agreeing with his correspondent, Horrall indicated that he too lamented changes made to the Force's badge in the early 1950s, and he decried this loss of tradition. But Horrall expressed a sense of realism in these matters:

> I doubt, however, if anything can be done to rectify this change. Under the present political and social climate in this country, I cannot see a department of the Government of Canada seeking authority from a British official to change its emblem. . . . One must also consider the question of Bilingualism. Our present Badge is authorized and defined in an Order in Council. This would have to be amended. *The present Government is far more likely to be concerned with whether or not the Badge is properly bilingual than with whether it accurately reflected our traditions.* We could end up, "Police Canada."[15]

As it turned out, the RCMP did not become "Police Canada," but it did, in many ways, become what those in favour of such a title had hoped for: an organization ostensibly more in tune with the times. It did this by opening its ranks to women, Native peoples, and ethnic minorities. It also did this by refashioning its history.

To succeed in applying this new historical makeup, the Force called upon advertising and promotional experts. Its experience with souvenir-makers and other private companies was not entirely without its problems. Commercial advertising in the RCMP *Quarterly* ended abruptly in 1974 as a result of "companies or individuals failing to fulfill their obligations."[16] Yet the overall success of contracting out much of the centennial events meant that this departure from the earlier, centralized approach to image control would be permanent. In late 1996, just a year after the Disney deal was signed, it was announced that the RCMP's historical section was being downsized and absorbed into the Public Affairs Directorate. History was now subsumed under the rubric of publicity.

Yet it is important to note that messages and stories about the Mountie could be resisted and refashioned as well as internalized. Jay Ward's Dudley Do-Right and Monty Python's "Lumberjack Sketch" are good examples of how, motivated by the social climate of the time, the classic Mountie image was challenged and unseated. Sometimes, however, attempts to appropriate or subvert the Mountie image fall flat.

New Democratic Party MP Svend Robinson discovered this at the 1995 NDP leadership convention. According to a newspaper report, as part of a tribute to outgoing leader Audrey McLaughlin, "Someone told a joke about McLaughlin being lonely for male company and having a special panic button in her apartment to summon handsome, Mountie bodyguards." In a speech Robinson later tried "to put a gay slant on the joke," saying outgoing party president Nancy Riche "tried to induce him to run as leader by mentioning that special button capable of summoning handsome Mounties." But his joke bombed.[17] Some aspects of the classic image linger on.

Liberalism and Modernity, Histories and Mythologies

Canada in the 1990s is a modern, industrialized nation. This, of course, was not always the case. Canada's industrial revolution occurred in the late nineteenth century and brought with it all of the trials and tribulations faced by other industrializing nations. The ushering in of modernity in the northern part of

CONCLUSION:
RE-MOUNTING THE
FORCE FOR THE
TWENTY-FIRST
CENTURY

182

North America was a messy and complicated undertaking. Indeed, it also produced a great deal of apprehension.

Like other industrializing countries Canada changed remarkably during the late nineteenth and early twentieth centuries. Railway construction expanded rapidly. Other forms of transportation, such as the bicycle and the automobile and truck, emerged. Telegraph and radio communications rapidly altered how people experienced time and space. The world, it seemed, was shrinking.[18] As Eric Hobsbawm suggests, the result of such technological innovations, was "a revolution in transport and communications which virtually annihilated time and distance."[19] Urbanization, secularization, and large-scale immigration transformed local communities.

As the federal government moved quickly to develop Canada's industrial potential through settling the West and setting up high tariffs to protect central-Canadian manufacturing, most Canadians were encouraged by the country's prospects. Some, however, were not. They saw modernity as dangerous and opposed many of the changes it was bringing with it. Like their American counterparts observed by Jackson Lears, some Canadians found themselves faced with the notion that their "sense of selfhood had become fragmented, diffuse, and sometimes 'weightless' or 'unreal.'" These "feelings of unreality were rooted in the corrosive impact of the market on familiar values, the dislocating impact of technological advance on everyday experience—and above all in the secularization of Protestantism, which by the turn of the century had become for many Christians a flaccid creed without force or bite or moral weight."[20] Into this void stepped advertisers and other proponents of a consumer culture offering authentic experience and tangible consumer goods.[21] Canadians expressed their antimodern sentiments in a number of ways, one of which included the genre of Mountie fiction.

Although most Canadians embraced, or at least tolerated, the changes ushered in by industrialization, they too found themselves actively responding to the new situations. Most people sought out new ways to cope with the ups and downs of industrial development. In the process they—in the company of other Western nations—rethought the underlying philosophies that governed their institutions and their laws. They rethought liberalism by discarding the laissez-faire liberalism that was so much a part of the Industrial Revolution in favour of an approach best understood as New Liberalism.

New Liberal thought emerged in Britain in the 1890s as an alternative to the harsh individualism of classical or laissez-faire liberalism. In Canada this transition gained a foothold several decades later and was consolidated during the reign of Mackenzie King's Liberal governments in the 1930s and 1940s. Its tangible achievements were very much a reaction to the economic Depression of the 1930s—a catastrophe that called into question old-style liberalism. Laissez-faire or classical liberalism had issued dire warnings about the effects of state intervention in the economy. It had preached the necessity of competition through rugged individualism, and it differentiated between the deserving and the undeserving poor. For many, the widespread horrors of the Depression suggested that this was no longer a workable—or desirable—model.

New Liberalism, on the contrary, recognized that problems such as unemployment were structural in nature. The Depression conditions had revealed all too starkly that people ended up being unemployed through *No Fault of Their Own*, to quote the title of one book on the subject. New Liberals articulated an organic ideal of community in which the government would play an important role. For them, state intervention in the name of community would allow all members (rather than just propertied individuals) to compete. Instead of freedom *from* government intervention, members of the public would be granted (at least in theory) the freedom to compete on a more level playing field. In Canada this New Liberalism was made concrete through such programs as unemployment insurance, public health care, and—later on—multiculturalism. These programs were often lauded by English-Canadian nationalists, who drew on them to make constant comparisons with the heartless individualism of the United States. The assurance of "common standards across the country"—a central tenet of Canada's welfare state—quickly became, according to Philip Resnick, "a key factor in the formulation of a common English-Canadian identity."[22]

Closely related to this increased government involvement in the daily lives of its citizens was the adoption of Keynesian economic policies in an attempt to

CONCLUSION:

RE-MOUNTING THE

FORCE FOR THE

TWENTY-FIRST

CENTURY

184

ward off another Depression. Increased government spending during times of economic recession helped keep money in the pockets of consumers. The result—a less volatile marketplace—ushered in an unprecedented era of economic growth in the Western world, lasting from about 1945 to the early 1970s.[23] Canada was among the first to adopt this stance and was quick to reap the benefits.

This era of growth was followed by what Eric Hobsbawm has termed the "crisis decades": a period of global economic instability that has so far befuddled economists (and even historians) around the world. Entrepreneurs, not surprisingly unwilling to wait for an answer to the economic slowdown of the period, responded on their own. Their answer, David Harvey argues, has ushered in a new era: an era some theorists are tentatively calling "postmodernity."

Anxious to maintain high profits, the business world in Canada and elsewhere embarked on a series of new strategies intent on finding profits anywhere and at any time. Embracing the technological capabilities of the computer age, they have become more flexible in their methods of seeking out business opportunities. This is truly the era of multinational corporations and extremely volatile currency markets in which billions of dollars are won and lost overnight. It is also an era in which the service and entertainment industries have increased exponentially in power and influence. And, finally, it is an era in which advertising has played an increasing role as companies attempt to create demand for the products and services they wish to sell.

This transformation shares some characteristics with the era of change that gripped Canada at the end of the nineteenth century. The world again seems to be shrinking. There is once again an air of ferment and instability. Yet there are differences too. The transition at the beginning of the century was very much a national process. Governments became increasingly involved in citizens' economic and cultural affairs. Today's world is marked by the withdrawal of government intervention in the economy and the dismantling of the social safety net.

Histories, I have argued, are central to the understanding of national identity and contemporary Canadian debates. In Canada, mainstream history textbooks have produced two irreconcilable versions of Canadian history: one in

French and the other in English.[24] Of these two narratives, the RCMP has a starring role in only one. Identified so closely with the opening up of the West, the story of the Force could not find an adequate place in Quebec histories that saw in Canada's westward expansion a "plot" to keep the French-Canadians out of the West.[25]

The Force's real duties, including its involvement in the Northwest Rebellion and in implementing conscription during the Second World War, combined with its depiction in popular culture, made it difficult for French-Canadians to relate positively to the image of the Mountie.[26] Recent literature concerning the seemingly endless battle between English-Canadians and French-Canadians often implies that only one side is nationalistic while the other is inherently rational—indeed, perhaps too rational to offer the needed recognition of the collective identity of the other group.[27] An obvious parallel can be seen between the "rational" laws of English Canada and the collective identities of Aboriginal peoples. English-speaking Canadians have not claimed to be distinct. Their claim has been much more hegemonic: to define the core traditions and values of the entire country. Theirs is a claim to an inherent attachment to the federal government, to the federal structure of the country. What better way to frustrate the claims of a rival collectivity than to deny any special characteristics of one's own? English-Canadians have relied upon the mythology of a rational and benign federalism to dismiss Quebec's claims as tribal and irrational.

Such arguments underscore the extent to which English-speaking Canadians do share an "imagined community." What Benedict Anderson argues persuasively for novels and newspapers seems equally appropriate for the icons of identity (such as the Mountie) that emerged from these media. After all, it is only because he supposedly says something about "us" that a Mountie in a turban or a cartoon mouse in a Mountie uniform becomes a matter of public debate. In coming to terms with our sometimes complicated (and sometimes ugly) past, we need to take a page from the scripts of Jay Ward and the Monty Python troupe; and to do this we must be prepared to question commonsense assumptions about our nation and about our past. After all, a healthy society is one that interrogates its all-too-comforting stories and national mythologies.

CONCLUSION:
RE-MOUNTING THE
FORCE FOR THE
TWENTY-FIRST
CENTURY

186

Notes

1 Introduction: Of Mice, Mounties, and Historical Magic

1 "Mounties Got Their Mouse," *Gleaner* (Fredericton), July 3, 1995.

2 Alan Fotheringham, "Taking Canada for a Musical Ride," *Maclean's*, July 17, 1995, p.52.

3 Interview by Peter Gzowski, *Morningside*, CBC-Radio, Sept. 10, 1996.

4 Paul Jackson, "Heck of a Deal for Our Mounties," *The Calgary Sun*, June 30, 1995.

5 Harvey Enchin, "Nothing Goofy about RCMP Deal," *The Globe and Mail*, June 29, 1995.

6 William Gold, "Walt's Boys Will Protect Our Icon," *The Calgary Herald*, July 6, 1995; reprinted as "Cry Me No Nationalist River for 'Mickey Mountie,'" *The Ottawa Citizen*, July 6, 1995.

7 "Mounties Got Their Mouse," *Gleaner*, July 3, 1995.

8 J. Bernard Pelot, ed., *Diary of a National Debate: Mounties in Turbans* (Orleans, Ont.: In-Tel-Ec Consulting, 1993).

9 E.H. Carr, *What is History?* ed. R.W. Davies (Harmondsworth, Eng.: Penguin Books [1961] 1990), p.104.

10 Royal Canadian Mounted Police (RCMP), *Memorandum on the Royal Canadian Mounted Police* (Ottawa: Queen's Printer, 1930), p.1.

11 Richard L. Neuberger, *Royal Canadian Mounted Police* (New York: Random House, 1953), p.32.

12 P. B. Waite, *Canada 1874-1896: Arduous Destiny* (Toronto: McClelland and Stewart, 1971), p.10.

13 Donald Creighton, *Dominion of the North* (Toronto: Macmillan, [1944] 1969), p.360.

14 RCMP, *Memorandum* (1930), p.1.

15 Ibid., p.2.

16 R.G. MacBeth, *Policing the Plains: Being the Real-Life Record of the Famous Royal North-West Mounted Police* (London: Hodder and Stoughton, 1921), p.78.

17 Neuberger, *RCMP*, p.67.

18 RCMP, *Memorandum* (1930), p.2.

19 RCMP, *The Royal Canadian Mounted Police* (Ottawa: Queen's Printer, 1961), p.5.

20 R.C. Fetherstonhaugh, *The Royal Canadian Mounted Police* (New York: Garden City Publishing, 1940), p.179.

21 Ibid., pp.183-4.

22 Delbert Young, *The Mounties* (Toronto and London: Hodder and Stoughton, 1968), p.145.

23 RCMP, *Royal Canadian Mounted Police* (Ottawa: Queen's Printer, 1969), p.10.

24 For a sweeping condemnation of the Force from its inception to the late 1970s, see Norman Penner, "How the RCMP Got Where It Is," in *RCMP vs the People: Inside Canada's Security Service*, ed. Edward Mann and John Alan Lee (Don Mills, Ont.: General Publishing Company, 1979).

25 Sarah Carter, *Lost Harvests: Prairie Indian Reserve Farmers and Government Policy* (Montreal and Kingston: McGill-Queen's University Press, [1990] 1993), pp.151-5.

26 Lorne Brown and Caroline Brown, *An Unauthorized History of the RCMP* (Toronto: James Lewis and Samuel, 1973), p.24.

27 Ibid., p.43.

28 Ibid., pp.69-73.

29 S.D. Hanson, "Estevan, 1931," in *On Strike: Six Key Labour Struggles in Canada 1919-1949*, ed. I. Abella (Toronto: James Lewis and Samuel, 1974), p.53.

30 On the Force's activities on university campuses, see Paul Axelrod, "Spying on the Young in Depression and War: Students, Youth Groups and the RCMP, 1935-1942," *Labour/Le Travail* 35 (Spring 1995), pp.43-63; and S.R. Hewitt, "Spying 101: The RCMP's Secret Activities at the University of Saskatchewan, 1920-1971," *Saskatchewan History*, Fall 1995, pp.20-31.

31 S.T. Wood, "Tools for Treachery," in *RCMP Quarterly* 8,4, quoted in Hewitt, "Spying 101," p.21.

32 Daniel Robinson, "Planning for the 'Most Serious Contingency': Alien Internment, Arbitrary Detention, and the Canadian State 1938-39," in *Journal of Canadian Studies* 28,2 (Summer 1993), pp.5-20.

33 Ibid., p.15. The day-to-day objectives and opinions of the Force during the Second World War are explored in Gregory S. Kealey and Reg Whitaker, eds., *RCMP Security Bulletins* (St. John's, Nfld.: Committee on Canadian Labour History, 1989). On the RCMP Security Service and its operations during the Cold War, see Reg Whitaker and

Gary Marcuse, *Cold War Canada: The Making of a National Insecurity State, 1945-1957* (Toronto: University of Toronto Press, 1994).

34 Daniel Robinson and David Kimmel, "The Queer Career of Homosexual Security Vetting in Cold War Canada," in *Canadian Historical Review* 75,3 (1994), p.321.

35 Ibid.

36 Ibid., p.320.

37 Ibid., p.325.

38 Commission of Inquiry Concerning Certain Activities of the Royal Canadian Mounted Police, *Freedom and Security under the Law*, 2nd report, vol. 1 (August 1981), Ottawa, p.347.

39 Ibid., pp.356-7.

40 Elmer MacKay, "Foreword," in Mann and Lee, *RCMP vs the People*, p.8.

41 See David Carr, *Time, Narrative, and History* (Bloomington/ Indianapolis: Indiana University Press, 1986), p.13.

42 There were, of course, many criticisms of the Force in working-class periodicals such as the *Unemployed Worker* and in the various publications of the Canadian Labour Defence League.

43 Fetherstonhaugh's account of the Winnipeg General Strike, however, is not one sustained by most historians.

44 Eric Hobsbawm and Terence Ranger, eds., *The Invention of Tradition* (Cambridge: Canto, 1983); Hobsbawm quotation at p.4.

45 Benedict Anderson, *Imagined Communities*: *Reflections on the Origin and Spread of Nationalism* (London: Verso, 1993 [1983]), p.6.

46 Ibid., p.36.

47 Raphael Samuel, "Continuous National History," in *Patriotism: The Making and Unmaking of British National Identity*, ed. R. Samuel, vol.1 (London and New York: Routledge, 1989), pp.10-12.

48 Anderson, *Imagined Communities*, pp.200-1.

49 Philip Resnick, *Thinking English Canada* (Don Mills, Ont.: Stoddart, 1994), pp.21-3.

50 Philip Resnick, "Free Trade, Meech Lake, and the Two Nationalisms," in *The Challenge of Modernity*, ed. Ian McKay (Toronto: McGraw-Hill Ryerson, 1992), p.458.

51 Eric Hobsbawm, *Nations and Nationalism since 1780*, 2nd ed. (Cambridge: Canto, 1993), pp.9-10.

52 Philip Resnick, *Toward a Canada-Quebec Union* (Montreal and Kingston: McGill-Queen's University Press, 1991), p.23.

53 Gilles Langelier, "The RCMP vs French Canadian Public Opinion," translated by J.M., unpublished manuscript, RCMP Historical Branch, RCMP Headquarters, Ottawa, 1971, pp.7-8. My thanks to Bill Beahen and Stan Horrall for leading me to this source.

54 Ibid., pp.12-19.

55 Ibid., p.21.

56 Ibid., pp.28-32.

57 Ibid., pp.33-4.

58 Alan Smith, "Introduction: The Canadian Mind in Continental Perspective," in *Canada: An American Nation? Essays on Continentalism, Identity, and the Canadian Frame of Mind*, ed. A. Smith (Montreal and Kingston: McGill-Queen's University Press, 1994), p.6.

59 Resnick, *Thinking English Canada*, p.56.

60 Ibid., p.57.

61 Howard Palmer, "Reluctant Hosts: Anglo-Canadian Views of Multiculturalism in the Twentieth Century," in *Readings in Canadian History: Post-Confederation*, 2nd ed., ed. R. Douglas Francis and Donald B. Smith (Toronto: Holt, Rinehart and Winston, 1986), p.198.

2   Fiction and Film: The Mountie as Antimodern Crusader, 1880-1960

1   *Manitoba Daily Free Press* (*MDFP*), March 15, 1886, p.4; *MDFP*, June 1, 1886, p.4; *MDFP*, June 18, 1886, p.4.

2   *MDFP*, Nov. 24, 1887, p.4.

3   *Winnipeg Free Press* (*WFP*), Oct. 25, 1875, p.3; *Winnipeg Daily Free Press* (*WDFP*), Feb. 4, 1875, p.3.

4   *MDFP*, May 25, 1880, p.1.

5   Sarah Carter, "Categories and Terrains of Exclusion: Constructing the 'Indian Woman' in the Early Settlement Era in Western Canada," in *Gender and History in Canada*, ed. Joy Parr and Mark Rosenfeld (Toronto: Copp Clark, 1996), pp.34-7, 44.

6   *MDFP*, April 11, 1877, p.3.

7   Harold Christie Thomson, "The North-West Mounted Policeman: A Character Sketch," *The Canadian Magazine* 8,1 (November 1896).

8   *MDFP*, April 21, 1880, p.1.

9   Keith Walden, *Visions of Order: The Canadian Mounties in Symbol and Myth* (Toronto: Butterworths, 1982), p.19. Two other important contributors to the study of Mountie mythology are Dick Harrison and Robert Thacker. See Dick Harrison, ed., *Best*

Mounted Police Stories (Edmonton: University of Edmonton Press, 1978); and Robert Thacker, "Canada's Mounted: The Evolution of a Legend," *Journal of Popular Culture* 14 (Winter 1980): 298-312; as well as Thacker, "The Mountie as Metaphor," *Dalhousie Review* 59 (Autumn 1979): 552-60. For a recent critique of what I have termed the "classic" mythology of the Force, see Daniel Francis, "The Mild West: The Myth of the RCMP," in Francis, *National Dreams: Myth, Memory and Canadian History* (Vancouver: Arsenal Pulp Press, 1997), pp.29-51. An early attempt by Robert L. McDougall at exploring the longevity of this classic mythology appears as "Public Image Number One: The Legend of the Royal Canadian Mounted Police," in McDougall, *Totems: Essays on the Cultural History of Canada* (Ottawa: Tecumseh Press, 1990), pp.125-42.

10 This is a common theme in Canadian historiography. See, for example, Craig Brown and Ramsay Cook, *Canada 1896-1921: A Nation Transformed* (Toronto: McClelland and Stewart, 1974).

11 Walden, *Visions of Order*, p.61.

12 For a detailed discussion of this masculine phenomenon of inheritance, see Michael Roper and John Tosh, *Manful Assertions: Masculinities in Britain since 1800* (London: Routledge, 1991), p.17.

13 Walden, *Visions of Order*, p.145.

14 For a discussion of how the Force employed the image of its officers to ensure social stability in the West and reproduce the social hierarchy of Eastern Canada, see Gerald Friesen, *The Canadian Prairies: A History* (Toronto: University of Toronto Press, 1987), pp.169-71; and R.C. Macleod, *The North-West Mounted Police and Law Enforcement 1873-1905* (Toronto: University of Toronto Press, 1976), pp.73-88.

15 See Lewis Jackson and Ian McKay, eds., *Windjammers and Bluenose Sailors: Stories of the Sea by Colin McKay* (Lockeport, N.S.: Roseway, 1993); Patrick Dunae, "Boys' Literature and the Idea of Race: 1870-1900," *Wascana Review* 12 (Spring 1977): 84-107; and Dunae, "Boys' Literature and the Idea of Empire 1870-1914," *Victorian Studies* 24 (Autumn 1980): 105-21.

16 For a detailed analysis of Canadian historians' infatuation with the frontier and its effects on the historiography of the Maritimes, see E.R. Forbes, "In Search of a Post-Confederation Maritime Historiography, 1900-1967," in *The Challenge of Modernity*, ed. Ian McKay (Toronto: McGraw-Hill Ryerson, 1992), pp.143-53.

17 Quoted in Harrison, *Best Mounted Police Stories*, p.154.

18 Quoted in ibid., p.48.

19 Quoted in ibid., p.34.

20 Walden, *Visions of Order*, pp.32-3.

21 Quoted in Harrison, *Best Mounted Police Stories*, p.175.

22 This construction supports the observation of Roper and Tosh that "Dominant ideologies of masculinity are also maintained through asserting their difference from—and superiority to—other races." Roper and Tosh, *Manful Assertions*, p.13.

23 Walden, *Visions of Order*, p.130.

24 James Oliver Curwood, *The Flaming Forest* (New York: Cosmopolitan Books Corporation, 1921), p.89.

25 Quoted in Walden, *Visions of Order*, p.174.

26 See Carl Berger, "The True North Strong and Free," in *Nationalism in Canada*, ed. Peter Russell (Toronto: McGraw-Hill, 1966); as well as Berger, *The Sense of Power: Studies in the Ideas of Canadian Imperialism 1867-1914* (Toronto: University of Toronto Press, 1976 [1970]).

27 Patrick Dunae summarizes the moral of these stories: "Since adult authorities were unwilling to take the lead, it was up to boys to prepare for the impending crisis." Dunae, "Boys' Literature and the Idea of Empire," p.119.

28 Quoted in Walden, *Visions of Order*, p.62.

29 Quoted in ibid., p.173.

30 See Walden, *Visions of Order*; Thacker, "Canada's Mounted"; Thacker, "Mountie as Metaphor"; and Harrison, *Best Mounted Police Stories*.

31 *The Canadian Encyclopedia*, 2nd ed. (Edmonton: Hurtig Publishers, 1988), p.912.

32 Friesen, *Canadian Prairies*, p.303.

33 David B. Marshall, *Secularizing the Faith: Canadian Protestant Clergy and the Crisis of Belief 1850-1940* (Toronto: University of Toronto Press, 1992), p.142.

34 Ralph Connor, *Corporal Cameron of the North West Mounted Police: A Tale of the Macleod Trail* (Toronto: The Westminster Company, 1912).

35 George Cotkin, *Reluctant Modernism: American Thought and Culture 1880-1900* (New York: Twayne, 1992), pp.xi-xii.

36 T. Jackson Lears, *No Place of Grace: Antimodernism and the Transformation of American Culture, 1880-1920* (New York: Pantheon Books, 1981), pp.xiii-xiv.

37 Brian J. Fraser, *The Social Uplifters: Presbyterian Progressives and the Social Gospel in Canada, 1875-1915* (Waterloo, Ont.: Wilfrid Laurier University Press, 1988), p.177.

38 Pierre Berton, *Hollywood's Canada* (Toronto: McClelland and Stewart, 1975), p.111.

39 Peter Morris, *Embattled Shadows: A History of Canadian Cinema 1895-1939* (Montreal & Kingston: McGill-Queen's University Press, 1978), pp.44, 107.

40 Berton, *Hollywood's Canada*, pp.118-9.

41 Gail Bederman outlines an interesting argument in which Victorian "manliness" (with its concern for "sexual self-restraint, a powerful will, [and] a strong character") was by the 1930s surpassed by "masculinity" (with its ideals of "aggressiveness, physical force, [and] male sexuality"). Citing the popularity of Tarzan novels and Rudolf Valentino movies such as *The Sheik*, she argues, "As Victorian formulations of manliness have gradually evaporated, 'the natural man's' primitive masculinity has increasingly overshadowed 'the white man's' civilized mastery." While some elites may have turned to the "savage" and the "primitive" in response to modernity, the persistent popularity of Mountie manliness in Hollywood films and beyond suggests that, in some genres, the prescriptive example of Victorian manliness persisted much longer than was previously assumed. See Gail Bederman, *Manliness and Civilization: A Cultural History of Gender and Race in the United States, 1880-1917* (Chicago and London: University of Chicago Press, 1995), pp.18, 19, 232. On the "savage" and the "primitive," see also Mariana Torgovnick, *Gone Primitive: Savage Intellects, Modern Lives* (Chicago and London: University of Chicago Press, 1990).

42 See Friesen, *Canadian Prairies*, p.230.

43 The fifteen chapters of *Dangers of the Canadian Mounted* were shown on the Space Channel in fall 1997. The serial was re-edited into the movie *RCMP and the Treasure of Genghis Khan* (1948).

44 Berton, *Hollywood's Canada*, pp.118, 121.

45 Ibid., p.123.

46 Joe Holliday, *Dale of the Mounted: Dew Line Duty* (Toronto: Thomas Allen, 1957), p.13.

47 Ibid., p.35.

48 Joe Holliday, *Dale of the Mounted* (Toronto: Thomas Allen, 1951), p.35.

49 Holliday, *Dew Line Duty*, pp.10-1.

50 Joe Holliday, *Dale of the Mounted in Hong Kong* (Toronto: Thomas Allen, 1962), p.11.

51 Joe Holliday, *Dale of the Mounted: Atomic Plot* (Toronto: Thomas Allen, 1959), p.8.

52 Holliday, *Dale of the Mounted*, pp. 93, 15, 31.

53 Holliday, *Dew Line Duty*, p.77.

54 T.A. Culham, "The Royal Canadian Mounted Police in Literature," Ph.D. dissertation, University of Ottawa, 1947, pp.3, 9-13.

3 The Mountie and the Culture of Consumption, 1930-70

1 A similar fate befell the so-called "fisherfolk" of Nova Scotia in the twentieth century. On this and the notion of "commercial antimodernism," see Ian McKay, *The Quest of*

the Folk: Antimodernism and Cultural Selection in Twentieth-Century Nova Scotia (Montreal & Kingston: McGill-Queen's University Press, 1994).

2   Roland Marchand, *Advertising the American Dream: Making Way for Modernity, 1920-1940* (Berkeley and Los Angeles: University of California Press, 1985), pp.xvii, xxi.

3   A.C. Shelton, Camera Club Department, ANSCO, Binghamton, N.Y., to Commissioner Wood, March 2, 1949; Wood to Shelton, March 7, 1949; Shelton to Wood, April 26, 1949; in Record Group 18, Access 85-86/612, Vol. 22, File G-575-2 (1953), National Archives of Canada (NAC), Ottawa. (Hereafter, cited by the abbreviation "RG" followed by Box and File numbers; information for which I have "inferred" the full citation because RCMP documentation was incomplete or out of order is indicated by inclusion in square brackets "[. . .]").

4   Interview with S.W. Horrall, Braeside, Ont., Nov. 3, 1995.

5   Bayfield to Mr. A.A. Bolte, Canadian Kodak Co. Ltd., Dec. 2, 1957; in RG 18, Acc 85-86/612, Vol. 22, File G-575-2 (1957), NAC.

6   M.J. Keough, Liaison Officer, to Mr. Martin Bersted, Bersted's Hobby Craft, Inc., Monmouth, Illinois, Sept. 12, 1958; Keough to Bersted, Sept. 19, 1958; in RG 18, Acc 85-86/612, Vol. 22, File G-575-2 (1958), NAC.

7   E.V. Brand, Canadian Wallpaper Manufacturers Ltd., Toronto, to Public Relations Officer, RCMP, Aug. 20, 1958; Keough to E.V. Brand, Aug. 27, 1958; in RG 18, Acc 85-86/612, Vol. 22, File G-575-2 (1958), NAC.

8   Keough to Mr. Warwood, Clover Farm Stores of Canada, Ltd., April 9, 1959; Keough to Warwood, April 23, 1959; in RG 18, Acc 85-86/612, Vol. 22, File G-575-2 (1960), NAC.

9   W.H. MacKay, International Playing Card Company Ltd., Windsor, Ont. to Holm, Jan. 27, 1961; Holm to MacKay, Feb. 2, 1961; in RG 18, Acc 85-86/612, Vol. 22, File G-575-2 (1961), NAC.

10 Gorman to MacKay, March 17, 1961; Gorman to MacKay, April 5, 1961; Holm to MacKay, May 11, 1961; MacKay to Holm, May 15, 1961; in RG 18, Acc 85-86/612, Vol. 22, File G-575-2 (1961), NAC.

11 W.J. Nash, Managing Editor, Monsanto Magazine to Commissioner Wood, March 8, 1948; in RG 18, Acc 85-86/612, Vol. 22, File G-575-2 (1953), NAC.

12 Marc T. McNeil, Public Relations Officer, CPR to Deputy Commissioner C.K. Gray, May 10, 1948; the request was approved by Commissioner Wood by a telegraph to o/c Edmonton, May 11, 1948; in RG 18, Acc 85-86/612, Vol. 22, File G-575-2 (1953), NAC.

13 J.D. Burk, Johnson's Wax to Gorman, March 6, 1964; in RG 18, Acc 85-86/612, Vol. 22, File G-575-2 (1967), NAC.

14 Commissioner A.B. Perry to Tom Mix, Feb. 18, 1919; in RG 18, Acc 85-86/612, Vol. 5, File G-556-2 (1944), NAC.

15 Superintendent Vernon Kemp, C.O. "O" Division to Commissioner, Nov. 3, 1939; in RG 18, Acc 85/612, Vol. 5, File G-556-2 (1944), NAC.

16 Ibid.; also Wood to Kemp, Nov. 6, 1939; in RG 18, Acc 85-86/612, Vol. 5, File G-556-2 (1944), NAC.

17 Commissioner Wood to W.T. Randall, Chairman, Canada Night Committee, June 14, 1941; in RG 18, Acc 85-86/612, Vol. 5, File G-556-2 (1944), NAC.

18 Wood to R. Travers, Secretary, Hespeler Old Boys' Reunion of 1947, April 30, 1947; in RG 18, Acc 85-86/048, Vol. 5, File G-556-2 (1959), NAC.

19 Cst. N. Craig to O.C. "O" Division, July 7, 1947; in RG 18, Acc 85-86/048, Vol. 5, File G-556-2 (1959), NAC.

20 Bayfield to O.C. "E" Division, April 6, 1956; in RG 18, Acc 85-86/048, Vol. 5, File G-556-2 (1959), NAC.

21 J.E.S. Biscaro, Security Officer in Charge, Belgium, to O.C. Security Section, Visa Control, Canada House, London, Sept. 28, 1956; in RG 18, Acc 85-86/048, Vol. 5, File G-556-2 (1959), NAC.

22 Oliver Clausen, TIME International of Canada Ltd. to Inspector M. J. Keough, Oct. 30, 1958; in RG 18, Acc 85-86/048, Vol. 5, File G-556-2 (1959), NAC.

23 J.R. Lemieux, C.O. "C" Division to Mr. J.H.R. Marois, Visa Control Section, Canadian Embassy, Belgium, Oct. 31, 1958; in RG 18, Acc 85-86/048, Vol. 5, File G-556-2 (1959), NAC.

24 Gorman to C.O. "O" Division, July 14, 1964; C.O. "C" Division to Commissioner, July 17, 1964; in RG 18, Acc 85-86/048, Vol. 5, File G-556-2 (1964), NAC.

25 *Sixth Annual Report*, 1951; in RG 5 Tourism and Publicity, File 1.3, Archives of Ontario (AO), Toronto. Many thanks to Karen Dubinsky for this and other references concerning tourism in Ontario.

26 Jørn Winther, Producer, TV, CBC Vancouver to Commissioner, Aug. 11, 1959; in RG 18, Acc 85-86/048, Vol. 5, File G-556-2 (1959), NAC.

27 E.H. Adams, address to Canadian Chamber of Commerce meeting, Vancouver, B.C., Sept. 9, 1937; in G.G. McGeer papers, Add. Mss.9, Box 14, File 6, British Columbia Archives and Records Service (BCARS), Victoria, B.C.

28 Marc McNeil, CPR to Deputy Commissioner C.K. Gray, Aug. 31, 1951; in RG 18, Acc 85-86/612, Vol. 22, File G-575-2 (1953), NAC.

29 *Niagara Falls Evening Review*, March 6, 1952, p.4.

30 W.K. Kiernan, Minister of Recreation and Conservation, Government of British Columbia to Commissioner McLellan, June 8, 1964; in RG 18, Acc 85-86/048, Vol. 5,

File G-556-2 (1967), NAC. The B.C. request got the support of Assistant Commissioner D.O. Forrest, who passed it on to the commissioner; but there is no documentation to show if the commissioner gave his approval.

31 Asst. Comm. C.E. Rivett-Carnac, Commanding "F" Division to Commissioner Wood, July 4, 1949; in RG 18, Acc 85-86/612, Vol. 22, File G-575-2 (1953), NAC.

32 Rivett-Carnac to Commissioner, Aug. 7, 1951; Deputy Commissioner Gray to Rivett-Carnac, Aug. 14, 1951; in RG 18, Acc 85-86/612, Vol. 22, File G-575-2 (1953), NAC.

33 C.H. Bayfield, Liaison Officer to Mr. Rupert Leach, Director of Photography, Sawyer's Inc., Portland, Oregon, Jan. 5, 1956; in RG 18, Acc 85-86/612, Vol. 22, File G-575-2 (1957), NAC.

34 Ibid.

35 Supt. J.H.T. Poudrette, c/o "A" Division to Commissioner, Aug. 8, 1956; in RG 18, Acc 85-86/612, Vol. 22, File G-575-2 (1957), NAC.

36 Post Order No. 11, Parliament Hill Day and Evening Shifts, Aug. 31, 1956; in RG 18, Acc 85-86/612, Vol. 22, File G-575-2 (1957), NAC.

37 S/Inspector for E.A.F. Holm, Inspector Liaison Officer, Memorandum for File, April 25, 1960; in RG 18, Acc 85-86/612, Vol. 22, File G-575-2 (1960), NAC.

38 D.O. Forrest, Asst. Comm., Commanding "E" Division to O.C. New Westminster Sub-Division, June 2, 1960; W.G. Hurlow, Insp. O.C. New Westminster Sub-Division to O.C. "E" Division, June 6, 1960; in RG 18, Acc 85-86/612, Vol. 22, File G-575-2 (1960), NAC.

39 Edwin Seaver, Little, Brown & Company to RCMP, March 19, 1957; C.H. Bayfield to Seaver, March 29, 1957; in RG 18, Acc 85-86/612, Vol. 22, File G-575-2 (1957), NAC.

40 Joe Holliday to Bayfield, Feb. 6, 1958; in RG 18, Acc 85-86/612, Vol. 22, G-575-2 (1958), NAC.

41 Superintendent H.A. Maxted, C.O. "Depot" Division to Commissioner, April 12, 1957; Bayfield to Maxted, April 23, 1957; in RG 18, Acc 85-86/612, Vol. 22, File G-575-2 (1957), NAC.

42 Bayfield to Mr. T. Landale, Editor, *Omaha World Herald*, Omaha, Nebraska, June 27, 1958; Bayfield to Landale, Aug. 7, 1958; M.J. Keough, Liaison Officer, to Landale, Aug. 15, 1958; in RG 18, Acc 85-86/612, Vol. 22, File G-575-2 (1957), NAC.

43 Paul Rutherford, *When Television Was Young: Primetime Canada 1952-1967* (Toronto: University of Toronto Press, 1990), pp.378, 511, 379.

44 W.J. Hepplewhite, Eaton's Merchandise Display Manager to Supt. P. Bazowski, O.C. Vancouver, July 11, 1968; in RG 18, Acc 85-86/048, Vol. 6, File G-556-16, NAC.

45 Insp. G.A. Kennedy, memo, Aug. 14, 1968; in RG 18, Acc 85-86/048, Vol. 6, File G-556-16, NAC.

46 "Eaton 100 Police Show"; in RG 18, Acc 85-86/048, Vol. 6, File G-556-16, NAC.

4 A Moment of High Nationalism (and Tension), 1968-73

1   Quoted in Lawrence Martin, *The Presidents and the Prime Ministers* (Toronto: Doubleday, 1982), p.216.

2   William Thorsall, "For Six Months, It Was Canada's Century," *The Globe and Mail*, April 26, 1997, p.C1; and "Expo 67's Happy Face Idealism Was Misleading," p.C5.

3   *FFFFF* (*Frostbite Falls Far Flung Flier*) 5,2 (December 1990), pp.1,4; and *FFFFF* 5,4 (June 1991), p.6.

4   Karl Cohen, Interview with Alex Anderson, *FFFFF* 4,1, p.4.

5   Personal Biography of Dudley Do-Right. Many thanks to Gary David and the folks at *FFFFF* for passing this along to me.

6   *FFFFF* 3,4, p.4.

7   Whiplash himself was coloured green in the cartoon, perhaps reflecting Ward's attempt to create a villain who was unrepresentative of any ethnic group.

8   *FFFFF* 5,2 (December 1990), p.12.

9   "Stolen Luck," in *Rocky and Bullwinkle*, Whitman, Ward Productions, 1973.

10 Harrison, *Best Mounted Police Stories*, p.15.

11 Rudy Weibe, *The Temptations of Big Bear* (Toronto: McClelland and Stewart, [1973] 1976), p.152.

12 S.W. Horrall, *The Pictorial History of the Royal Canadian Mounted Police* (Toronto: McGraw-Hill Ryerson, 1973), pp.118-9.

13 Young, *The Mounties*, p.116.

14 RCMP, *Royal Canadian Mounted Police*, p.1.

15 On the emerging Native rights movement of the period, see J.R. Miller, *Skyscrapers Hide the Heavens: A History of Indian-White Relations in Canada* (Toronto: University of Toronto Press, 1989), pp.230-66. For a recent study highlighting the emerging Native nationalism *before* the 1969 White Paper, see Richard Kicksee, " 'Scaled down to Size': Contested Liberal Commonsense and the Negotiation of 'Indian Participation' in the Canadian Centennial Celebrations and Expo '67, 1963-1967," M.A. thesis, Queen's University, Kingston, 1995.

16 Ruth Roach Pierson et al., *Canadian Women's Issues*, vol.1 (Toronto: James Lorimer and Company, 1993). In the preface to this work (p.ii), Marjorie Griffin Cohen points to 1967 as the time "when women's issues began to be recognized as a political force with the potential to change the existing power dynamics."

17 Robert Jackson and Doreen Jackson, *Politics in Canada: Culture, Institutions, Behaviour and Public Policy*, 2nd ed. (Scarborough, Ont.: Prentice Hall Canada, 1990), p.110.

18 Donald Swainson, "Rieliana and the Structure of Canadian History," in *Louis Riel: Selected Readings*, ed. Hartwell Bowsfield (Toronto: Copp Clark Pitman, 1988), p.36.

19 George L. Mosse, ed., *Police Forces in History* (London: Sage, 1975), pp.1, 5.

20 C.W. Harvison, *The Horsemen* (Toronto: McClelland and Stewart, 1967), pp.156, 243-61.

21 Brown and Brown, *An Unauthorized History of the RCMP*, pp.154-81.

22 "Indians Plan Mass Demonstrations," *Province* (Vancouver), Feb. 25, 1972, p.22; "20 Angry Teen-agers Demonstrate against Alleged Police Brutality," *The Vancouver Sun*, July 15, 1972, p.11.

23 *Province*, Jan.12, 1973, p.12.

24 Jack Ramsay, "My Case against the RCMP," *Maclean's*, July 1972, pp.19, 58, 65, 68.

25 "Return to BC Police Force Threatened," *The Vancouver Sun*, Feb. 25, 1972, p.12; "Mountie Insignia Stays, Trudeau Tells Albertans," *Province*, April 28, 1972, p.6.

26 Interview with S.W. Horrall, Nov. 3, 1995.

27 Interview with John Bentham, Ottawa, Ont., Sept. 24, 1996.

28 RCMP, "Annual Report of the Royal Canadian Mounted Police 1971-1972," in *RCMP Centennial 1973: A Background For Editors*, Ottawa, 1973, pp.11-39. No women uniformed members entered the Force until 1974.

29 Hugh A. Dempsey, ed., *Men in Scarlet* (Calgary: Historical Society of Alberta/ McClelland and Stewart West, 1974), p.ix.

30 Interview with S.W. Horrall, June 7, 1996.

31 *Scarlet and Gold*, 54th ed. (Vancouver), p.1.

32 RCMP to Treasury Board, May 16, 1972; in RG 18, Acc 80-81/315, Box 22, File G-180-8-38, NAC.

33 Ibid.

34 Ibid.

35 D.B. Dewar, Deputy Secretary, Treasury Board, to Ernest A. Coté, Deputy Solicitor General, June 9, 1972; in RG 18, Vol. 22, File G-180-8-38, NAC.

36 Memorandum, S/Insp. J.C.Y. Turgeon to "D.S.S." June 22, 1972; in RG 18, Vol. 22, File G-180-8-38, NAC.

37 Ibid.

38 Memorandum, D.T. Saul to Deputy Commissioner Bazowski, Dec. 11, 1972; in RG 18, Vol. 26, File G-180-8-75-1, NAC.

39 Interview with John Bentham, Sept. 24, 1996.

40 D.T. Saul, *Ride a Black Horse: The RCMP Centennial Review* (Victoria, B.C.: Review Editions 73, 1989), p.12.

41 Interview with S.W. Horrall, Nov. 3, 1995.

42 *RCMP Quarterly* 39,1 (January 1974), p.3.

43 Memorandum, Bazowski to S/Sgt M.J. McInnis, March 9, 1973; in RG 18, Vol. 27, File G-180-8-75-2, NAC.

44 "Proposal to Ronalds-Reynolds and Company Limited Re: RCMP Centennial Travelling Exhibit-1973," from Robin Bush and Associates, Aug. 5, 1972, p.2; in RG 18, Vol. 23, File G-180-8-45-Supp "A," NAC.

45 Letter, Lawrence Marshall to McInnis, Oct. 25, 1972; in RG 18, Vol. 24, File G-180-8-46, NAC.

46 Draft Script of audio-visual presentation, Oct. 17, 1972; in RG 18, Vol. 24, File G-180-8-46, NAC.

47 Ibid.

48 Saul to Jim McKibben, Oct. 16, 1973; in RG 18, Vol. 26, File G-180-8-75-1-pt.2, NAC.

49 Letters requesting copies of the souvenir booklet that accompanied the Centennial Review could usually expect a response from the Force signed by Saul, although occasionally a lower-ranking officer would respond. Letters critical of Centennial projects inevitably reached the Commissioner. All correspondence between the public and the Force is contained in RG 18, Vol. 27, NAC.

50 See Telex, Feb. 26, 1973; in RG 18, Vol. 24, File G-180-8-49, NAC.

51 Saul to members of Review, May 7, 1973, emphasis added; in RG 18, Vol. 26, File G-180-8-75, NAC.

52 Commissioner Higgitt, Administrative Instructions, Serial Number 1247, Dec. 28, 1972; in RG 18, Vol. 26, File G-180-8-34-Supp "A"-vol. 2, NAC.

53 Brown and Brown, *An Unauthorized History of the RCMP*, p.127.

54 Thacker, "Canada's Mounted," p.304.

55 See memo, Nov. 16, 1972, Saul to Bazowski, concerning lecture kits; in RG 18, Vol. 24, File G-180-8-46, NAC.

56 Rolph-McNally Ltd. to Saul, March 21, 1973; in RG 18, Vol. 27, File G-180-8-75-3, NAC.

57 Letter from Higgitt to Marcel Blais, June 25, 1973; in RG 18, Vol. 27, File G-180-8-75-29, NAC. The complaint concerned the performance of the Centennial Review in Moncton, N.B., being conducted only in English. The Force maintained that this was the decision of the local sponsors.

58 This was the opinion of a Mr. Dubé as it was forwarded to members of the Steering Committee in a letter from Collette Locas, Oct. 12, 1972; in RG 18, Vol. 23, File G-180-8-41, NAC.

59 The company's plans for the Montreal exhibit, including the film "What If None?" were rejected by Information Canada. The late date of this cancellation, March 20, 1973, meant that the project was taken over by Information Canada/Exhibitions which made use of exhibits already in design or production for other cities. See Government of Canada memo, J. Creighton Douglas to Guy D'Avignon, March 28, 1973; in RG 18, Vol. 23, File G-180-8-41, NAC.

60 Design and Communication letter to D.T. Saul, March 20, 1973; in RG 18, Vol. 23, File G-180-8-41. George Arthur French was commissioner Oct. 18, 1873 to July 21, 1876, and James Farquharson Macleod from July 22, 1876 to Oct. 31, 1880; Horrall, *Pictorial History*, p.248. Henry Larsen was Captain of the *St. Roch*.

61 CPIC telex, from "C" Division to the Commissioner's office, May 4, 1973; in Rg 18, Vol. 27, File G-180-8-75-22, NAC.

62 Langelier, "RCMP vs French Canadian Public Opinion."

63 This advice came from Design and Communication Inc.; see correspondence in RG 18, Vol. 23, File G-180-8-42-Supp "A," NAC.

64 "Dual Centennials," in *RCMP Quarterly* 39,1 (January 1974), pp.12-16.

65 "Report of the Coordinator of the Alberta-RCMP Century Celebrations Committee 1973-1975"; in RG 18, Acc 85-86/048, Vol. 45, File K-180-12-pt.3 (1974), NAC.

66 News Release, Mid-Night Twilight Tourist Association (Zone 14), Oct. 24, 1973; in RG 18, Acc 85-86/048, Vol. 45A, File K-180-12-2 (1974), NAC.

67 "$32,100 to Saddle Lake Reserve Century Celebrations Projects," News Release, Alberta-RCMP Century Celebrations Committee, May 27, 1974; in RG 18, Acc 85-86/048, Vol. 45A, File K-180-12-2 (1974), NAC.

68 In organizing the Flare Square Exhibit in Calgary, for instance, the Force kept to its economic plan. The exhibit was on budget and on time. Meticulous record-keeping meant that receipts were kept for everything and excess materials were sold off once the celebrations were over. Interview with John Bentham, Sept. 24, 1996.

69 See Higgitt's handwritten comments on Centennial Advisory Committee memorandum, July 4, 1972; in RG 18, Vol. 22, File G-180-8-37, NAC.

70 RCMP memo for file, Jan. 15, 1973; in RG 18, Vol. 23, File G-180-8-40-I, NAC.

71 W.F. MacRae to "Depot" Division, Jan. 26, 1973; in RG 18, Vol. 26, File G-180-8-75-I-pt.I, NAC.

72 Stanley Public Relations to Saul, March 29, 1973; in RG 18, Vol. 27, File G-180-8-75-2, NAC.

73 Memo from Saul to Bazowski, Nov. 16, 1972; in RG 18, Vol. 24, File G-180-8-46, NAC.

5 Embracing Modernity, Liberalizing the Past: The 1973 Centennial Celebrations

1 Gregory S. Kealey, "State Repression of Labour and the Left in Canada, 1914-20: The Impact of the First World War," *Canadian Historical Review* 73,3 (1992), pp.281-314, quotation at p.289.

2 S.W. Horrall, "The Royal North-West Mounted Police and Labour Unrest in Western Canada, 1919," *Canadian Historical Review* 61 (1980), p.190.

3 See, for an interesting discussion, Kenneth C. Dewar, "Where to Begin and How: Narrative Openings in Donald Creighton's Historiography," *Canadian Historical Review* 72,3 (1991), pp.348-69.

4 A copy of the official centennial place mat can be found in RG 18, Vol. 22, File G-180-8-37-pt.43, NAC, while the calendar was produced by the Regina Chamber of Commerce with the approval of the Force.

5 RCMP, *An Historical Outline of the Force* (Ottawa: Queen's Printer, 1967), pp.1-4.

6 Ibid., p.4.

7 Dudas, Kuypers, Adamson Ltd., "Report on Concept for RCMP Toronto Exhibit," Nov. 1, 1972; in RG 18, Vol. 22, File G-180-8-40, NAC.

8 Ibid.

9 Folio Creative to Saul, Dec. 29, 1972; in RG 18, Vol. 26, File G-180-8-75-1-pt.1, NAC.

10 See Carter, *Lost Harvests*, p.151.

11 See computer printout of panel no.47; in RG 18, Vol. 22, File G-180-8-40, NAC.

12 "Memo for File" from Sgt. Zyveniuk regarding March 9, 1973 meeting concerning Montreal exhibit; in RG 18, Vol. 23, File G-180-8-41, NAC.

13 Henry Klassen, "The Mounties and the Historians," in *Men in Scarlet*, ed. Dempsey, p.178.

14 See final draft of script, pp.1,6; in RG 18, Vol. 23, File G-180-8-45, NAC.

15 See place mat in RG 18, Vol. 22, File G-180-8-37-pt.43, NAC.

16 See, for instance, Friesen, *Canadian Prairies*, p.153.

17 Dudas, Kuypers, Adamson Ltd., "Report on Concept for RCMP Toronto Exhibit."

18 Horrall, *Pictorial History*, p.113.

19 See computer printout of panel no.52; in RG 18, Vol. 22, File G-180-8-40, NAC.

20 *RCMP Gazette* 36,7-8 (1974), pp.1-2.

21 E.C. Morgan, "The North-West Mounted Police: Internal Problems and Public Criticism," *Saskatchewan History* 26 (Winter 1974), pp.41-2.

22 Ibid., p.41.

23 Quoted in ibid., p.56.

24 See computer printout of wall panel no.43, Toronto exhibit; in RG 18, Vol. 22, File G-180-8-40, NAC.

25 Horrall, *Pictorial History*, p.112.

26 Carl Betke, "Pioneers and Police on the Canadian Prairies, 1885-1914," in *Lawful Authority*, ed. R.C. Macleod (Toronto: Copp Clark Pitman, 1988), p.105.

27 Ibid., pp.105-6. A realistic (and complicated) depiction of an officer's attitudes and duties is found in William M. Baker, ed. *Pioneer Policing in Southern Alberta: Deane of the Mounties 1888-1914* (Calgary: Historical Society of Alberta, 1993).

28 Quoted in ibid., p.111. Perry's concerns reflected the imperative of "less eligibility." See James Struthers, *No Fault of Their Own: Unemployment and the Canadian Welfare State* (Toronto: University of Toronto, 1983).

29 Ibid., p.112.

30 See computer printout of panel no.47; in RG 18, Vol. 22, File G-180-8-40, NAC.

31 R. Quinn Duffy, *The Road to Nunavut* (Kingston and Montreal: McGill-Queen's University Press, 1988), pp.114, 198.

32 Henry Larsen, *The Big Ship* (Toronto: McClelland and Stewart, 1967), p.104. See also Klassen, "Mounties and the Historians," p.182.

33 Regina Chamber of Commerce, *Royal Canadian Mounted Police Centennial Calendar*.

34 Horrall, *Pictorial History*, pp.178-9.

35 Horrall, "Royal North-West Mounted Police and Labour Unrest," pp.185-6.

36 William M. Baker, "The Miners and the Mounties: The Royal North West Mounted Police and the 1906 Lethbridge Strike," *Labour/Le Travail* 27 (Spring 1991), pp.55-96.

37 Steve Hewitt, "September 1931: A Re-interpretation of the Royal Canadian Mounted Police's Handling of the 1931 Estevan Strike and Riot," *Labour/Le Travail* 39 (Spring 1997), p.161.

38 Regina Chamber of Commerce, Royal Canadian Mounted Police Centennial Calendar.

39 See insert for souvenir program in RG 18, Vol. 27, File G-180-8-75-3-1, NAC.

40 Avery is mentioned in D.T. Saul, "Centennial Review Tour," in *RCMP Quarterly* 39,1 (January 1974), p.40. For information on Saul's campaign to combine the two shows, see memorandum from Saul to Bazowski, Dec. 11, 1972; in RG 18, Vol. 26, File G-180-8-75-1, NAC.

41 Saul, "Centennial Review Tour," pp.40-1.

42 Copy of Saul's dedication speech; in RG 18, Vol. 27, File G-180-8-75-13, NAC; emphasis added.

43 See the script for "March West," June 28. 1973; in RG 18, Vol. 27, File G-180-8-12, and G-180-8-75-1-Supp "A"-pt.1, NAC.

44 *Centennial Review Handbook*; in RG 18, Vol. 27, File G-180-8-75-12, NAC.

45 Macleod, *North-West Mounted Police*, pp.74, 78, 82.

46 John Tobias, "Canada's Subjugation of the Plains Cree, 1879-1885," *Canadian Historical Review* 64,4 (1983), pp.530, 531.

47 See scripts in RG 18, Vol. 26, File G-180-8-75-1-Supp "A"-pt.1, NAC.

48 Bederman, *Manliness and Civilization*, pp.18-19. On ideals of masculinity within the RCMP itself, see Steve Hewitt, "The Masculine Mountie: The Royal Canadian Mounted Police as a Male Institution, 1914-1939," *Journal of the Canadian Historical Association*, new series, 7 (1996), pp.153-74.

49 The Musical Ride was suspended from 1939 until 1948 and again suspended several times in the 1960s.

50 See, for instance, "Centennial Review Adds New Facet to RCMP Image," *The Leader-Post* (Regina), July 3, 1973, p.3.

51 *Daily Times* (Victoria), Sept. 7, 1973, p.3.

52 "Mounties To Present Show of the Century," *Daily Colonist* (Victoria), Aug. 30, 1973, p.44.

53 "RCMP Centennial Revue Opens K-Days," Klondike Days Insert, the Edmonton *Journal*, July 12, 1973, p.4; the Edmonton *Journal*, July 17, 1973, p.1.

54 See letter from Saul to Dudas, Kuypers, Adamson Ltd., May 11, 1973; in RG 18, Vol. 22, File G-180-8-40, NAC.

55 See computer printout of wall panel no.51; in RG 18, Vol. 22, File G-180-8-40, NAC.

56 Calgary Stampede, *News Release*, May 9, 1973; in RG 18, Vol. 21, File G-180-8-34-pt.2, NAC.

57 *The Ottawa Citizen*, May 23, 1973, p.2.

58 Letter to Saul from Smith, March 13, 1973; in RG 18, Vol. 26, File G-180-8-75-pt.1, NAC.

59 See correspondence, Feb. 16, 1973; in RG 18, Vol. 22, File G-180-8-40, NAC.

60 Calgary Stampede, *News Release*, May 9, 1973; in RG 18, Vol. 21, File G-180-8-34-pt.2, NAC.

61 Centennial Advisory Committee, Report; in RG 18, Vol. 22, File G-180-8-37-pt.2.#16, NAC.

62 [Centennial Advisory Committee, Report; in RG 18, Vol. 22, File G-180-8-37-pt.2. #20, NAC.]

63 [See Centennial Advisory Committee, Report, Oct. 15, 1973; in RG 18, Vol. 21, File G-180-8-32-1, NAC.]

64 S. Horrall and J. Bentham both outlined the Force's opposition to the Winchester proposal; interview with S. Horrall, Nov. 3, 1995; interview with J. Bentham, Sept. 24, 1996.

65 [Centennial Advisory Committee, Report; in RG 18, Vol. 22, File G-180-8-37-pt.2.#39, NAC.]

66 [Centennial Advisory Committee, Report; in RG 18, Vol. 22, File G-180-8-37-pt.2.#35, NAC.]

67 [Centennial Advisory Committee, Report; in RG 18, Vol. 22, File G-180-8-37-pt.2.#3, NAC.]

68 [Centennial Advisory Committee, Report; in RG 18, Vol. 22, File G-180-8-37-pt.2.#7, NAC.]

69 See pamphlet; in RG 18, Vol. 21, File K-180-3-5-pt.2, NAC.

70 See letter, Higgitt to President of the American Society of Composers Authors and Publishers, Feb. 22, 1972; and his letter to the National Arts Centre, July 24, 1972. Higgitt declared the Force in favour of such a show but stated that the Force could provide no financial help in the endeavour. In the end, the Centre was unable to obtain the rights to the show. RG 18, Vol. 22, File G-180-8-37-1, NAC.

6 Upholding the Image, Maintaining the Rights: The Mountie Enters the World of Postmodernity, 1973-97

1 Benjamin Barber, *Jihad vs. McWorld: How Globalism and Tribalism Are Reshaping the World* (New York: Ballantine, 1996 [1995]), pp.6-7, 17. Barber also sees Disney's "It's a Small World" attraction as a metaphor for globalization. See Barber, *Jihad vs. McWorld*, p.109.

2 Ibid., p.298.

3 Ibid., p.89.

4 *Province* (Vancouver), Oct. 16, 1974, p.1; "RCMP Fact or Fiction," *Province*, May 31, 1977, p.4; "A Sad Chapter in RCMP's Noble History," *The Vancouver Sun*, Nov. 9, 1977, p.A6.

5 "Pro-Mountie Backlash Proves Trap for Tories," *The Vancouver Sun*, Nov. 12, 1977, p.A1.

6 Canadian Institute of Public Opinion, *The Gallup Report*, Jan. 14, 1978, pp.1-2.

7 Walden, *Visions of Order*, p.2.

8 "Women RCMP Urged for Traffic Duties," *The Vancouver Sun*, March 6, 1972, p.15; "RCMP Won't Be Hiring More Women," *Province*, March 7, 1973, p.6; "Women Seek Equality in RCMP Enlistment," *The Vancouver Sun*, June 9, 1973, p.10.

9 *RCMP Gazette* 37,7-8 (1975), pp.3-10.

10 "Ms to Join the Crimebusters," *Province*, May 25, 1974, p.1.

11 "Women Break Tradition," *Daily Times* (Victoria), Sept. 16, 1974, p.15; *Province*, May 10, 1975, p.10.

12 *Winnipeg Free Press*, July 28, 1973, p.9.

13 "Five Indians Join Mounties under New Program," *Province*, March 25, 1976, p.13.

14 *The Leader Post* (Regina), July 7, 1973, p.9; "Visit More Successful than Expected," *The Leader Post*, July 6, 1973, p.1.

15 "Queen Assured Indians Pacts to Be Honoured," *The Edmonton Journal*, July 5, 1973, p.1.

16 "Treaties Get Royal Pledge," *The Leader Post*, July 6, 1973, p.27.

17 "Mounties in Work Clothes Watch over Ottawa 'Circus,'" *The Vancouver Sun*, Aug. 31, 1973, p.1; "A Little Soul-Searching in Order," K. Bell letter to the editor, *The Vancouver Sun*, Oct. 17, 1973, p.5.

18 For Vancouver exhibit figures, see telex, Aug. 9, 1973; in RG 18, Vol. 23, File G-180-8-44, NAC. For total attendance figure for Vancouver and Kelowna, see correspondence, Oct. 10, 1973; in RG 18, Vol. 26, File G-180-8-75-Supp "B," NAC. For Toronto figures, see similar correspondence; in RG 18, Vol. 22, File G-180-8-40-Supp "C," NAC.

19 *North* 16,3 (1973); *Atlantic Advocate*, January 1973; *Province*, Dec. 9, 1972, p.5.

20 Janet Timm and Annette Jaenen, Winnipeg, Man., to D.T. Saul, July 30, 1973; in RG 18, Vol. 27, File G-180-8-75-9, NAC.

21 R.G. Strickland, Winnipeg, Man., to Commissioner Higgitt, Aug. 8, 1973; in RG 18, Vol. 27, File G-180-8-75-9, NAC.

22 David Wm. Hankinson, CKXL News, Calgary, to Commissioner Higgitt, July 18, 1973, RG 18, Vol. 27, G-180-8-75-9.

23 CFRN, Edmonton, "Minitorial for Thursday, July 19, 1973"; in RG 18, Vol. 27, File G-180-8-75-9, NAC.

24 Donna Marie Scorer, Annapolis County, N.S., to Commissioner Higgitt, June 19, 1973; in RG 18, Vol. 27, File G-180-8-75-9, NAC.

25 Joan Lloyd, Chatham, Ont., to Higgitt, Sept. 23, 1973; in RG 18, Vol. 27, File G-180-8-75-9, NAC.

26 John S. Holdstock, Victoria, B.C., to Assistant Commissioner, G.C.Cunningham, "E" Division, Sept. 10, 1973; in RG 18, Vol. 27, File G-180-8-75-9, NAC.

27 Jean E. Pigott, Ottawa, Ont., to Commissioner Higgitt, June 21, 1973; in RG 18, Vol. 27, File G-180-8-75-9, NAC.

28 Mrs. J. Ann Liddle, Regina, Sask., to RCMP Headquarters, Regina, July 4, 1973; in RG 18, Vol. 27, File G-180-7-75-9, NAC.

29 Letter to Commissioner Higgitt (signature illegible), June 20, 1973; in RG 18, Vol. 27, File G-180-8-75-9, NAC.

30 R.H. Reid, Moncton, N.B., to Commissioner Higgitt, June 1, 1973; Mrs. Nettie Leaman, Moncton, N.B., to "Commanding Officer," June 4, 1973; in RG 18, Vol. 27, File G-180-8-75-9, NAC.

31 Mrs. C. King, Maple Ridge, B.C., to Higgitt, Sept. 3, 1973; in RG 18, Vol. 27, File G-180-8-75-9, NAC.

32 Bernard and Brigitte Doughton, Richmond, B.C., to Higgitt, Sept. 3, 1973; in RG 18, Vol. 27, File G-180-8-75-9, NAC.

33 On the more general obsession with youth in the 1950s and 1960s, see Doug Owram, *Born at the Right Time: A History of the Baby-Boom Generation* (Toronto: University of Toronto Press, 1996).

34 John Story, Dartmouth, N.S., to Higgitt, June 11, 1973, and Higgitt to Story, June 14, 1973; in RG 18, Vol. 27, File G-180-8-75-9, NAC.

35 W. Motiuk and N. Van Horn, letter to the editor, *Province*, Sept. 19, 1973; in RG 18, Vol. 27, File G-180-8-75-9, NAC.

36 CFRN, Edmonton, "Minitorial."

37 Rev. James Montgomery to Commissioner, RCMP, July 18, 1979; in RG 18, Vol. 28, Acc 85-86/612, File GH-180-3 (1980), NAC.

38 T.R.G. Fletcher, Assistant Deputy Minister, Tourism to Commissioner Nadon, Aug. 29, 1975, and accompanying documentation; in RG 18, Vol. 30 Acc 85-86/612, File GH 1510-120, NAC.

39 Detachment Investigation Report, June 6, 1981; telex, EXTOTT to CNBRA, May 11, 1981; in RG 18, Vol. 28, Acc 85-86/612, File GH 180-3, NAC.

40 D.C. Arnould to Commissioner, Nov. 3, 1981, RG 18, Vol. 28, Acc 85-86/612, File GH 180-3, NAC.

41 Interview with S.W. Horrall, Nov. 3, 1995.

42 Paul Palango, *Above the Law: The Crooks, the Politicians, the Mounties, and Rod Stamler* (Toronto: McClelland and Stewart, 1994), pp.245-6.

43 Roger D. Landry, Montreal Baseball Club Ltd., to R.H. Simmonds, Oct. 3, 1980; in RG 18, Vol. 28, Acc 85-86/612, File GH-180-3 (1980), NAC.

44 Simmonds to Landry, Oct. 14, 1980; in RG 18, Vol. 28, Acc 85-86/612, File GH-180-3 (1980), NAC.

45 [Tourism Dept] Request For Travel Approval Outside Canada and U.S.A., Oct. 19, 1982; and Memo to File, Dec. 10, 1982, from Cpl. W.J. Kazmel, Public Relations Branch; in RG 18, Vol. 4608, File GH 1510-120, NAC.

46 Memo to File, Dec. 10, 1982, from Cpl. W.J. Kazmel, Public Relations Branch; in RG 18, Vol. 4608, File GH 1510-120, NAC.

47 Paul Michaud, Manager, Special Products, Canadian Government Office of Tourism (CGOT) to Supt. J.R. Bentham, Public Relations, RCMP, Jan. 4, 1983; in RG 18, Vol. 4608, File GH 1510-120, NAC.

48 Commissioner Simmonds to The Honourable Bob Kaplan, Feb. 1, 1983; in RG 18, Vol. 4608, File GH 1510-120, NAC.

49 Memo to File from Cpl. J.R.E.S. Carrière, Public Relations Branch, June 28, 1983; in RG 18, Vol. 4608, File GH 1510-120, NAC.

50 Mel MacDonald, Director, Market Development-Overseas, CGOT to Supt. John Bentham, RCMP, June 24, 1983; in RG 18, Vol. 4608, File GH 1510-120, NAC.

51 D.R. Turner, Manager, CGOT to R. Desjardins, Director, Marketing Operations, USA, Department of Industry, Trade and Commerce, May 2, 1980; in RG 18, Vol. 28, Acc 85-86/612, File GH-180-9, Supp "A," NAC.

52 Simmonds to Solicitor General Kaplan, March 30, 1984; in RG 18, Vol. 4608, File GH 1510-120, NAC.

53 Kaplan to Simmonds, June 6, 1984; in RG 18, Vol. 4608, File GH 1510-120, NAC.

54 Memorandum from D.J. Wright to "H" and "J" Divisions, June 27, 1978; in RG 18, Vol. 30, GH 1510-120, NAC.

55 RCMP Transit Slip, undated; in RG 18, Vol. 30, GH 1510-120, NAC.

56 T.R.G. Fletcher to Commissioner Simmonds, Sept. 10, 1979; in RG 18, Vol. 30, GH 1510-120, NAC.

57 T.R.G Fletcher to Commissioner Simmonds, Sept. 19, 1979; in RG 18, Vol. 30, GH 1510-120, NAC.

58 RCMP, *News Release*, June 30, 1995.

59 Ibid.

60 "Canadian Pacific Railway From Iron Horses to Musical Rides," The Pony Express, courtesy of RCMP Public Affairs Directorate (PAD).

61 IEG Sponsorship Report, courtesy of PAD.

62 Solicitor General of Canada, "Launch of the RCMP Product Licensing Program," *News Release*, Ottawa, Jan. 27, 1995.

63 RCMP, *News Release*, Jan. 30, 1996.

64 Mounted Police Foundation (MPF), *Press Release*, Feb. 1, 1996.

65 Kevin Fowler, "Mounted Police Foundation to Help Fund RCMP Programs," MPF *Release*, January 1995.

66 "Gross audience," *The Vancouver Sun*, June 8, 1995, p.C6.

67 Paul Welsby, "Our Cops Are Cool," *TV Guide*, Nov. 5, 1994, p.16.

68 Interview with B. Beahen, Ottawa, June 11, 1996.

69 "Seeing Red," Opening Notes, *TV Guide*, Nov. 5, 1994.

70 Welsby, "Our Cops Are Cool."

71 Carolyn Abraham, "RCMP-Disney Deal Works like Magic," *The Ottawa Citizen*, June 30, 1996, p.A1-2.

72 Dana Flavelle, Business Reporter, "Mounties Disney-fied/ Official RCMP Merchandise Beginning to Hit Store Shelves," *The Toronto Star*, June 29, 1996.

73 A 1997 Dominion Institute quiz found that one-third of Canadians between the ages of eighteen and twenty-four did not know that the economic hardships of the 1930s were known as the "Great Depression"—a finding that, considered in the context of the marketing of Mountie and Canadian history in general, is cause for more than a little concern.

7 Conclusion: Re-Mounting the Force for the Twenty-First Century

1 Mary Ann Kletter and Lloyd Wagner, Minnesota, to R.A. Tweedie, Director, N.B. Travel Bureau, 1956; in RG 415 R 2b, Public Archives of New Brunswick, Fredericton, N.B. Many thanks to Andrew Sackett for passing this reference along.

2 MacBeth, *Policing the Plains*, pp.58, 68, 108.

3 Ibid., pp.158, 162, 188, 189, 206, 222, 228-9, 248, 299.

4 Marc Tetro, *The Royal Canadian Mounted Police* (Richmond Hill, Ont.: Scholastic Canada, 1994), pp.3, 19-20.

5 Even books by "hard-hitting" journalists shy away from the more controversial aspects of the Force's past. Hence, Alison Griffiths and David Cruise, in *The Great Adventure*, offer a detailed analysis of the trials and tribulations of the Great March, but avoid sustained comment on a more contentious issue such as Native-white relations. Alison